Libya's Unknown Atrocity

The true story of one woman's
20-year fight for justice after the death
of her husband in Libya

T0096934

Libya's Unknown Atrocity

The true story of one woman's
20-year fight for justice after the death
of her husband in Libya

Felicity Prazak

BOOKS

Winchester, UK
Washington, USA

First published by O-Books, 2013
O-Books is an imprint of John Hunt Publishing Ltd., Laurel House, Station Approach,
Alresford, Hants, SO24 9JH, UK
office1@jhpbooks.net
www.johnhuntpublishing.com

For distributor details and how to order please visit the 'Ordering' section on our website.

Text copyright: Felicity Prazak 2012

ISBN: 978 1 78099 445 1

A CIP catalogue record for this book is available from the British Library.

Design: Stuart Davies

Printed and bound by CPI Group (UK) Ltd, Croydon, CR0 4YY

We operate a distinctive and ethical publishing philosophy in all
areas of our business, from our global network of authors to
production and worldwide distribution.

CONTENTS

Prologue	1
Chapter 1	6
Chapter 2	13
Chapter 3	21
Chapter 4	28
Chapter 5	36
Chapter 6	40
Chapter 7	48
Chapter 8	54
Chapter 9	62
Chapter 10	72
Chapter 11	75
Chapter 12	83
Chapter 13	90
Chapter 14	96
Chapter 15	103
Chapter 16	109
Chapter 17	117
Chapter 18	126
Chapter 19	134
Chapter 20	143
Chapter 21	151
Chapter 22	159
Chapter 23	169
Chapter 24	176
Chapter 25	184
Chapter 26	190
Chapter 27	198
Chapter 28	205
Chapter 29	212
Chapter 30	222

Chapter 31   231
Chapter 32   238
Chapter 33   243
Chapter 34   249
Epilogue   256

This book is written in the Memory of:

Victor, my larger than life husband.
Isabel, my pioneering, spirited mother.
And Danny.
ALL WE HAVE LOVED AND LOST

Acknowledgements

When I started to count the men of the Church who have sustained me, the list went on:

Tony Powell of the Shaftesbury Church, Battersea. Delroy Powell of Junction Church, Clapham Junction. Reverend Paul Kennington of St Marys, Battersea. Reverend John Mosey from the Lockerbie group, Pastor Hamdy and Michael Starr of the Anglican Church Tripoli and Dr Rowan Williams, Archbishop of Canterbury. These are true men of God and I have been privileged to be their captive audience.

When I think of friends that have listened to my pain, there are too many to name. I thank each one of you.

When I remember colleagues that have supported me, I know you have seen the real me.

When I have spoken to the press I have found caring and dedicated professionals and to name Ayesha Burkes, Dipesh Gadher and Martin Fletcher is only a small recognition to the journalist who give their lives so that we know the real truth. Especially Martin, you changed my world.

To Dr Jim Swire: Jim, I thank you for your words of endorsement for my book. Without the Lockerbie group I would have stayed in limbo.

But without my children, Theodore and Tallena I would have no reason to live.

Reader, I thank you for reading my testimony. It could happen to any of us.

LIBYAN PROVERBS

'If you fear, you are safe'
'Silence is the door of consent'.
'Murder rectifies nothing'.

BIBLE QUOTATION

25 She is clothed with strength and dignity;
she can laugh at the days to come.

26 She speaks with wisdom,
and faithful instruction is on her tongue.

27 She watches over the affairs of her household
and does not eat the bread of idleness.

28 Her children arise and call her blessed;
her husband also, and he praises her:

29 "Many women do noble things,
but you surpass them all."

30 Charm is deceptive, and beauty is fleeting;
but a woman who fears the Lord is to be praised.

31 Honor her for all that her hands have done,
and let her works bring her praise at the city gate.

PROVERBS 31:10-31 given to me after my Baptism at the
Shaftesbury

Prologue

Cambodia, 2006

I was alone when it happened, though there were nameless faces all around me. It was one of those private moments that touch your life and make your soul cry out in despair. Without warning, the thief struck: Tonlé Sap.

We were on our way to the ancient city of Angkor Wat; a strange choice for a holiday for a single mum and her two teenage children, admittedly. We were living in China at the time and intent on exploring Asia. My choice would have been Thailand: we had been there for the Christmas break and I had thought I would never tire of it: the smiles on the people's faces, the elegant flowers that adorned the bed at night, the crystal blue waters of the sea – as close to heaven as I could imagine. But now the Easter holidays had come around, and my son had unexpectedly requested we visit Cambodia next. The thought intrigued me, though the location did not, but I was determined to foster a sense of democracy in our family. The three of us.

Clouded in a blanket of faded memory, the former Kampuchea, now known as Cambodia, had stayed a war-torn territory in my mind until my son brought it back from being forgotten to my memory. Imprinted on my mind back from my own teenage years, in the early seventies, was the crackle of the static as the Bakelite radio spewed out the six o'clock news in the background while we ate our tea off the red Formica table. I couldn't remember a tablecloth ever coming out in my house, and the crumbs spilt over onto the worn-out linoleum flooring in the kitchen. I knew differently now, yet growing up I had thought we were well informed of world events. My father would put the radio on as he served up the evening meal; background fodder to block out any conversation and the perpetual rows of my parents. The broadcaster would fill us in on news of events of the Viet Cong advancing down the Mekong Delta and count the casualties of the Australian troops. He would continue with sparse news on neighboring Kampuchea, also embroiled in a civil war. We would listen attentively as we ate our tea with hearty appetites. I was a teenager in Australia – the land of plenty. War and violence and death: these things were alien, light years away.

Then we landed in the humidity at Phnom Penh airport and my children were the teenagers now, stepping off the plane into the history I had listened to so many years before. And it was beautiful: the din of the motor peds carrying lovers riding pidgin along the street, the tuk-tuks passing, constantly ringing their bells, the colorful clothes of the local people complementing the smiles on their faces, the open bars, with their veranda settings giving a colonial atmosphere, the blood of history washed away in the murky brown rivers.

Then, the Killing Fields. We rode out some 30 kilometers of the capital in a local tuk-tuk. The Khmer guide was chatty, and as far as I could gauge, well-informed. Whether he was a victim of the regime or part of it was no longer an issue. He was friendly and pleasant, and I was pleased to let him take charge of our day. He perceptively guessed that my teenage children would be interested in the firing ranges that the guidebooks mistakenly said had gone underground. Handling AK-47s and relic handguns was now a tourist attraction; one that bizarrely appealed to my children. For a few dollars, the guide explained, we could buy some bullets and fire them in an earthen dugout. Sparks flew out from the handgun as it kicked back, and as the blast sounded the damp earthen floor trembled. I was glad to get out of there, but not before taking photos of my gleaming-faced children with the artillery.

The driver continued and the rustle of the breeze through our hair brought some relief from the heat. As he rode through outlying villages the local children, elated by the opportunity of seeing foreigners, threw flour at us: a Khmer New Year tradition that was said to bring good luck. Then the road narrowed and overgrown vegetation filled the ditches at the sides of the road. The skeleton and cross signs warning of land mines sobered us from our laughter following the playful antics of the local children, and we rode on in silence until we reached the Killing Fields. It was the greenness of the neatly manicured pastures that surprised me at first. There was even a white picket fence, so oddly out of place.

We walked slowly down the path in near silence, speaking only when we stopped to read a sign or view the statues of human skulls piled high in a sculptural monument. I had only heard of the atrocities from the old radio; now my eyes were wide open to the butchery that had happened only a few decades ago. Before us stretched the fields, the land undulating into the distance where mounds of earth testified to the bodies that were buried below. The air cried out with ululating howling and wailing at the torture that the fields had born witness to. If the news had been sketched in my formative years, the horror had not been painted until this moment.

It was an important place to visit, but harrowing. My son complained bitterly about being there. He had wanted the holiday, not the realism. Because for him, and for his sister and for me, the mass graves were a connection to our own personal torture. Standing in the Killing Fields, we were plunged thousands of miles away to another mass grave in whose concrete embrace rested the remains of Victor. Father. Husband.

I was washed over with the same nausea with which I had struggled upon first seeing my husband's burial place some years before – when the Libyan authorities finally granted me permission to visit the grave: a stark expanse of concrete in a barren graveyard. I looked at the neat precision of the Killing Fields. Not a blade of grass was out of place. A lush deep green colored the grass, outlined by the path that led to the area where the human skulls were piled on top of each other. I tried to imagine the scene as it would have been decades ago, in the reign of terror. The grass would have been stained with blood, the paths nonexistent, the picket fence would have been where the Khmer Rouge guards stood enclosing the captives as they slaughtered their people, and there would have been pits full of decaying bodies. I decided it would have been better if they had left the area alone, let the overgrown lawn take over, let the skulls fall and topple over in the heap where they lay. Then maybe the tourist would see the raw pain that I knew existed in this place, beneath the veneer of calm.

The next day brought with it a renewed desire to adventure and to journey away from the past that had revisited us at the Killing Fields. But it also brought with it the thief.

We took a seven-hour boat trip up the Tonlé River, into the huge expanse of Tonlé Sap Lake and on to Siem Reap where the treasure of the ancient ruins of Angkor Watt awaited us. The river meandered along and the pace of life drifted back to a near normality for its people that had been unchanged for centuries: a rural scene of buffalos and fishing villages. Then we entered the lake, and visibility was infinite; just water stretching for miles all around.

The heat inside the boat cabin was stifling, and I knelt on the wooden seat and leaned my head out of the window to clear my head. Water sprayed up from the lake, suggestively inviting me to play with the water. I reached with my left hand to play with the water, just to stroke it and feel the coolness on my skin. I had hardly realized the shock of the warmth of the water and the sheer power of the force behind it before I screamed out with all the pain that was left in my heart. I stayed facing the water, gripping my hands as my fingers nervously wove in and out, going over and over each digit. My body rocked from side to side and the passengers near me stopped their chatter mid-sentence. I could feel their eyes on me but I kept my back to them as the tears rolled uncontrollable down my face.

It was gone.

As the ground had claimed my husband, so the water of Tonlé Sap had taken the very symbol of my love: my precious diamond engagement ring, hand-crafted to Victor's own design, lay at the bottom of the lake. Even if I had cried out to stop the boat and the crew had jumped overboard to search the lurid water below, there was no hope of finding it.

Unvoiceable pain made my body tremble. I hadn't been allowed to go to my own husband's funeral, to witness his burial; his body had been encased in a mass grave without my consent, without my blessing. And now I had buried his ring.

I cried until I ran out of tears. A kind passenger came with tissues to see what had happened. She had no words that could console me. Someone else went up on deck to get my children. Clutching my finger, I looked at the mark that had imprinted on my second finger. The woman asked if I was insured; I didn't bother to answer. The half-carat diamond set in 18-carat gold had been priceless. It was a token of love and commitment that symbolized our unity, which even in death had not been lost.

I looked at the water that had stolen my ring and felt an evil chill come over me. And I heard the soft words of comfort that my daughter spoke as she gently put her arm around me.

'It could mean a new beginning, Mum.'

Just as Cambodia deserves a new beginning, I thought.

But the thief had slipped away. Uncaught. Unjudged. Free.

Chapter 1

London, 1992

In my thirties, I painted a self-portrait. I stand in the center, my arms outstretched. On one side my daughter Tallena, aged three, pulls on my arm, enticing me to come. Her other hand clings to a cloth doll her grandmother made her of a guardsman; his felt bearskin peeps out from under her arm. Pulling me in the opposite direction is my son Theo, aged four. Familiar objects of our everyday life are scattered on the canvas: free McDonald's toys to represent my regular walks up to McDonald's and letters, lots of love letters, to represent my husband – absent from the picture as he often was from our daily lives then. On my feet are huge slippers: a reminder that I had just finally passed my driving test after I had broken two of my toes and had to wear men's slippers that were two sizes too big for me. And then there is my hair – an enormous, electrifying riot of flame red that conceals my face. A representation of a disorderly and tumultuous life.

The painting was born of art classes I began in London once the children were old enough for crèche. It helped pass the long afternoons while my life was on hold, waiting until my husband returned home.

We had met nine years before, in 1983. I had come to London from Australia when I was not yet twenty: running as far as I could from my parents who fought and hated each other, from the boys at school who mocked and persecuted me, from a township behind whose closed doors lurked secrets I couldn't bear. I'd decided to do an electronics course; a subject I knew nothing of. I was the only female in a room of men, and I struggled to make sense of the course content. Victor – also on the course – was a willing tutor. He was incredibly handsome, in his black leather jacket sitting behind the wheel of his black Sirocco sports car. Cautiously, I resisted any flirtation at the beginning of the course, but when I aced an exam and Victor offered to buy me a congratulatory drink, I accepted. And the rest, as they say, is history.

Victor had nearly always worked abroad; that's part of what had made him so interesting for me, a girl who'd been desperate to travel from her little Aussie township all her childhood. He had worked in Libya, Saudi, Holland and even Russia, which I thought was particularly alluring. Now that we were married with children, Victor was working in Libya. He was happy in his job as an analytical chemist, a petroleum inspector; he liked and respected the Libyan people. Earnestly, he sought to have his young family accompany him, and I would have gone anywhere to be with my husband. I pictured living in the portacabin that he shared with his co-workers, saving the washing up water and throwing it over a small patch of flowers or vegetables outside. I tried to get a job out there; I even went to the doctor in London and asked about sun cream for our young baby. I was naïve but I believed we could make anything work, as long as we were together. But it was never going to happen. The visa issues were one insurmountable problem, but also wives just never accompanied their husbands to their workplace. It just wasn't done in the early nineties.

So I had to trade off our life together for the next best scenario, which was that he would work in Libya for two months straight and then have a month's leave. It was hard being apart, but the arrangement worked well. We lived in a plain flat packed with cheap furniture in Battersea, London; we had bought our home from the council, and the estate was a notorious dumping ground for problem families. Escape required the earnings of a decent job. So when the offer of a post in Libya came, there were no second thoughts. The money was good, the eight long weeks away were hard but there was nothing to replace the excitement of him coming home or even his love letters falling on the hallway mat. The phone calls were an extra bonus that I treasured; sometimes I rushed in to hear the answer phone switching off and then I would replay his messages as if listening to my favorite record.

I had begun the art foundation course without any real seriousness in art, so I was amazed when the painting was chosen for the opening of a new art gallery in Battersea Park. The Royal Academician who chose my paintings was so excited by my work that he embraced me in a bear hug as if he had found a long-lost relative. I modestly hid a tinge of acknowledgement that perhaps I was talented in a subjective way. I was pleased by the praise. Without realizing it, I had found a passion that would set me up for my future.

When Victor was home he didn't mind the odd evening I spent at the classes. It gave him time alone with his children, even if he was just bathing them and putting them to bed. He would then prepare a meal for us to have together and busy himself around the house with the man jobs that needed doing: fixing a light, replacing a washer in a leaking tap.

Then, after a couple of days in London and maybe a visit to his mother's, we would pack up and travel to France where we had bought a not-too-run-down property. Well, at least the main part of the house was livable, and there was plenty for Vic to spend his energy on. It was an amazing property dating back to 1692; La Houdrie, a chateau with a turreted tower housing delightfully uneven wooden stairs, three-foot-thick walls, original wooden beams and an enormous fireplace across the center of the living room. We had fallen in love with it when we first laid eyes on it. I loved the setting: it was perfect for the children with its huge garden and barns to play in, and it was rife with inspiration for my painting. But what I loved most was that my husband was so excited and happy at being lord of the manor. This was our special place; this was where we would build our lives together.

I marveled at my husband and his ability to get things done.

His French was less than schoolboy standard but his smile and hardy handshake were universal. They spoke anyone's language and the local French residents took to him. They were probably somewhat amused to watch an Englishman come in and try to rebuild La Houdrie, but to their credit they were always happy to help.

Victor had such energy, such determination, which was appealing and maddening in equal measure. One particular afternoon the children and I looked on – from the safety of the house – as Victor eagerly set about pulling down a huge electric pylon that had been dormant for some length of time; an eyesore on our land. Undeterred by the size of the pylon, and its concrete base, Victor charmed the local farmer into helping him pull it out of the ground using his tractor. Pretty soon Victor was rolling his sleeves up and drilling away at the concrete to break it down, squinting through his safety goggles. Hours later the pylon was down, though quite what he thought he would do with it next I'm not sure – it was too heavy to take anywhere. Leaving the metal contraptions upended by the barn, Victor and the farmer toasted their engineering feat with a Pernod. I took him a cup of tea to wash down the Pernod after the farmer had gone, thinking he would sit down and relax now, but Vic was on a high and argued that there was still another hour of daylight left and there was no point sitting idle when there was work to be done. He rummaged through his tools, found the angle grinder and set to work chopping up the enormous concrete rod.

Victor worked until long after sunset and I became marginally annoyed at his determination. 'Come in, darling,' I shouted out to him more than once. It was possible that he didn't hear me as the tool was deafening as it made contact with the concrete and then the steel pipes that were encased inside it. More likely he was focused on one thing: finishing the job. He rigged up some floodlights to continue with his mission. I peeped out of the kitchen window every fifteen minutes to see the silhouette of my industrious husband beavering away.

'Surely you could finish it tomorrow?' I called out to him. I looked at the extension lead and considered pulling it out of the socket. It was past nine by now and I had fed, bathed and settled the children in bed. I didn't want my husband to eat alone; he did that too many times when he worked away. I walked over to him, wrapped in my coat to fight the chill of the night air. 'Darling, the kids have gone to bed, they missed you. Why don't you stop and come in now? Let's have dinner.' My voice was disapproving; I couldn't help it. I just wanted to nestle up in front of the fire and enjoy my husband; was that too much to ask when I didn't see him for months at a time? As soon as the words were out I regretted my tone. We had our fair share of married rows, as do any couple. Have a little tiff and get it over with, and then clear the air. Victor answered back he would come in when he was ready and I knew not to go further.

He finally came in after ten, not because he had got the job done but because the blade on the angle grinder had given out. I was a little annoyed, but there was no point harping on any longer. As usual, I ended our fight with, 'Say you're sorry,' and Victor replied, 'No, you say you're sorry.' To which I retorted, 'I'm sorry if you're sorry,' and in parrot fashion he recited, 'Well, I'm sorry if you're sorry.' And that was the end of any disagreement: he held me in his arms and I knew I could never be happier.

The next day, I did my chores in the morning and my drawing in the afternoon and came back to the house to make tea. Theo and Tallena had been helping their father move straw from one of the barns that used to be a piggery. Victor was proud of his little helpers. They had put on their Wellingtons, which I always called gum boots, and spent the afternoon in cahoots with their father. I caught sight of Theo laughing his head off and there was a gleam in Tallena's eye. I was walking past the three of them, wondering what they were up to, when my husband called to wait a minute; they had something to show me.

'What is it?' I wanted to know.

'Close your eyes,' Theo said.

'What for?' I asked.

Victor found it hard to hide his smile. 'Just close your eyes, darling,' he persuaded me. 'The children found something you might like to see.'

It was no use trying to filter the information from them; I had to play along with whatever the joke was going to be or else be a bad sport.

'Hold out your hands,' Theo said, 'and keep your eyes shut.'

I said no but did it anyway; I wasn't sure what I was letting myself in for. Nervously, I extended my hand, keeping it bent and close to me. I felt a wet blob make contact with my palm and instantly opened my eyes and screamed. The three of them practically fell on the floor in laughter. The small brown frog hopped off on its tiny webbed feet, I jumped up and down screaming and they all laughed until they cried.

'You are horrible, horrible, horrible,' I told my family. I had entertained them just as they had predicted. 'I hate you,' I told them lovingly.

Victor was bemused by his conquest over my dignity. I patted down my trousers, wiping the imaginary slime off my hands, then clapped my hands loosely to wipe away the last bit of the joke.

'I'll get you back, don't worry,' I told them, not knowing how or when, and went to walk away. I wasn't sure if I was going to make tea or not now.

With one sweeping move, Victor put his strong arms around my waist and used his foot to bring me to the ground. We lay there in full view of any passing farmers, unable to move for the laughter we shared.

'Oh, yeah, how are you going to get me back?' Victor asked, knowing he was in full control. I wiggled and squirmed and jostled around but there was no getting away from the loving arms of my husband.

'Like this,' I said as I kissed him and laughed at my predicament. The children thought this was the funniest wrestling they had ever seen and jumped in on the action. Tea was forgotten.

There wouldn't have been a pot of gold big enough to buy that moment from me. Was it right that I had so much love? How had I been so lucky?

I had no way of knowing then that it would be one of my last few memories of happiness. We had the French house together for just one year. The dreams we had and the plans we made turned into nightmares and emptiness.

Chapter 2

Certain events in life, just a handful of them, are branded into your mind for ever. You remember what you were doing, even what the weather was like that day. The first such event for me was the assassination of JFK when I was seven. I ran to the neighbor's house to announce that John F. Kennedy, the seemingly invincible president of the United States, had been shot dead in Dallas. It was the first shattering, unbelievable event in my life. Of lesser impact, some fifteen years later, but equally memorable, was sitting by a keyboard in an office in Amsterdam, punching data into the system, when the radio blared out in Dutch that Elvis Presley, the legendary king of rock and roll, had died. It wasn't until a decade later that another such tragic event was broadcast over the television network to the shock of the nations on either side of the Atlantic.

The Lockerbie disaster was breaking news. In the early evening I had put my baby son Theo to bed. My mum was staying, while Victor worked abroad. I flicked on the TV and was about to start dinner when my attention was drawn to the newsreader's somber tone. A plane had come down over the Scottish town of Lockerbie. 'Mum, Mum!' I shouted in disbelief. 'Come quickly! There's been a bomb! It's exploded over Lockerbie.' Mother and daughter stood and watched the television; we didn't even manage to sit down on the sofa. I stood gaping at the news flooding in, unable to believe that such an event had taken place, and just days before Christmas. It was 21st December 1988. Those poor families, I thought.

I could never have imagined that Lockerbie would come to mean so much to me.

Because four years later, nearly to the day, on 22nd December 1992, I watched the midday news and saw the same thing again. Only this time the newsreader wasn't talking about the Pan Am air disaster over Lockerbie; unbelievably, he was talking about a plane being brought down by a fighter plane in Libya. In *Libya*.

My ears pricked up at the five letter word. Instead of half-listening to the news in the background while I busied myself with chores, I stopped immediately and turned up the volume. A Libyan Arab Airline passenger jet had been hit in mid-air by a Libyan fighter plane, a MiG the newsreader called it. I knew enough to know a MiG was some sort of military plane; I thought they were Russian. The first report was sketchy, but it was enough to send a chill through me.

I had woken that morning to a strange sight. I had looked first at the bedside clock that sat on the chest of drawers. It said eight thirteen a.m. (ten thirteen a.m. Libyan time). Then I had looked next to where I lay, knowing my husband would soon be nestled there beside me, where he belonged. But in my husband's place I saw a green vapor, like an aura, with a tubular, sort of oblong appearance. How strange, I had thought to myself.

Another two days and Victor would be home. He was flying that morning from Benghazi. I was looking forward to seeing him as always, not least because we needed to clear the air after a silly row. Victor had called before the weekend to explain that, although he should have been heading home for Christmas, his company were making him work a couple more days. I had protested: it was cutting it fine to be home for Christmas with all the running about and present and grocery shopping, not to mention a little time for ourselves. I let my husband know I was not happy. It may have been hard for him, alone in the desert, but he had his work colleagues. In the evenings, after I had put the children to bed, I felt completely alone. The art course at least helped me get through two of the evenings, and I would go to a prayer group sometimes, so really I had no reason to complain; but none of this was the same as being with my husband.

I had never fought on the phone with my husband before; the time was too precious and there was no way to make up a fight over the phone as I could do when we were together. But this was too much for me: Victor had missed last Christmas, and my heart sank at the thought that my children would not get to see their father on Christmas morning. I wanted them to experience that joy. They were three and four now, and they wouldn't understand that he had to work. I couldn't help myself; I was cranky.

So we argued, and I hung up on him after a terse goodbye. I regretted it the second I did it. There was no callback, though I stared at the phone, begging it to ring. A friend called a little later and uncharacteristically I said, 'I can't talk, I have to get off the phone.' I didn't want to hear my friend's voice; I wanted to hear my husband's. He could still ring back. Perhaps he had had to wait for someone else to make their call. Surely he wouldn't leave it like that? Who knew the next time he would be able to get to the phone exchange. Sometimes a few weeks would go by before he had the opportunity to go there. The phone calls were my lifeline and now I had cut him off. I should have been more supportive, more understanding. The fact was, I didn't know the desolation that my husband felt, being so cut off from his family and normal life. Things were okay when they were busy at work, but in the quiet times there was nothing to do.

The United Nations' embargo on international flights – part of its sanctions against Libya in an effort to force the handover of two suspects in the Lockerbie bombing – had meant Vic lost nearly a week of his leave. He had to take the internal flight from Benghazi to Tripoli and then the overnight ferry to Malta. The boat arrived the next day but the connection for the flights was not good and sometimes it meant another overnight stay in a one-star hotel in Malta. It was the same coming the other way: what would have been just over a three-hour direct flight from London to Tripoli or Benghazi was now an epic journey. Vic would have to take a flight to Malta, and with an overnight stay there in order to make the early departure of the boat the next day. If he caught the morning boat from Valetta to Tripoli he would sometimes be able to make the night flight in time to Benghazi, but it didn't always work out like that and there would be a further delay and overnight in Tripoli. At least in Malta the lads could get some beers in, but Tripoli offered no such reprieve.

The lads from his work had complained bitterly to the head office, but they got nowhere. They asked about other routes into Libya, either from Tunisia or Egypt, but they weren't workable. The UN sanctions were causing havoc for the three thousand or so British expat workers there, mainly oil workers. And yet Libya still continued to produce and sell as much oil as ever. The sanctions did not affect its income, just its people.

After our phone call, I paced up and down the living room, looked to the phone in the hallway intermittently. It stayed silent. I picked up the receiver once or twice and heard the dial tone I hoped was missing; that would explain why my husband had not called again to soothe my ruffled feathers. Finally, I slumped in front of the television, aware that I only had myself to blame for being so snaky. I should have been more understanding, I told myself. This night was the first night of our nine years together that I would let the sun go down on an unresolved argument.

The hours dragged by all weekend, and then Sunday morning brought a promise of hope: the phone rang but there was no one at the other end. That sometimes happened when he rang from Libya. I waited for the callback but it didn't happen. Finally, I decided that holing up in the house wasn't doing me, or the children, any good, so we went to church.

A boisterous buzz swirled around the modern church hall as the congregation sang out praises. This church was so different to my Catholic upbringing, and I loved it for its vibrancy. All these years I had searched for God, and I had found him on the edge of our council estate. The preacher read the notices about the Carol Service and the Christmas Day Service. There were five days to go til Christmas, and usually I would have listened with excitement. Now I didn't know if my husband would be home in time. I rushed the children out of the door the moment the service concluded, anxious to get home and check the answerphone. And when I did, hallelujah! A message: Victor had called, and would try to reach me again later.

I was home a little more than an hour when the phone rang again. Victor had even allowed the coffee time after church before calling back. He knew me so well. I grabbed for the phone, ejecting a quick hello before settling on the stairs by the phone.

'Hello, darling,' said the dear voice at the other end. 'Do you still love me?'

'Of course I love you, darling,' I told my husband, our fight completely forgotten.

'I have to work tomorrow, that's all,' Victor went on to explain. 'It's cutting it fine but I'll still be home for Christmas. I'll try to ring you from Malta once I've confirmed a flight.'

We talked for a few more minutes, neither of us wanting to hang up. Then, after we finally said goodbye, and 'I love you' again, I took a few minutes to compose myself. I was purring like a cat that had just been stroked. There was so much to say to him still; a letter, yes, I would write him one of my long, rambling letters about how much I missed him and how much I looked forward to seeing him. Never mind that I'd just told him this on the phone; I would put it in writing, as was our habit. I stood up from my cramped seat on the bottom step, and stretched, arching my back and then smoothing down my tummy. Perhaps we would have another child, I thought. I wanted more children; we had agreed that four was a good number. Victor was keen to have more, but I had held back, just allowing a little breathing space. Now Tallena was three, perhaps I would give him what he wanted this time.

For the next couple of days I bustled about preparing for Christmas and to welcome home Victor. On the Tuesday I planned to take the children to the park and then run some errands, but first I'd finish up some housework. The television was on, just background noise, as I worked, and the word jumped out at me in the quiet of the room as I turned off the vacuum: *Libya.*

Slowly, I moved over to the television and turned the knob of the volume control up. The sunlight streamed in from the windows across the length of the outside wall, but it wasn't the blinding light obscuring a clear view of the television set that made me slump to the floor. A map of Libya was on the screen and, emblazoned across it, the route from Benghazi to Tripoli.

'There are reports of a Libyan fighter plane colliding in mid-air with a civilian plane. It is not known how many casualties they are, but the pilots of the MiG military war plane have ejected to safety.'

The newsreader didn't have many details; an archived photo of the Russian-built warplane appeared on the screen. As he rambled on about Gaddafi's ageing military fleet I began to scream.

The children came rushing in to find me doubled up on the lounge floor. Their happy, smiling faces turned to stone when they saw me.

'What's wrong, Mummy? Mummy, what's the matter?'

I looked at my children, but I didn't know what to say. As young as they were, they could perceive something was seriously wrong. I tried to speak to them but all that seemed to come out were frantic, wrenching cries.

'Mummy, I'm scared,' Theo said. They stood flanking me on both sides, their anxious eyes peering into mine as I stayed hunched down on the floor, unable to move or speak. My son tried again, 'Are you hurt?' He was going to be five in a little more than a month's time and his father had often said to him, 'Look after Mummy while I'm gone.'

I don't know how long I sat on the floor. My children didn't move from my side. Their faces were grim and they knew something was terribly wrong. I rocked back and forth, waiting for some words to come. Finally, I pulled my little girl and little boy into my arms and said bleakly, 'I'll get you some lunch,' then added, 'Mummy and Daddy love you.' I kissed each in turn on the forehead, then got up and walked to the kitchen.

My young son called out to me, 'Mummy, are you sure you're alright? Do you need a doctor?'

I had completely forgotten my doctor's appointment. I had made arrangements to have my IUD out so we could try for another baby. I thought about the appointment for a few seconds. 'Yes, that's a good idea, darling. Maybe I'll go after lunch.'

I busied myself in the kitchen, all the time thinking furiously. I knew Vic was due to take an internal flight today from Benghazi to Tripoli, where he would connect to the ferry to Malta. But perhaps he had been forced to work a little longer. To avoid my annoyance, he wouldn't have rung to tell me. I needed more information. There was no point panicking, I told myself firmly; after all, hadn't I convinced myself once before he'd been involved in an air disaster, only for him to walk in the door and kiss me hello?

That time, two years before, with Theo just a toddler round my knees and my stomach swollen with pregnancy, my sister Elaine had sat with me through news footage of a Korean airliner crash-landing at Tripoli Airport. I knew Victor was flying home that day. My sister and I called everyone we could think of – the news station, Reuters, the Foreign Office. Finally, Elaine got through to someone who delivered the words I was desperate to hear: 'There were no Westerners on board the Korean airline.' My life, which had been on hold for the past few hours, resumed, and then later that day my husband arrived home safe and well.

As I gave the children their lunch, I thought, this just cannot be happening again. Another air disaster just when my husband was travelling home from Libya. What were the odds? The newsreader didn't really have many details, and now it was nearly one p.m. so I decided I would watch the news in a few minutes to see whether there was any new information.

Theo was not impressed that he had to forgo *Sesame Street* to watch a boring guy in a suit drone on about planes, but I overruled his objections. As I switched on the television I gasped in horror: they were actually showing the wreckage of the plane and emergency services pulling bodies from the burning wreckage and placing them onto makeshift stretchers. The workers wore muslin masks as if to block out the burning stench of flesh. I could not look away from the charcoal ground, the burning embers of soil, as the camera panned over the crash site. The announcer read out more details this time; it was just an hour later but more information had been relayed.

The mid-air collision had happened at ten fifteen a.m. local time.

I remembered looking at my bedroom clock that morning. I remembered the time, and the strange shape on my husband's side of the bed. And I remembered his answerphone message of two days before, played several times already; the next best thing to speaking to him. And I wondered whether I would ever hear his dear voice again.

Chapter 3

When the news report finished, leaving me none the wiser as to the fate of my husband, I was galvanized into action. The next news wasn't until after five o'clock, and I needed information fast. I jumped up from my seat and fumbled through paperwork in a drawer until I found my husband's business card, on which was the head office number in Essex. I would ring them. What would I say? I knew I could barely talk. I struggled between reason and panic. I had been through all this before and everything had been alright. Would they think I was an eccentric wife? I didn't care; I had to phone them. A receptionist answered the phone and I didn't know whom to ask for. I hadn't thought that far ahead. Struggling to put two words together, I blurted out something incomprehensible about the midday news and a plane crash in Libya. Finally I got through to a manager, and with a smattering of composure I recounted what I'd seen on the news.

'Calm down, Mrs. Prazak,' the man ordered; his conviction that I was overreacting was clear. 'I'm sure Victor is alright. We haven't heard anything is wrong here.'

'But Victor is flying from Benghazi today. He was told by your office to work the weekend and to come back on Tuesday. Don't you have someone you can ring?' I begged.

'You don't know Victor was on the plane, just wait and see,' said the manager. He was not going to put himself out, and besides, he knew calls to Libya were difficult to make and costly.

'I'm not going to wait for anything,' I told him through my mounting tears. 'I want you to ring your office in Ras Lanuf and see what you can find out.' I was unaccustomed to giving directions but I had to do something. If it was all a false alarm like last time, they would tick Victor off for his wife making a nuisance of herself and I didn't want that, but this man just didn't seem to believe me. Had it been real? Had I mistaken what I had seen on the news? But I had seen it twice.

The manager promised to phone if he heard anything. It was clear he was pushing me off the phone so he could get on with his day. If I hadn't been so shocked I would have been furious at the man's nonchalant attitude.

I went again into the living room and sat down. The children, on the verge of tears themselves, nestled in beside me.

'Has something happened to Daddy?' asked Theo.

'I don't know, darling. I hope not.'

It was little comfort; their usual laughter and cheeky smiles had evaporated. Just for a moment I lingered with my children. Who knew what was in store for them in the next few hours.

'I just want to make some phone calls,' I explained to them as I got up from the lounge. The children stayed seated together, hugging each other.

I dialed directory enquiries, and asked for the number for the Foreign Office. As I listened to the ring tone, I pictured myself sitting that night to write my letter to Victor, looking back in gratitude for his survival, telling him all about the unnecessary worry his family had been through. The Foreign Office operator was indifferent.

'Please can I speak to someone?' I pleaded with her.

The operator repeated my question, then asked her own, pausing uncomfortably between the words: 'Who... do... you... want... to... talk... to?'

What sort of intellect did these people have? I had said I had seen the news report. I had said I knew my husband was flying that day. I had explained it was an internal flight because the sanctions were on. What else could I tell her? Surely the operator could recognize the panic and concern of the distraught person at the other end of the phone? Why wasn't she helping me?

'I need a name or a department to put you through.'

Between sobs I told the callous operator I would ring back. I tried to find a number for Reuters, but the directory enquiry operator said she couldn't find it. What about the BBC or ITV? They had both reported on the event.

'Well, which one do you want?'

'Any will do, both of them, then, it doesn't matter which one.' I was losing my coherency and had to pull myself together. I was not making sense to people and they simply either didn't care or weren't taking me seriously. The number the operator gave just presented the same brick wall I was getting from everyone.

This was unbelievable, and I was beside myself. From the whimpering sounds emanating from the lounge, I knew the children were crying too.

I decided to ring my husband's work again. The receptionist put me through to the senior boss I had spoken to before.

'We haven't heard anything, Mrs. Prazak,' he said dryly.

'Well, have you phoned Libya yet?' I demanded.

'No, not yet. We would hear something if there were any problems,' he said in a bored tone.

'You didn't see the news; I did,' I snapped. 'Can you phone your office in Libya and ask someone, please?' Why was I having to beg everyone to help me?

I decided to try the Foreign Office again too. It was only a few minutes since I had called them, but I didn't let that deter me. I retold the story to the operator – the same one? The monotonous, disinterested tone made it hard to tell.

Finally, the operator conceded, 'I'll put you through to the North Africa Desk.'

I explained my dire situation to the man on the North Africa Desk. 'We haven't heard anything here,' he told me.

'But it's nearly two, and it was on the midday news. Surely you should know about this if it was on the news!' I couldn't hide my frustration and hurt any more. 'I want someone to find out if anything has happened to my husband.'

'You can try phoning your husband's work,' suggested the

man.

For someone working on the North Africa Desk, I gauged that he knew very little about phoning Libya. The best my husband's work would do was send a telex, and they hadn't even bothered to do that yet.

'I've done that and they tried to fob me off as well,' I told him sternly. My voice was shaking and my emotions were all over the place and I didn't accept that this was the best that these people could do for me. 'Can I leave my details and you can ring me back if you know anything?' I trusted him just enough to take down my phone number. It was in the era before mobile phones, but at least I had the answerphone.

Suddenly, I felt I had to get out of the house, it was smothering me. The children needed to go outside and try to salvage some normality. 'We'll go to McDonald's,' I told the children. 'Let's get your shoes and coats on.' I left the house in such a hurry it could have been on fire. I couldn't sit, or phone, or speak to another tactless human being.

Yes, I thought, looking at my glum children, a Happy Meal was in order. They had not long ago eaten lunch, but the way the day was going I wasn't sure I would be up to cooking supper. But the frisky mood they were usually in for their outing to Maccy D's frosted over to a quiet, reflective time. The children barely spoke as they ate their meals. I stared out of the window, cradling my coffee in my hands. My face was red from crying. I don't know how long we stayed there – it could have been twenty minutes; it could have been two hours – but finally I strapped Tallena into the buggy and took a firm hold of Theo's hand.

What next? I was numb.

A friend caught sight of me, but the last thing I wanted to do was tell anyone because then word would spread and the phone would be going. 'I can't stop,' I told my friend, 'I've got a doctor's appointment.' I wasn't lying to my friend. I did have an appointment at five p.m. I hadn't planned on keeping it, but now

I had said it, I didn't like to lie.

I asked the receptionist if she would keep an eye on the kids while I went in. I left the children sitting outside reading their books; I knew I wouldn't be long. I didn't know what I was going to tell my doctor. Like the receptionist, he went to my church.

In the doctor's office I slumped in the chair, exhausted. He noted the strained emotion on my face and said at once, 'What's the matter, Felicity?'

I recounted the very little I knew, and he said he would get his wife to ring me when he got home. 'I'm sure everything will be alright,' he tried to reassure me.

I knew he would use his discretion, as his wife would. I was glad that I had come; that I hadn't had to fight to be believed.

When we got home I checked the messages at once. My husband's company had called to say they had sent a telex to their office in Libya and were waiting for someone to get back to them. The only concrete fact they had found out was that there were two flights from Benghazi that morning within about an hour of each other. There was also a message from the Foreign Office; they knew of the plane crash by now but did not have a casualty list yet. At last, I was being taken seriously.

The call from Victor's company should have given my some hope. I knew my husband; I knew he would have opted for the earlier plane. But which plane had come down? The information was too sketchy. I watched Newsround, but they gave more or less the same version I had heard on the midday news. The doorbell went: it was Ellen, the doctor's wife. She took over with the children; just what I needed as the six o'clock news was about to commence.

The crash was now the top story. A Libyan fighter plane had collided in mid-air with a passenger plane, and they were now saying that a hundred and fifty-seven people had been killed. The newsreader was making a connection between this disaster · and Lockerbie: Pan Am flight 103 had gone down at 7.03 p.m. on

21st December 1988; this flight, LN1103, had gone down on 22nd December 1992. But what brought me to my knees was the newsreader announcing that the United Nations' sanctions had imposed an embargo on Libya buying any maintenance equipment or spare parts for its civilian fleet. I couldn't believe my ears: it was bad enough to hear that a plane had been brought down by a military aircraft while the pilots had ejected safely, but now to hear that Libya's civilian airlines were not allowed to buy any parts to maintain their planes to safety standards! They couldn't buy the equipment from abroad, and there was no home industry in making airline parts. Was the plane substandard? Had that contributed to the collision?

My mind was exploding; there was so much information to digest. How had the MiG pilots ejected in time? If they'd known they were on a collision course, why didn't they try to divert? Why was the Libyan fighter plane in civilian airspace? There were too many questions.

Ellen came down the stairs with the children, freshly bathed and in their nightclothes. I sat for a while in the lounge, cradling my two children and saying, 'Mummy and Daddy love you' over and over. Then I let Ellen lead them upstairs and listened to my friend's voice softly lull my children to sleep.

I waited. Whom could I call? I didn't want to worry my mother-in-law, and my mother's cries of 'Lord, don't let it be true' would not have helped at this point. I looked at the phone, willing it to ring. Willing it to be Victor. Willing the life we had built together to go on. Yes, he should have rung by now; he should have called to reassure me. But if his journey was on schedule he would be on the ferry now. Perhaps he didn't know of the air disaster; perhaps he couldn't find a phone to use. He would ring and put my mind at rest first thing tomorrow when he docked in Malta. It was the only hope I had.

Ellen came down the stairs from reading a bedtime story to the children. The TV was off now; there would be no more news broadcasts until nine o'clock. We sat quietly. Ellen wasn't in a hurry to go, and there wasn't anything else I could do.

The shrill of the intercom buzzer pierced the hush, blasting through the air and disturbing the only quiet moment I had had all day. I looked over at Ellen. I didn't want to hear the intercom buzz. I would have run if the phone had gone, but the buzzer had alarmed me. The heavily plumed voice at the North Africa Desk of the Foreign Office had offhandedly mentioned that if they heard any details in the night they often sent the local bobby around to inform the families. I didn't want a visitor. I didn't want to hear the news they might bring.

Chapter 4

There were no policemen at my door. But there were three men in suits, their faces bloodless; a grey, lifeless color. They were from Victor's work.

I motioned them into the lounge room. The children's toys littered the room and unwashed cups and plates lay randomly around. I went to pick them up and offered tea. They accepted, and I went into the kitchen to put the kettle on. Two of the managers followed me and one stayed in the living room to talk to Ellen. I could hear him thanking her for staying with Mrs. Prazak.

'What does he mean?' I said to the men who had followed me.

'It's not good, Mrs. Prazak, I'm sorry. Victor was driven to Benghazi airport by one of our employees this morning…' one of the men started.

I had troubled focusing. The manager was looking at a widow's face, my face. He looked into death itself: that moment I was dead.

He had to try to tell me what he knew. 'We contacted our man in Tripoli to find out what he could. He went to the airport and asked around. The second plane landed safely at Tripoli Airport but the driver was sure Victor had taken the first plane of the day, the one that the military plane struck. He found out it came down on its approach to Tripoli Airport. It crashed fifty kilometers south of the airport.'

I looked pensively at the manager's face. This still didn't mean they knew Victor was dead. He could be alright. He might have missed the first plane and taken the second plane. It was only an hour later.

'No one saw him at the airport,' continued the man, 'so our men went to the dock. Usually they wouldn't be allowed in as it's a restricted area, but he talked his way in. He searched for an hour and didn't see him.'

I wasn't going to concede so easily. 'No,' I said, 'that doesn't prove anything. Maybe he missed him.' But I knew the man at the docks couldn't easily have missed my husband. Victor was larger than life; if he grew his red fiery beard he was like a Viking warrior. It would be easy to spot him among the dark-skinned and olive tones of the local Libyan people, and even among expats he was distinctive.

Mechanically, I made the tea, and the other manager joined us in the kitchen. I didn't have any energy left to even move back to the lounge. They sipped their tea but didn't drink it; it was just a prop in a scene in a play.

The third manager offered his condolences, saying, 'I'm very sorry, Mrs. Prazak.'

The managers stayed in the kitchen for the best part of an hour. Before they went to go, I had to concede that if they were right I had to ask difficult questions. I managed to get out the words: 'If he was on board that plane, would you arrange to bring the body back home?' They promised they would. Promises are only made to be broken, but I have no doubt they meant what they said in that moment.

They left, and I lapsed into an automated state. One minute my only worry had been getting up to Northampton to be at my mother-in-law's in time for Christmas. Now I was wondering about getting my husband's body home.

'They said they would take care of everything,' I recited to Ellen. 'But they're not certain it's Victor, they're not sure. No one's said they've seen his body. There's nothing official yet.'

We watched the nine o'clock news, and then the ten o'clock news, and finally Ellen turned the TV off and put her arm around my shaking shoulders. 'Don't watch any more, this is eating you up,' she said. She prayed with me. I didn't mind: God's words were always beautiful to me, and Ellen meant well. But God couldn't save him if he was already dead, so what was the point in praying? I wanted to say.

When Ellen left I sat all night on the sofa. I must have drifted off to sleep at some point because I was awoken by Tallena crying out. I went upstairs to comfort her and to check on Theo. Then I made a cup of tea for something to do, and I sat down to wait for my husband – my life, my soul mate, my whole world – to call. For there was still some slight shred of hope in me.

With the time difference I worked out that he would ring between eight and nine as soon as the boat docked. The tears came and went; the clock seemed to tick away my hope. Maybe the ferry was a bit late. That happened sometimes in choppy seas. I would give it a bit longer, between nine and ten, I told myself. The children came down, and I left them in their bedclothes; I didn't even bother to get them breakfast. I tried to imagine him getting off the boat and walking through passport control. I thought of him picking up his suitcase, always filled with presents for us. Victor had a knack of finding unusual mementos – huge pieces of petrified wood, desert roses, gold bangles, so many I had to beg him not to buy any more for I could only fit ten on my arm.

The phone interrupted my thoughts, and I dived for it.

'Hello…' my next word was going to be 'darling', but then a man, a man I didn't know, said, 'Hello, Mrs. Prazak?'

I choked out a barely audible, 'Yes.'

'This is the Foreign Office…' He hadn't finished but I didn't want to hear any more. No, I thought, I don't want to talk to you; I don't want to hear anything you have to say. Don't talk to me now; you didn't want to know me yesterday, don't try to pretend you want to help me now.

'What is it?' I asked.

'I'm afraid I have very bad news for you…'

The phone dropped out of my hand and I slumped down on the hallway stairs. I let the cord dangle in the air and the receiver bobbed up and down. I could hear the man calling, 'Hello, Mrs.

Prazak? Are you there?'

Finally, I caught hold of the receiver and put it to my ear. 'I'm here,' I whispered.

'I'm sorry, but your husband's name is on the manifest for yesterday's air crash. He was the only Westerner. I'm very sorry.' The offhanded tone I had come up against yesterday had now dissolved into pity.

'But who has identified him?' I wanted to know.

The man said he was sorry but the bodies had been badly burnt in the explosion and it was hard to recognize anyone. 'I'm terribly sorry, but his name is on the list,' was all he could offer.

I stared through the lounge door to the Christmas tree, standing bare, ready for a family to decorate. He wasn't coming back.

The man from the Foreign Office gave a few more details and then left his number. I managed to get myself together sufficiently to explain that my husband's work would repatriate the body for burial. I asked if I could give them his number to contact to make arrangements. 'Of course,' he said. I didn't bother to hang up the phone; I left it dangling in limbo. I fell back down on the hallway steps and cried my heart out.

The children were alerted by my inconsolable crying on the stairs and came out to hug me. I didn't know what to say to them. How do you tell a three- and four-year-old that their father is dead?

As soon as I replaced the phone it rang. It was Ellen. I tried to get out the words, but all I managed was, 'He's... he's... he's...'

'I'll be right over,' Ellen said.

I hugged my children and waited for my friend to arrive. Ellen took one look at me and pulled me into her arms, saying, 'I'm so sorry.' Noticing the tears in the children's eyes, and my inability to say anything to them, she quickly bundled them off to the park to give me some space.

The restless night and the state of my clothes made me look

and feel like a wreck; I would have to get myself together for the children's sake, I decided. Truthfully, I wanted to do nothing but cry, but I made myself shower and dress. I turned on the TV to see the midday news and watched blankly. There was nothing, no mention of the plane brought down. It was yesterday's news.

The phone went and I answered it, although I did not feel like talking to anyone.

'Hello, Mrs. Prazak,' the voice said, 'this is the Foreign Office again.'

I think I managed a 'yes'.

'I have to inform you that your husband is being buried this afternoon in two hours' time, in a mass grave.'

I was startled from my comatose state. Ice had cracked on the frozen lake beneath my feet, suddenly dunking me in freezing water. I went under the surface into the inky-black depths and as I came up I shouted, 'NO! NO!' Then I was submerged again, my lungs filling with water. 'No!' I said over and over again. 'No, they promised they would bring the body home! My husband's firm is going to fly the body home. They promised me they would!'

'I'm sorry, Mrs. Prazak,' said the man. 'It's very hot over there.' As if that meant anything to me. 'He's being buried at two p.m. local time. It's the custom to bury the dead within twenty-four hours.'

I didn't think to ask, whose custom? What about my custom? What about my right to go to my husband's funeral? What about my right to bury my husband? Why hadn't they even asked me to attend?

'There is nothing any one can do,' said the man as I desperately argued. 'We don't have an embassy in Tripoli.'

There was no point in belaboring the conversation any longer; the Foreign Office official had delivered his message.

I was stunned and traumatized. The latest news had been a bigger shock than hearing of my husband's death. I had at least had the best part of twenty-four hours to let this sink in before it had become the official line. The suddenness and finality of being told he was going to be buried in a mass grave in two hours left me mortified.

I heard small footsteps and children's laughter coming from the outside corridor. It had been a good move to take the children outside; at least they seem to be enjoying themselves. Their faces dropped when they saw me; the atmosphere was immediately subdued and they walked in quietly. Ellen took one look at me and gauged something else was terribly wrong.

'I'll take the kids tonight,' Ellen offered. 'I'll send Don around with a sedative.'

'I'll be alright,' I said, knowing I was lying.

I waved goodbye to the children and looked at the clock: it was after one p.m. I just knew I couldn't be alone when they were burying my husband. I grabbed my car keys and drove to a friend in Clapham.

'What's the matter?' Terry asked as soon as he opened the door.

Inside, as I related the story, he sipped his scotch and said softly over and over again, 'Jesus, Mary and Joseph. Jesus, Mary and Joseph.' By the time the clock had passed two p.m., burial time, he had moved on to, 'Bloody Jesus, Mary and Joseph. Bloody Jesus, Mary and Joseph.'

A little over 24 hours since the disaster struck and now my husband was buried in the ground in some remote arid location in the Libyan sub-terrain dessert. They had buried all the crash victims at one site. One day he was alive and well and full of anticipation at being with his family, and the next he was wrapped in sack cloth and thrown into the ground.

Back home that night, I sat on the sofa as I had the night before. The longest night of my life. The newsreader the previous day had recounted that the Lockerbie bombing had occurred on 21st December, the longest day. But the cusp of the winter solstice was between the 21st December and 22nd December, and it was not the longest day. It was the shortest day. How could they get that wrong? I thought. The disaster had happened on the darkest day of the year.

My mind worked furiously. I had been stripped of my right to go to my husband's burial. No one had invited me to the gravesite to watch the bodies being buried. No one had said a few words in his honor. Victor had been left to rot as if he meant nothing. The Foreign Office had said nothing of counseling. Didn't they arrive in the town of Lockerbie in their hordes? The official had said nothing of a trip to Libya. Didn't Pan Am fly the relatives over from America within hours of the disaster? Didn't the families of Lockerbie put them up and offer them condolences and anything else they could do for them? Had no Libyan family thought anything of the foreigner who had died along with them? Or his family?

I wanted to ask the Foreign Office a dozen questions. I knew I had no hope of speaking to anyone now and chances were the office would be shut for Christmas tomorrow. Why hadn't they left me an emergency contact number? Surely someone had to be on duty?

I had to tell the children. How could I tell the children? I had been scathing of Victor's mother's failure to tell him that his father – an officer in the Czech army, possibly a spy – had died when Victor was a boy until weeks later. But now I understood. Saying the words to the children would make it too real.

I found my mind drifting back to a holiday we had taken the year before. Snow was deep on the ground as we drove up the mountain pass on our journey to Czechoslovakia. Victor was an excellent driver and I trusted him implicitly at the wheel. We gazed at the magnificent scenery; the pine trees heaped with snow scattered randomly over the mountain terrain. In the back, the children munched biscuits as they, too, took in the breathtaking views.

We were beginning our descent on one of the highest points of the range when we hit the ice. There was no salt on the road; it had not been gritted since the last snowfall. Before I could form a thought we were skidding into a crash barrier, then plunging down the road. Victor expertly maneuvered the vehicle, keeping off the brakes and instead changing down the gears and letting the car flow. We travelled the next few hundred yards at top speed, swerving and gliding over the iced road as if on an ice rink. Finally, Victor took control of the car again. He pulled over as soon as he could and we rested on the side of the mountain, looking over the edge, knowing we could have been at the bottom. Certainly, if the crash barrier hadn't been there, we would have plummeted over the side and down to the rocks below. It was hard to tell if the children were screaming from delight or panic. Both I and Victor said nothing and hugged each other and then the children, who decided it was time to cry.

Later, at the hotel, Victor described the near accident in detail from his perspective. 'As if travelling through space,' he had said. Was that how it had been for him, at the end, on the plane? I wondered.

It was not the right time for death on that icy mountain road. Had it been Victor's time yesterday? Or was it evil that had taken him? The evil of man: nothing to do with God. It was a question that would plague me for many years to come.

Chapter 5

The news spread fast. The phone rang off the hook; the house was full of people coming in and out to offer condolences – friends, family, members of the church. The words that were supposed to comfort me in the following days were thrust deep into scripture that poisoned my spirit. The Lord taketh away? Why? I wanted to yell back at people, 'How is he in a better place!' My husband was buried in a mass grave in the Libyan Desert! But my husband had taught me not to snap at people. So for him, in his memory, I listened and thanked people for their kind words; they meant well.

Toby, the pastor, had planned many funerals before. 'Do you want to talk about the funeral arrangements, love?' he asked delicately when he came to visit.

I looked at him blankly, unable to say anything. I would have no hand in planning or organizing my husband's funeral. 'It's all over!' I blurted out. 'I couldn't even go; they didn't even ask me. They have already buried Victor.'

'You could still do a service,' Toby began to explain.

'Yes, of course.' I slouched my shoulders forward, not convinced that I could do anything at the moment.

'It's very important to hold a service, even if you weren't able to go to the burial,' he said as gently as he could. He had worked somewhere in Scotland where the main income for the area was fishing, he explained. Sometimes, in the rough seas and gale-like conditions a fisherman was swept overboard. There was little or no chance of survival in such treacherous conditions and the body was sometimes lost to the mercy of the ocean. Toby knew what families needed in such circumstances.

I agreed. It would be very meaningful to those who grieved Victor's passing. I thought very deeply and quietly prayed to God to help me do the right thing. Finally, I said, 'I would like it to be a thanksgiving service. I want to thank God for Victor's life. I can't do anything else.'

When Ellen returned with the children, I knew it was time to tell them. As I sat with them, crying, I struggled to form the words. I thought of starting with 'Daddy's gone', but that seemed inadequate; no finality. 'Daddy's not with us any longer' sounded like a divorce scenario. The words 'Daddy's in Heaven' entered my mind, but I didn't want any confusion. But simply saying 'Daddy's dead' was beyond me. Ellen looked on as I tried so earnestly to explain to my children that their father was dead, the children looking up at me, tearful and silent. Finally, she stepped in and knelt down, all four of us huddled together on the floor. 'Your Mummy wants to tell you that your Daddy has died,' she said. 'He died in a plane crash and they buried him near the plane.' The worst had been said. My children clung to me, hugging and kissing me. I had no doubt they understood what they had been told.

Christmas Day. I had offers aplenty to spend the day with friends, but I turned them down. I needed space. I wrapped the presents for the children with silver foil from the kitchen and brown paper – I hadn't got around to shopping for wrapping paper. When the children descended the stairs they looked timidly at the tree. 'Why don't you open your presents,' I said lovingly. They looked at each other and then asked if it was alright. I hugged them and said, 'Daddy would want you to be happy.' Their faces lit up with the mention of their father and they took the few presents under the tree and handled them delicately as if they were breakable.

A friend came at lunchtime and took the children out. With the children having some semblance of a normal Christmas, and having barely slept for the past three days, I lay down on the sofa and shut my eyes. The peaceful sleep that I had yearned for soon took over my aching body, but rest did not come as the nightmares I had been afraid of attacked me.

I was in a different universe and I was violently tossed about in a galaxy that was God's battleground. I physically reached out to hang on to every good deed and every wonderful work that my husband had done, while a beast of another realm brought up evidence against him – that this faith was not strong. I couldn't let go, I had to fight with all my might and every prayer I knew to save his soul. This wasn't an imaginary world; it was a spiritual world that human forms didn't enter. The attacks continued to rage in darkness; in limbo. I battled along with God's warriors to save Victor's soul. I knew all the good things he had done since we had met. This alone should be enough to save him. Faith had nothing to do with it. How good, how kind, how loving he had been was what counted at this moment.

When I woke up, I couldn't move. The phone rang and I tried to get up, but nothing worked. I couldn't move my legs, my arms, I couldn't turn my head. If I was crying there were no tears flowing down my cheeks. The nightmare swelled with hallucinations and had left me completely drained and in a frozen paralyzed state. I felt like death myself. My husband was dead and no one could bring him back. I could feel my mind screaming but no sound came out of my lips; everything was locked inside. Hours later, I felt a release in the hold over me, and I staggered to the kitchen to get some aspirin and something to eat. I had not given my body any fuel to sustain itself in the past few days and I knew I had to take better care of myself in order to look after the children.

The pastor phoned with a date for the Thanksgiving Service: 3rd January 1993. I threw myself into arrangements as a way to cope. There were hymns and readings to choose, the order of service to prepare and invitations to send out. Those who were at our wedding would have recognized the invitation: we had bought a job lot and had loads left over, but now, instead of writing of a union, I wrote of a separation, a final farewell.

The day arrived, and for the first time and only time in my life my young son and my tiny daughter and I sat in the front row of the church. The choir sang as people took their seats and the pastor welcomed the congregation to the thanksgiving service for Victor Charles Prazak. Extra chairs were brought out for the people at the back and after that they stood – a congregation three-hundred strong. Our focal point was a large black and white photo of Victor mounted on a thick grey paving stone and surrounded by petrified wood and desert roses: Vic's treasures of the desert. On one side stood a smaller framed photo of Victor with me and the children; on the other I had placed one of Victor with his mother and two brothers.

The crowd was silent as I rose to read my scriptural passage: John 14:2: In my house there are many rooms... I managed to speak without crying. I wouldn't allow myself to fall to pieces; it was not an option. It comforted me to see the many faces there, and afterwards so many commented on how lovely the service was. I knew that Victor would have been looking down, smiling at his family, and be so proud of me.

He would do the same, I was sure, some seventeen years later, when, surrounded by bishops of the Church of England in the heat of the Libyan Desert, I finally stood before his grave and committed his soul to God.

Chapter 6

Aged thirty-six, a widow with two young children, I had no choice but to retrain to be the breadwinner. Teaching seemed to make sense as it would allow me to be there for the kids after school and in the holidays. The foundation course I had done as a fill-in to pass the time while my husband worked abroad was actually the stepping stone for my access into university. I threw myself into my studies; it gave me an opportunity to work some of my grief out through my artwork. My paintings were raw, full of pain and sorrow. Then I progressed to the PGCE teaching training certificate.

It was a hellish time. We were all grieving, I was ill and exhausted and the children missed me while they were with the childminder – I refused offers of help from members of the church; I did not want to be dependent. The doctor saw my exhaustion and suggested anti-depressants. 'What good would that do?' I said. I knew I had to keep going and I didn't want any drug to help me cope. I wanted to feel the pain; I needed to feel the loss. I didn't want to wipe it away and walk around in some daze pretending it didn't exist, or the suffering I was going through wasn't real.

My children were my everything, but mothering alone while trying to carve some kind of career was hard, so hard. Like the time, right before I completed my PGCE, that Theo broke his arm badly and needed to be hospitalized. I blamed myself for buying him rollerblades two sizes too big so he would grow into them. I blamed myself that he had to stay in a strange place without me. I blamed myself that I was letting down the school I was training at by taking time off to visit Theo; that I was falling behind with my coursework. I blamed myself for leaving Tallena with the childminder who was registered and known to the school, but not warm and caring, without her big brother there to watch out for her. As hard as I tried, it was impossible to please everyone, to manage life without Victor.

Money was a concern. When Victor's final salary payment was made into his account, it was half of what I was expecting. His work had automatically stopped any salary being accrued the day he died, even though he was due leave pay: he had just served two months in Libya and the third month leave would have accrued when he was on holiday.

All that was in his bank account was exactly enough to pay the mortgage in France. The French bank wanted proof that Victor was on a commercial, not a private, airline in order to pay off the mortgage for the French property (under French law, I was not allowed to sell the property, part of which now belonged to my children, until they came of age). They also wanted the death certificate, which the Foreign Office said could take three to six months to receive from the Libyans and would be in Arabic. It took months of legal red tape to prove to the French bank it was a civilian plane, and in the meantime I still had to make the monthly repayments of over a thousand pounds or else I would be severally penalized under French law – I could have gone to jail.

These were the worst weeks of my life. I was struggling to get up in the morning and feed and clothe the children, let alone think about payments and mortgages. I wondered about selling the council house to cover the French mortgage payments, but it was worth so little – and where would we go? I mustered up the first payment, and then a letter arrived from the Department of Pensions with a check of a thousand pounds: an unexpected one-off payment for the death of a spouse. This covered the second payment, but by the time the third month came around other debts for the London flat were mounting, and there was still no news on the death certificate. I knew I would receive a widow's pension in time, though it was a pittance; it was staggering that the government thought a woman could bring up two very young children on such a measly amount. Then I remembered Victor had once told me about the benevolent fund of the Institute of Engineering:

'I pay my dues every year,' he had said. 'If anything ever happens to me, you can claim up to a thousand pounds.'

'I don't want to talk about any such things!' I had retorted.

'Yes, but you should know about it,' he told me lovingly.

I wouldn't entertain any thought or mention of death and dealing with it. Why was he even telling me? He was only thirty-six.

Six months after that fateful conversation, I found myself calling the Institute. A gentleman sat in the lounge for two hours and grilled me, taking reams of notes. But to my relief, they granted me the full one thousand pounds, which covered the next payment, and then the death certificate arrived and I was released from the mortgage in France.

Once the dust settled, I found myself a lawyer to deal with my husband's death. The payout from the airline company finally came three years after my husband died. I was devastated by the amount: sixty thousand US dollars, which converted at the time to forty thousand pounds.

'That's just one thousand pounds for each year for the children until they reach their twenty-first birthdays, and nothing for me,' I told the lawyer when he phoned to ask whether I would agree to the settlement. 'What if I don't agree?' I wanted to know.

'If you don't agree to the amount, we would have to find a lawyer in Libya,' the lawyer informed me. 'I must admit I've never done that before, and I don't know anyone who has. With the sanctions in place, there are no diplomatic relations with Libya and it's virtually cut off from the Western world. There isn't even an Embassy, since the policewoman Yvonne Fletcher got shot outside the Libyan Bureau in 1984.' He was keen to unfold all the pitfalls of finding a local Libyan lawyer. 'Who knows how much English he would know? His fee would have to be considered, and the time frame would have to be reconsidered. This offer is on the table now. They could come back with an even lower offer.' He had to be realistic. We had waited nearly three years, and as it was money had to be passed by the Bank of England to come into England from Libya. The fact that it was airline insurance money and not Libyan money was in my favor now, but they might take a different view of things if relations continued to spiral downhill with Libya.

'How would you go about suing in Libya?' I asked.

'I have no idea,' the lawyer told me honestly. 'Both the civilian airline, Libyan Arab Airlines and the military are owned by the state. The supreme leader of the state for both institutions is Gaddafi.' He paused to let this sink in and then continued, 'You would effectively be suing Gaddafi, who is answerable to no one.'

What hope did I have? In truth there wasn't a choice. Would any lawyer in Libya actually take a stand against Gaddafi? It was a lottery I had no chance of winning. And if a law case dragged on for years, how would that affect me and the children? At least if I settled now I would be able to move from the rough council estate into a modest house with a small garden, away from the painful memories that haunted me in our flat, and get some maintenance work done for the house in France the French system was forcing me to keep, though I neither wanted it nor could afford it. Perhaps if there were a normal relationship with Libya... But I was led to believe the governments were completely cut off from each other. I couldn't even get my children into Libya to visit their father's grave. How could I possibly sue the state that hadn't even done the right thing and offered a passage for us to travel to Libya?

Signing the affidavit to release the money felt like a betrayal. I didn't want to admit that my husband's life was worth just sixty thousand dollars; it wasn't true. I wanted to scream and tear up the paper. 'I'm so sorry, darling,' I whispered to the air as I signed, as if an angel had come to take the message to Heaven for me.

I thought about Victor, and the manner of his death and burial, constantly. At first, I struggled to accept he was gone. With no body or remains, not even his clothing from a suitcase, something I knew was his, there was no evidence that he been killed in the disaster. Why hadn't they removed his wedding ring, or his gold chain from around his neck? I had heard of scavengers, even at crash sites. Had someone taken these items from him as they hurled his body into the pit where all the victims of the crash were buried? What had they done with his luggage? Some precious T-shirt or novel, even his Bible would have been the proof I craved so that I could fully believe my husband was dead. I imagined him being saved from the fall from space by landing on a tree that had acted as a safety net. He could have lain unconscious for days before anyone found him. What if some nomadic tribe had found him in the desert and nursed him back to health and he had lost his memory? I wanted to clutch on to anything that had an ounce of possibility. Love would return. He would return. I knew I was being absurd; that I had to bring myself back to reality. I needed to accept that he was dead. But I only felt half alive; like my life was meaningless without him.

The part of me that could accept reality clamored for answers. Why was the MiG in civilian airspace? Had Gaddafi commanded the MiG to set a collision course for the passenger plane? If so, why? Had the MiG fired missiles as was rumored? Could this have been an attempted coup against Gaddafi, whose plane was due to be in that airspace at the same time, orchestrated by the West to get revenge for Lockerbie, as George Bush Senior had fervently promised before he went out of office? Time after time I asked the Foreign Office to request the crash report. But they hid behind the curtain of sanctions and shrugged their shoulders and said there were no diplomatic relations with Libya.

For the last four years I had contacted many people in my quest for answers. I even tried writing to Colonel Gaddafi himself. In my naivety, I thought he would respond with compassion and offer me some resolution. Finally, an answer to one of my many letters: the Head of Missions for the Libyan Bureau finally agreed to meet me. The meeting, in Harley Street, London, was not the battleground I had expected. The Acting Ambassador invited me into his leather-bound office, gently nodded for me to sit down and charmingly asked if I would like tea. He had received my letter and understood my position and he would do what he could to help, he said. He would ask the Libyan Government what they could do, and felt they wouldn't be opposed to offering scholarships for my orphaned children, as he put it. I was pleased with the meeting, but when I rang a few weeks later to check to enquire of the Head of Missions' progress, a secretary bellowed, 'He is not here anymore; don't ring this number again,' and then hung up.

Not long after this I learned that the Libyan diplomat had been thrown out of the country by the British Government. It was an era of tit for tat. If one of their diplomats had been expelled from Libya then the cycle was set in motion. Though I had never made a political statement in all my life, I was caught up in a game of politics.

This episode knocked me for six, and I slowed down my pace in seeking justice and answers. Then, one day, I was trawling through the loft, looking through the many papers I had received and deemed to be fob-off letters from the Foreign Office and various ministers who had sent sympathy but not facts. Maybe I had missed something, I told myself; perhaps there was a name or fax number of someone who may be able to help me. By the light of the lamp my husband had crafted years before – the result of the electronics course we had attended – I sifted through papers. I put aside Victor's old love letters, unread since his death; I could not bear to look at them now. I scanned through the old official paperwork, blue for the Foreign Office, yellow for the MPs. Suddenly, the words 'identified from his passports' caught my eye. I would have seen the letter before, but now the words finally sunk in. How had I missed it? Why had I gone all these years fantasizing that he would be found alive, that somehow the mid-air collision and the missiles that were reportedly fired from the warplane had not blown him to smithereens? I stared at the letter until I knew it all by heart. The Foreign Office had the proof I needed to accept the finality of Victor's death.

My conversation with the Foreign Office that afternoon was frustrating; as were all dialogues with officials in my experience since Victor's death. They were poorly informed, lacking in compassion, indifferent and reluctant to help. The conversation ended with the noncommittal words, 'I'll see what I can do.'

I had never had anything back of Victor's at all. A few months after the air disaster that killed my husband one of his co-workers from the camp in Libya had phoned me to say they had recovered his Bible and he would send it to me, if I wanted it. I was awestruck. Had they found it in the desert? Was it on him? Had he gone to Tripoli and recovered anything else of Victor's? I could think of no other way that the Bible would be in his possession unless it had been found at the crash site. His name would have been in the inside, as I had written it there when I gave it to him. But when the parcel from the colleague arrived, I felt my world destroyed all over again as I tore open the wrapping to find a hardback blue cover of the King James Version. The Bible I had given Victor was red and the New International Version. This was the Bible Victor had left behind at his camp. It was a cruel blow to me.

But now I had the chance of something concrete. Finally, the Foreign Office called to say that they had Victor's passports (he had two, as did all expat workers in Libya at the time) and would I like to collect them. And so I made the journey to a sterile office.

It was such a personal moment; I wanted to give it respect and reverence. It was a moment to be at peace, or at least be as near to my husband's last day on earth as I could.

'We need you to sign for them,' the official said carefully to me once I was seated across the desk from him. 'This old style of passport was designed to withstand a nuclear blast, so they're fairly intact. But you might want to brace yourself a bit; they were quite damaged in the fire.' I waited while he opened the sealed envelope. Pausing for a moment, he carefully let both passports slip out of the manila envelope onto the table.

Picking up one of the passports that were lying on the table, I found immediately my hands and fingers were covered in soot. The burnt embers were as fresh as the day of the disaster. Turning the pages slowly, I saw that some corners of the first few pages were charred and burnt away but the rest of the pages were there. All the details and the photo were still there, even *Tallena Prazakova* written in my handwriting under *enfants*.

The Foreign Office official handed me a tissue. How thoughtful of him to have a box ready to blot my tears, I thought, until he picked up the passports, put them in a clear plastic bag and then wiped his hands distastefully. I left his office clutching the last piece of my husband.

Chapter 7

Finding the passports was like reclaiming some of my life. The years of pretending he wasn't dead were over. And so were the years of avoiding questions I did not want to ask.

Had that UN embargo on buying any spare parts or maintenance equipment for their civilian airlines contributed to the disaster? Were the pilots able to read their equipment accurately? Or had the equipment used by the air traffic controller at Tripoli Airport malfunctioned? Had the warplanes carrying live missiles misfired? It was rumored that Gaddafi's private jet had been due to approach Tripoli Airport at that time; had the passenger plane been mistaken for Gaddafi's jet and fallen victim to an attempted coup? I had heard George Bush Senior had said he would get revenge for Lockerbie before he went out of office. Were the Americans involved? The Foreign Office were not impressed by my questions, and dismissed them, keeping to the official line, which was that the mid-air collision was a tragic accident. I was supposed to accept this, though there was no inquiry or crash report to confirm this interpretation of events.

I didn't know what had caused the air disaster; I needed evidence. How could I, a lone woman, caught in the immediate aftermath of shock and tragedy, stand up to a regime that had caused terror in the Western world, and now the United Nations, which controlled the puppet strings? I was up against two giant warlords.

Because my husband was the only Westerner on board the doomed plane, there was little interest; in marked contrast to the Lockerbie bombing, which often cropped up in the news. A year after Victor's death, I had got in touch with Dr. Jim Swire, the spokesperson for the British families of the Lockerbie disaster. Libya was the common thread between the two atrocities. I attended some of the Lockerbie meetings; I went to a remembrance service for the families at the chapel at Heathrow for the fifth anniversary. I was honest with Dr. Swire about my feelings towards the UN for their sanctions that prohibited the importation of airline parts; although I didn't believe this was the only explanation for what had happened, it was important for me to be transparent. Jim said, 'Something very sinister happened there. We are all very shocked and sorry if what we have done has contributed in any way to your husband's death.'

All the members of the Lockerbie group were welcoming. I would listen to the business at hand and the next piece of evidence for the Lockerbie families to unravel. The conspiracy theories abounded, and who was to say there was no weight to them? The CIA was deemed to have been smuggling drugs through mules from Palestine and the whistle was about to be blown on them. The revenge attack for the downing of the Iranian Airbus by the US naval warship *Invincible* also surfaced more than once. They never gave up and they never let themselves be fobbed off with all the lies they heard. It was evidence they needed, though. Tirelessly they campaigned, overturning every stone and piecing together the jigsaw puzzle.

The blame eventually came to rest on Libya. In a political climate where no one admits to doing deals with a terrorist, Jill Morrell stopped campaigning for her 'boyfriend's' release that week and the two headlines that dominated the papers were the release of John McCarthy, Terry Waite and Brian Keenan, and the blame cast on Libya for the bombing of Pan Am 103. The media had coined the phrase 'Mad Dog' in association with Gaddafi, and painted a picture of a vicious beast. The West began to persecute him for this crime and many others – from the La Belle disco bombing in Germany to the French UTA flight that exploded over the Sahara Desert. I wondered why they had stalled so long before shifting the blame onto Libya. Libya had become a pariah state, allegedly sponsoring terrorism and supplying arms to the IRA. But weren't the Americans also doing that? Wasn't it contradictory to say that one source could supply the arms, but if you waved a green flag, it was forbidden? I wasn't condoning the supply of arms; it just seemed a double standard to me.

Three years down the road, did the Lockerbie families feel any relief that the blame had finally come to rest on the culprit who had destroyed their lives? Or did they too start to question what they were being fed through the media and the politicians?

Dr. Jim Swire had already picked up on the comment in Margaret Thatcher's memoirs that 'the truth will never come out' with regard to who was behind Lockerbie. He, rightly so, wanted to know why. What truth was so horrible that they couldn't tell the relatives' families, or the press, or the public? What was so frightening that it had to be hidden from everyone?

A key piece of the puzzle was that the Pam Am flight had been only half full when it was bombed; what plane is half full at Christmas time? Then I met a man – a policeman and an Oxford graduate – who recalled he should have been on that ill-fated flight Pan Am 103 flight to New York, but had been bumped onto a United flight leaving at a similar time. He hadn't questioned the move; he'd just done as he was told. Was it just a random act that had spared his life, or had his connections in the police force – which the Lockerbie group suspected had received a warning of the bombing – acted in time and saved his life?

My mouth gaped open at the revelation. The speculation was no longer just a rumor; this was hard evidence. 'Did you keep your boarding card? Or ticket? Anything?' I urged the man to tell the Lockerbie families of his displacement that day, but he wasn't interested in helping 'fuel their fantasies'. He wouldn't, or couldn't, talk. Still, my discovery helped confirm what the Lockerbie group had long suspected and would later come out: that the CIA had received a warning of the attack. On 5th December, sixteen days prior to the bombing, a man with an Arabic accent had called the US Embassy in Helsinki, Finland,

and warned that a Pan Am flight bound for the United States would blow up.

Through the Lockerbie meetings I got to know a number of people with whom I had an immediate bond. I exchanged telephone numbers and e-mails; occasionally I went to a gallery or a show with people I clicked with. Most of the members of the group were parents of victims just touching adulthood, but I did meet bereaved spouses, some of them, like me, mourning victims of other disasters than Lockerbie. One of the most moving testimonies I heard was from a widower who had been on the plane that had come down on the motorway in Manchester. Many had been killed on board, but he had been among the survivors. The man had been in the back of the plane, and his wife next to him had died. He was torn up with guilt; why had he survived when so many others hadn't?

I met a widow of Lockerbie at the launch of the documentary on the disaster, and we struck up an unusual friendship. Art was a common bond. She was an artist, and like me she explored her grief on canvas. Caitlin invited me on many occasions to private views of her art exhibitions. There people would ask inanely, 'How do you know Caitlin?' I wanted to tell them the truth: 'Our husbands were both killed in plane crashes.' But it was unwarranted to expect people to cope with such a commonality.

I clung to the friendship with the Lockerbie families. They were a support network for me. I remember a speaker in the group saying one day, 'There are two types of people in the world: those who have been through a terrifying tragedy, and those who haven't.' The words stuck with me. I belonged in the first category; I knew the pain of losing a loved one so violently and inhumanely. The question I asked myself was, what was I going to do with this knowledge?

A lady from the group had set up Disaster Action, a support organization for those affected by devastating catastrophes. She asked if I would speak to people from time to time who may be able to identify with me and with my experiences. I agreed, and some days later a young student studying art phoned me. She had lost her mother in a plane crash in Nepal. I encouraged her to express her pain and loss through her artwork, and I attended her art shows. It was some consolation to know I could be of comfort to someone else.

Contact with the Lockerbie families helped focus my own search for answers. But try as I might, the Foreign Office continued to tell me their hands were tied because the British and Libyan governments didn't talk to one another. I was not convinced. 'Of course you talk to each other,' I told an official who was weary of me, as they all were. 'How can there be any progress if you don't talk to each other?' Nelson Mandela had flown to Libya to intervene and persuade Gaddafi to hand over the two Libyans suspected of blowing up Pan Am flight 103. 'How can you not be talking to them if Nelson Mandela is there as mediator?' I pressed.

How could they channel their resources into one air disaster, but deny me any help at all? I understood that Lockerbie had caused the death of forty-three British citizens, while the collision in Libya had taken just one British life – but to me, Victor's life was just as valuable, and justice just as essential. With Lockerbie, it was so clearly a terrorist act that had caused the loss of life. But it seemed to be easier, somehow, to dismiss the Libyan Arab Airline disaster as an accident – a mid-air collision caused by faulty equipment, or perhaps human error. To this day, sources such as Wikipedia list the collision of Libyan Arab Airlines Flight LN1103 with the MiG as an accident. But I was convinced otherwise; as would be any rational person surveying the (limited) evidence.

I was pleased the Lockerbie families were making progress; they deserved the truth. They learned how to ask the questions, and there has probably not been one minute in their lives since the atrocity that they have accepted what they have been told by officialdom. The compensation they would later secure of ten million dollars each for their loved ones paid by Gaddafi to bring retribution for the sanctions didn't bring closure or truth. The campaign to know the truth fueled their lives, and so it became their life. They effectively lost their own lives to pursue justice.

I admired their stamina and I tried to justify my own shortcomings at not always spending every minute of my life locked in a battle to open doors to know the truth. Many families had lost sons and daughters. The Syracuse students returning to the US were a prime example. Their parents were established in life, many powerful and wealthy. Their loss was as great as mine, but their position in life meant they had the means to fully dedicate themselves to seeking the truth. Most had a partner to rely on, they had their careers established and they were financially secure. I had lost my partner, my best friend and soul mate, and I had to bring up and support two very young children on my own. I did what I could to plead for justice and compassion, but I didn't have the option of dedicating my whole life to the cause.

Dealing with Libya was like wolves devouring sheep. I was the sheep who had strayed from the flock. There was safety in numbers if the sheep stayed together, but a lone sheep stood no chance against the ravenous wolf. The shepherd, the British government, should have helped; but instead it closed the pen, leaving me shut out, totally alone.

There was no one to depend on or even fight my cause with. My husband had been the only British citizen on that flight – mostly they were Arabs, from Egypt, Sudan and Chad, and of course Libyans themselves, who were largely from Benghazi. That was why the Foreign Office wanted to close their eyes to what had happened. They called it an accident, but they didn't know that. There was no inquiry or crash report to confirm this.

I had to continue to fight for answers as to why and how my husband had died, but, as Victor would have wanted, I also had to continue to live my life, and to build a future for our children.

Chapter 8

Botswana, 1998

We arrived at a barren wasteland, open plains all around, nothing but baobab trees and tumbleweeds that blew when the wind stirred a little. It was like seeing true wilderness for the first time. We were coming to the end of our ten-hour journey from London, via a refueling stop at Johannesburg, to Gaborone, the capital of Botswana. I sat with the children – eight and nine now – in silence in the hot car, just looking at the vast open space, nearly devoid of any life apart from the sparseness of the vegetation that reminded me of the Australian bush landscape of my childhood.

It was a new beginning. Better schools and a better life, I repeated to myself. Unable to cope with my life in London any longer, I was looking for a more relaxed pace of life. I didn't want to read newspapers that told stories of six-figure payouts to people who couldn't take the pressure of their jobs, or had been called a name, or branded a racist, or had to cope with repetitive strain injury. Britain had become a sue-happy culture; there was big money to be made from litigation. The last straw had come when a worker who had lost two fingers in an accident was awarded forty thousand pounds; the same sum I'd been awarded when I was left a widow and single mother to two young children when my husband was blown to bits by a Libyan warplane. I had become jaded, cynical, sick of fighting the British government, exhausted, demoralized. It was time to regain my life, and I felt I could not do that in London. So I took up my first real role in teaching for the Botswana government on a two-year contract.

We spent our first two weeks at the Sun Hotel, while I attended workshops and basic language classes. The five-star luxury was to cushion the fall into basic school accommodation at the end of the induction fortnight. Teachers were assigned anywhere in the country. The married couples, whether teaching couples or accompanying spouses, nearly all ended up in Francistown, the second largest town in Botswana after Gaborone. It was an exciting location, right by the Zimbabwe border and the gateway to the Okavango Delta. A lone teacher might find him- or herself in a remote village hundreds of miles from anywhere.

'We have to keep you in Gaborone,' an official from the government told me, to my relief, 'because of your children, Mma.'

I was pleased they had given it some thought. But unpredictably, the children's schooling was causing some concern. Had I booked places? Were their names on the waiting list? Where would they be going? I hadn't considered any of these questions; I had understood places were guaranteed for my children. Private education was part of the package I had signed up for. The salary was not much more than was paid to local staff, and the reason I had decided to try teaching abroad was so that my children would get a good education.

The two-week induction period at the hotel was an opportunity to meet the other teachers recruited at the same time and establish some friendships. Fitting in was difficult for me. There were thirty-five teachers, and I was the only one with children. Most were young, right out of university, just twenty-three years of age and beginning the most exciting phase of their life in Africa. In the evening, after the daytime classes were over and dinner eaten, a large group of them would join up a few tables and sit in the warmth of the air around the patio, drinking large quantities of Castle beer. You could hear them talking and laughing until the small hours of the morning and then the next day, bright as a button, they would be up early for the workshops. I liked a drink as much as any of them, but I preferred sitting at the outside bar by the pool. It was always difficult for me to be in crowds: I was tongue-tied, hated attention and self-conscious if I ever spoke. I got to know some of the others, though, chatting quietly to whoever sat by me, and the chuckles of laughter that infiltrated the youngsters' conversation always caused an eyebrow to raise or a glimpse over their shoulder to see what the commotion was.

Once the honeymoon at the hotel was over we moved on to our schools. The transition bordered on regressing back to colonial days and the first settlers. Taking a deep breath I looked around before charging into my new abode. The large, open-sided yard was typical dirt, not a blade of grass insight. A few trees and hedges provided some greenery but not much shade. An overgrown vine that extended onto the roof would have to come down for fear of snakes and vermin living in it. The furniture comprised a cupboard, a dresser and a bed in each of the two bedrooms, a two-seater sofa with two single chairs and a table with four chairs and TV in the lounge; three people in a two-person house was going to be a squeeze. There was no fridge, no washing machine, no hot water. I had packed all sorts of kitchenware and mats and homely items to make our compound house a home, but it would be another four weeks before the luggage arrived. We would have to make the best of our new surroundings, and for tonight at least I would be sharing my single bed with my daughter; a little like sleeping with a dancing octopus, I discovered.

The next day I was to start work at the school at six fifty a.m. The children still weren't enrolled in a school, so I had to leave them in the school compound and check back on them during my morning break. The school day ended at two, and it was the first opportunity to meet the head.

'No, Mma Prazak,' the head said in answer to my request for a larger house, or at the very least a third bed, 'this is unacceptable. You can't see me without making an appointment. And anyway, we do not provide three beds. A two-bedroom house has two beds, that is the way it is.'

'Well,' I said calmly, 'I would not have come here, Mma

Jwaneng, if I had known you expected me or one of my children to sleep on the floor for two years.'

But it was impossible to reason with the woman, so, after another restless night's sleep tangled up with my daughter, I decided to sleep on the small couch.

A friend from the teacher workshops at the Sun Hotel, Drew, came to stay at the Cresta Lodge hotel opposite the school compound while he waited for his apartment at another school to be ready for habitation. I began to visit him at the hotel with the children in the long, hot afternoons, and we would sit and share horror stories of settling in while the children frolicked in the cool water of the pool, getting some relief from the fierce sun and tediousness of the afternoon. So began a routine I would continue once Drew moved on: I would walk across with the children and take afternoon tea while the children swam; the staff would assume I was a guest staying there.

The first long week of school finally came to an end. This Saturday was the school sports day to be held at the stadium, and I was told to report there at six fifty a.m. When I woke at eight a.m., late, I considered throwing on my clothes and dashing off to the stadium. But while it was all very well leaving the children in the house while I was working, when I could easily check on them in a free period or break time, being off site was another matter. It wasn't sensible to take the children to the stadium; they had suffered one severe bout of sunburn when they first arrived in Gaborone. Had the head been more accommodating in granting me another bed, which I saw as a necessity and part of the package that I was entitled to, then maybe I would have felt a sense of responsibility to stick to the six-day week imposed on me. But right then, I was sick of sleeping on the sofa, I was tired of forcing down rancid butter and sour milk spoiled by the lack of a fridge, and I wanted to buy Theo, whose birthday was the next day, the bike he so badly wanted.

I decided the sports day would manage without me; maybe I

would call in for an hour or two to show my face mid-afternoon. I didn't seek permission from the head; I had not made an appointment, I told myself, and it was Saturday when I should have been off, not going to a sun-drenched stadium. I would face the head's wrath on Monday, but today I was going shopping.

My stomach churned from the sour milk; it hadn't even kept overnight without a fridge. I thought I should have felt a little better, though, with the sleep-in until eight o'clock. The children thankfully had declined any offer of cereal or toast, so they weren't feeling the same ill effects I was. At least, I thought, I had a valid reason to give Mma Jwaneng for not attending the sports day.

Had the phone in the house been working properly I would have ordered a cab to collect us from the house. As it was, we had to walk to the main road to go in the cramped combi bus, the local form of transportation. We made it to the shops, but the trip soon proved to be an ordeal: the uneasy feeling in my stomach gave way to cramps of increasing intensity. Finally, I could take the pain no longer and slumped to the pavement.

'Mum, you're sitting in the gutter,' Theo said.

'I can't get up, I can't stand.' I tried to mask the alarm in my voice. I must have food poisoning from the rancid food, I thought. All I could do was lean over and rock to and fro. Time seemed to stand still. Theo and Tallena didn't know what to do to help.

Theo sat down beside me and put his arm around me. 'Don't die, Mummy, don't leave us,' he begged.

'I'm not going to die, darling,' I reassured him. I couldn't bear the expression on the children's faces; the same one I had seen the day I told them their father was never coming home.

A taxi pulled up by the curb. 'Are you alright, Mummy?' the taxi driver asked.

'Can you take us home, please,' I stuttered.

'Are you sure you don't want to go to Princess Marina?' This was the state hospital, and I had heard how the AIDS patients were laid out in the corridors.

'No, just take us to the school by Cresta Lodge, please.'

Back home, the children made me a cup of tea with powdered milk we had bought, and I slept. When I awoke an hour or two the pain had gone. But that evening, it returned with a vengeance. Now I was scared. Three weeks before leaving the UK I had found myself in hospital with the same acute pain. I had stayed in for three days on a drip while the hospital ran tests, but eventually the pain subsided and the medical staff assured me I was okay. Besides, they said, they were sure there were very good hospitals in Africa, should I need them.

I lay down on the bed, clutching my stomach and rolling about in agony.

'What can I do, Mummy?' Theo asked.

'Maybe I should ring Rhoda at the British Council. I might have acute food poisoning,' I told them. But the blasted phone didn't work, not for outgoing calls.

'What about May and Peter's phone?' Theo suggested. May was an expat who also worked in the art department; Peter was her husband.

It was now nine p.m., and I was reluctant to let the children go out in the dark. Dogs sometimes roamed about in packs and the night noises could startle them. But they were more scared of their mother's current plight than any bogey man in the bush. So I let them go.

Thankfully, Peter burst into the house ten minutes later, and an hour later I found myself in the nearest private hospital facing a long, dark night that was a blur of agony and pleas for more pain relief. At some point they wheeled another trolley into the room bearing a young girl who was bloodied and sobbing and crying out a name I couldn't make out. It was torture listening to her. In hushed tones I was informed that the girl had been gang-raped and her boyfriend beaten to within an inch of his life. It was his name she kept calling.

Finally, around sunrise, a nurse took my blood pressure and temperature and immediately paged the doctor. He arrived, and then called another doctor at once. I listened, in a haze, to their exchange.

'We're losing her.'

'We need to get Doctor Wilkinberg here now.'

'But it's Sunday. He doesn't work on Sundays.'

'This isn't work; this is saving a life. Get the theatre ready now and call him, we can't wait.'

It was all dreamlike, fuzzy. My husband was sitting at the end of my bed. I looked solemnly at him and thought, why doesn't he come closer? Deliriously, I thought about a verse someone had shared with me when my husband died: 'I am going to make a place for you, and I will come back and take you with me' (John 14:2). Had I misunderstood the message all these years? Was my husband coming back to take me with him?

Then, nothing.

I woke up that afternoon dazzled by stark white walls that illuminated a brilliant and blinding light that seemed to be shining right at me. A surgeon approached me and lowered his face mask; he still had on his surgical gloves, cap and apron. He said gently, in a South African accent, 'We nearly lost you. You're a lucky girl.'

I did not feel lucky; this was not quite the new start in Africa I had envisaged. But I was alive, albeit with one heck of a scar. The surgeon had sliced me open from four inches under my breast to my lower abdomen, going right through my belly-button, a full twenty inches from north to south, and then from hip to hip, travelling east to west, another incision of twenty inches right across the lower part of my body, in his effort to clean out all the poison that had invaded my body from my burst appendix. I was proud of my war wound, my souvenir of Africa. It was symbolic of my life that I was still alive: a reminder of how thin the line is between life and death. I had beaten death; I had stayed with my children. I had done what my husband had been unable to do.

Chapter 9

Tripoli, Libya, 2000

Seven years after the crash, the Foreign Office called, just before I finished the contract in Botswana, to tell me that the Libyan government had offered to allow me and the children to visit Victor's grave. I felt like I'd won a bout in a boxing ring. All the letters to members of Parliament and foreign secretaries over the years had finally paid off. A new British Ambassador, Richard Dalton, was in place in Tripoli, and I had met him with the Lockerbie families once or twice in London. He had been able to persuade Libyan Arab Airways of their sense of duty to all of the victims' families, not just the Libyans. His promise that he would see what he could do had been honored, and I felt some redemption for mankind: at last, someone had stood up and helped me.

I had become aware that after any air disaster the airline offers free passage for the victims' families to travel to the place of the disaster, to aid with the grieving process. Libya had offered me nothing. I learned later that Libyan Arab Airlines did charter a plane in the early years to travel from Benghazi, where many of the victims came from, to Tripoli for the day on the anniversary of the disaster. It is customary in Muslim culture to mourn the dead once a year and stay all day at the gravesite. But never had I been invited to this annual pilgrimage. It was as if I didn't exist. My husband was buried in the mass grave along with all the victims. I needed to be at the cemetery as much as anyone.

Finally, though, my children were to be permitted to pay their respects to their father. They were eleven and twelve now. Theo had some memories of his father, which I thanked God for, though Tallena was just too young to remember. I would remind my children constantly what a lovely father Victor had been, and that he still loved them. I was sure his love had never died, and I wrapped my children in it.

The Foreign Office recommended that I take up the offer sooner rather than later. Reading between the lines, I knew they were dubious as to whether the offer would last: relations were still tense. But times were busy: my contract finished in Botswana, and we moved back to London. Then, finally, in May 2000, the children and I boarded a Libyan Arab Airlines jet as guests of the airline. It unnerved me a little to take my children on the same carrier on which my husband had died, but I couldn't turn down an offer that I had spent seven years fighting for.

As we touched down at Tripoli International Airport, I unclenched my eyes. I no longer sat at window seats; I was haunted by the thought that the last thing my husband had seen as he peered out of the small plane window was a Libyan warplane coming directly at him. The heat was overwhelming as we stepped off the aircraft, but it was the vastness and emptiness of the surroundings that possessed me. Once before I had encountered that sense of isolation in the wilderness, when I arrived at Botswana to start a new life there. Now I was back in Africa, and I let my soul be overtaken by nature. No one really owns anywhere, I thought. It is all God's. The Botswana savannah had captivated my heart, and the Libyan Desert could do the same.

It was a rude beginning to the trip to be interrogated by a passport control official at the airport.

'Why have you come to Libya? Where is the children's father? Is he Libyan? Have you come to see him?' he demanded of me in his heavily-accented English. A young, white, Western woman with two young children was an oddity in this desolate place.

I explained the purpose of my visit, but the man's English education had never covered such vocabulary as 'grave' and 'killed'.

The fifteen minute grilling could have turned into hours of

interrogation had an airline employee not stepped in and spoken to the passport officer in Arabic. I watched the severe expression on the official's face transform into one of contrition, and he said to me, 'I am very sorry,' then stamped the passports and waved us through. Whatever mask the airline officials may have been wearing, I took them at face value. To me, they had a duty of care, and the passage of time had not diminished their responsibility.

Four men from Libyan Arab Airways took us to a moderate hotel where we checked in to an ample room. Nothing was ostentatious, but it was adequate. We unpacked – I hadn't known quite what to pack, because I didn't know how long we would be staying; no one had discussed the length of the trip and I hadn't asked – and got what rest we could in preparation for the next day.

The next morning breakfast was served to the room. The tepid soft-boiled eggs, processed cheese triangles, indescribable meat and black, cold coffee were unappealing, so the children and I made do with orange squash. As I waited for the call I knew would come, I thought back seven years to when I had first been here, in Tripoli, waiting to visit my husband's grave.

Back then, I had waited six months for a visa to travel to Libya. I came via the ferry from Malta, chaperoned by a work colleague of Victor's. It was during the sanctions, and I was only allowed three days in Tripoli, alone, without the children. When the phone had rung in the hotel bedroom on my first day I had assumed it was the work colleague ringing to see whether I was up. Instead there was a man on the line who said he was from the insurance company. I hadn't even remembered whether I had told my lawyer I was travelling to Libya, and certainly the work colleagues would have no interest in contacting him. Yet this man knew I was in Libya and what hotel I was staying in. He asked to meet for coffee at half ten at the hotel coffee shop, and, intrigued, I agreed.

The Arabian style coffee shop was quite tastefully done up.

My main concern was whether the coffee was drinkable. I sat down and ordered a cappuccino. When it arrived, I took a sip and smiled in relief.

A man approached me and asked, 'Mrs. Prazak?'

I looked around the coffee shop; a few people were scattered about. I was the only Western woman; in fact, I was the only woman. It wasn't hard to identify me; but then, I was sure he already had a good idea who I was.

'May I sit down please?'

The waiter approached and he ordered coffee and looked politely over at my full coffee.

'Yes, I'll have another one,' I said, determined to be polite.

The man introduced himself; even though he had said his name on the phone I hadn't caught it. He handed me a card and it was much easier to visualize the pronunciation when I saw it in writing. He did not elucidate how he had known I was in Libya, or how he had known the hotel and room number. He explained that he was a lawyer who represented the airline, and he had some papers for me to sign and a copy for my lawyer. He didn't need me to sign right then, and I was grateful for that. He was polite and efficient, and having passed the papers to me, he quickly took my leave.

I stayed for another coffee after he left and tried to fathom out the meeting. Were they just checking me over? Was my every movement being watched? I had called my children to let them know I had arrived okay – had they listened to that call? I came away from the meeting not knowing what information he had gleamed, or what to make of the encounter. I never saw the man again.

Now, seven years on, the phone rang, piercing my thoughts. A very friendly, polite voice welcomed me to Libya. The man's English was excellent, and something about his manner set him apart from the people I had met the day before. The man, Mohammed, said he was waiting downstairs in the lobby for me.

He left me with no clue as to what to expect of the day ahead.

By the time I had walked down the flight of steps to the small reception area there was no one there. I had left the children sleeping; there was no point waking them until I had an idea what was going on. It was a pleasant enough hotel, although small, but it had no pool. I knew the secret of a successful holiday with my children was if the hotel had a pool so they could spend the day splashing about in the water.

Hearing my name being called, I looked around the reception area. The voice was coming from outside on the patio. As I stepped outside a man who commanded authority, in his late forties or early fifties, invited me to sit down. He introduced himself as Mohammed, and said he was in charge of customer relations for Libyan Arab Airlines.

In excellent English he asked me, 'How do you like the hotel?'

Had we been staying for only one or two nights, I would have said everything was fine. I blame the lack of a decent cup of coffee for my response: 'I don't.'

Not one hair moved out of place and he continued to smoke his cigarette and coolly said, 'I am very sorry, Mrs. Prazak. We will find you another hotel.' He didn't even ask what was wrong or why I had decided to give the thumbs down on what otherwise was a pleasant hotel.

Hopefully, I considered us moving to another hotel, this one with a pool to occupy the children. They would become bored otherwise, and boredom always led to fights. Was it natural for a brother and sister to fight so much? It was as if he had read my mind.

'How are the children?' Mohammed enquired. 'Did they sleep alright? We will find a large hotel with a pool. It will keep them happy.'

Mohammed had arranged for me to meet with the chairman of Libyan Arab Airlines. It was my chance to ask questions and seek answers. I was unsure what I would ask him, but I knew I needed him as an ally. I knew that, if I wanted this man to help me, my best approach was to tell him what he wanted to hear, not my views. But I wasn't good at playing the game; I had proved so in job interviews where I stood up for my principles and my beliefs about education rather than demurely deferring a headteacher's ego.

Later that day – after a move to a new hotel – I found myself granted an audience with the chairman of the airline company whose aircraft my husband had died in. As I sat in the leather armchair across the desk from the chairman of Libyan Arab Airways, I was aware of the power game playing out in the room. Just a few minutes into the meeting, I knew it wasn't going well, and it spiraled downhill rapidly from there.

I knew the airline itself had no money, and I was not asking them to compensate me. The forty thousand pounds I had received as settlement had come from the insurance company registered under Lloyds, not from the airline or from Libya. But I tried to open a discussion about the money that Libya had paid to compensate families for actions they were considered liable for. There was the UTA flight that had taken off from Chad and had exploded en route to Paris. I had read that France had held a court case and found Libya guilty *in absentia* even though Libya had not been represented in the courtroom. Libya had paid compensation to the victims' families. Libya had also compensated the family of the policewoman shot outside the Libyan Embassy in London: they had quickly and quietly given the money to the police fund for the disadvantaged. And then there was Lockerbie. I knew these were facts, not just journalists' claims; my contacts at the Lockerbie meetings had confirmed that these payments took place.

The chairman shook his head in disagreement. No, Libya would never pay any such money for something they did not openly accept was their responsibility.

'But Libya has done this,' I argued.

He did not believe me and said, 'You have to go back to the insurance company if you want more money.'

I had no intention of doing so. I knew there was no chance of getting the insurance company to offer more money. What I was looking for was an advocate to speak on my behalf to the Libyan authorities, to make them understand that the payment I had been given was totally inadequate for our life in London and an insult to my husband's life.

The chairman could not be budged, and I knew I had rubbed him up the wrong way. He patently had no clue what his government did in the West. He thought it outrageous that his country would pay for a crime they would never admit to. And the woman sitting in his office had the affront to mention Lockerbie. What was that in connection to my loss? He might have given his apologies to me when I first entered the room, but Lockerbie, UTA or any other atrocity was nothing to do with the airline.

I felt I was sinking into a bigger black hole and didn't know how to climb out of it. Trying to salvage what I could of the meeting, I implored him again to help. I mentioned the promises that had been made previously: my children's education, for one thing. Perhaps I could do a commission for the airport, I suggested. I was confident that my art was good enough to go in the Tate Gallery. It could be to honor everyone who lost their lives on board flight 1103.

'We would have to ask the relatives whether they would agree to anything like that,' the chairman retorted.

I was getting nowhere. I was starting to wonder what I was doing here, in this office, in Tripoli, in Libya. My eyes rolled over to Mohammed for help.

'We could fly Madam Prazak and the children to Benghazi for a few days. She could visit her husband's place of work in Ras Lanuf and then go and see the ruins at Cyrene,' Mohammed proposed.

'Yes, yes, of course,' the chairman said, waving his hands about. He appeared to suddenly remember the role he was to assume: to be seen to be playing nice with the widow and the two children who had lost their father. 'You are very welcome any time you want to visit Libya, madam. Anytime. You can come as our guest and stay as long as you like. Please. We will arrange everything. Visas, accommodation, flights.'

It was clear this was the final offer on the table and time to make a move. I looked at Mohammed and he echoed the chairman: 'Just let us know when you would like to come. You are welcome any time.'

On the way back to the hotel Mohammed started making plans for the trip to Benghazi. As we pulled up outside the hotel he announced, 'This is the program…'

I hid a smile as he outlined an itinerary; now we had a 'program' of events. It was my first smile since the tense meeting that I was still mulling over.

'… I will look after you while you are in Benghazi and take care of you,' finished Mohammed.

That evening I surveyed my appearance anxiously in the mirror in our hotel room. The British Ambassador had invited me to the Queen's birthday celebration. It was the event of the year in Tripoli, and a host of people would be attending.

'You look lovely, Mummy,' Tallena complimented me.

I smiled, but inside I was shaking. This event was way out of my league, and my comfort zone. Still, I enjoyed people watching, and the opportunity to have a glass of wine was also very pleasing in a dry country.

When I arrived, the garden was full with an array of people in beautiful cocktail dresses and dashing partners. The Ambassador recognized me straightaway and I was delighted when he directed his broad smile at me and he said, 'Ah, Felicity, a friendly face.' At that moment I forgot my attire, which didn't measure up to the splendor of the other ladies', and felt a million dollars. I decided then that I would paint a picture to give to the Ambassador, to express my gratitude for his help in bringing me and the children to Tripoli.

During the course of the evening I found myself in conversation with an officer of Libyan Arab Airlines, who had noted the special interest Mohammed took in my case.

'Mohammed thinks he's number two in Libya,' said the officer scornfully. He went on to insinuate that Mohammed was on good terms with the leader of Libya, Gaddafi.

It was a comment that lingered with me and I laughed awkwardly but said nothing. It was an interesting idea. Perhaps Mohammed would forget me as soon as I left Libya: did he really think I would want to come again once I had seen the country that had robbed me of my husband and our life together? Still, I would keep in mind that Mohammed would be a powerful ally.

After the party, I found myself feeling buoyant, almost. There was a feel of being on holiday, of make believe. I was unaccustomed to being looked after so carefully: nothing was too much trouble for Mohammed. He took the children horse riding; he took Theo to a specialist shop to get his PlayStation chipped and to buy games for next to nothing at the flea market. In what could have been an inhospitable city, he showed us hospitality along with compassion and consideration. He would come and see us nearly every day to make sure everything was alright and to see whether we needed anything. The children liked him too; he had a way about him that commanded respect. Tallena commented that when Mohammed told the other workers from the airline to do anything, they jumped. One night we saw him on the news on Libyan television; he was a commanding presence in his handsome Libyan attire.

Mohammed made our stay in Tripoli one to remember, and without meaning to, I fell in love with the city. It was a love that wasn't understandable; the type instigated by chemistry, not sense. I adored the ruins and the old souks; they lent themselves to spending hours and hours drawing and painting scenes from history as if captured in it.

Then it was time to go to the grave, and Mohammed brought flowers for us to take there. Now we would put frivolity aside, and make the journey for which we had come so far: to Victor.

Chapter 10

We entered through a big iron gate set in tall walls that enclosed the whole cemetery. Dirt paths scrambled off in all directions. There was no order to the haphazard arrangement: newly marked graves mingled with older, white-washed mud slabs among the patchy, straw-like grass. The horizontal rectangles of the graves stood barely a foot off the ground. The dead lay under them. No plaques, no names. Some had a date scratched onto the surface or a word written in Arabic that had been carved out before the wet mud had dried. The families, I was told, knew where their loved one was buried, and it was customary not to put a name. Families came once a year, and stayed all day. That was the Libyan way.

I looked out at the vast expanse around me. It was still fairly early in the morning and the heat was bearable; the sun was not yet in its full glory. Already my shoes were covered in sand and dust. I jumped a little at unexpected movement as tumbleweeds lifted off with a slight wind. There was no other soul there, just the three of us and our Libyan guide.

To one side of the cemetery I could see a small white mosque with a green-painted roof. Some trees gave a little shelter from the sun, casting a shadow that became sinister if you looked too long at it. Beyond the walls of the cemetery, I could see the dry land outside. We seemed to be standing in a basin, and I felt completely engulfed by the landscape. Sheep or goats could be heard in the distance, and then I saw them move across the rocky terrain outside. And there was a lone herder, walking a few paces behind his flock or herd. A buzzard encroached on my space, flying in and out of the trees scattered around the cemetery. This was a lonely place, full of isolation and abandonment. There were no tombstones to read, no mourners, no fresh flowers to bring color or life to this desolate wasteland. How had this become my life?

I carried my Bible with me. It may have been a Muslim cemetery, but my husband was a Christian. I took a red rose from the bouquet I'd brought. I opened a page – it didn't matter which page, they were all God's words – laid the delicate flower between the pages and rested the book on a rock that had pushed itself up through the ground and lay exposed to the world, the dry grass edging its outline. I took a photo for a keepsake. Sometimes I did this type of arrangement to use later in my artwork. This one was just for the moment, just for remembrance, just for love.

We moved on a little further to where the mass grave was. As we walked I pictured the bulldozers taking this path, loaded with bodies. The plane had come down a few miles away, and the bulldozers had come in to lift the bodies and scattered limbs that the Muslim faith prohibited the rescue workers from touching. Finally, we were there. A vast concrete area. Paint on some lines and it would look a lot like a car park. A tall brick wall enclosed two of the sides. It wasn't even a neat bricked wall, but a substandard effort put up with no care. There was a railing at the front, to stop people walking directly onto the grave, and I was pleased by that, but the third side was open, protected only by a few graves that had been there before the mass grave was marked out. By the railing was a marble slab, a little out of place, and next to it stood a plaque listing the names of the crew of the airline with the date (not of the disaster, strangely, but of the following day, the day of burial) and the flight number, engraved in Arabic.

A wave of despair shook me. I had been forbidden to lay the brass plaque I had made for my first visit, seven years ago; forbidden to mark my own husband's grave. Thankfully Bishop Martinelli at the Catholic Cathedral allowed me to place it there, along with a photo of Victor. I didn't want to appear ungracious, and I was careful not to say anything, but I was devastated to see there was now a plaque at the site commemorating the flight crew who had lost their lives. It was allowed for them but not for us. I was careful to hide my trembling in front of my children. They laid the large bouquet down and took a white rose each from the cellophane that encased it. Theo stood with his arm around his little sister and we prayed together, thanking the Lord for Victor.

As we walked back to the car, arm in arm, my mind played over and over in a constant loop the words that should have been on the grave we were leaving behind:

Victor Charles Prazak
Born 1st March, 1956. Northampton, England
In memory of a loving husband and father
Tragically killed in a plane crash in Libya, 22nd December, 1992
'At home with the Lord' 2 Cor. 5:8
Our eternal love, Felicity, Theodore and Tallena.

Chapter 11

London, 2002

The applause was nearly deafening, and there were only some thirty people in the room. Elation swept through the air, circling the crowd who were standing by now. The morning had been incredible: we were in an audience with one of the most famous men in modern history.

The Lockerbie families had sought a meeting with Nelson Mandela, who had been instrumental in getting the Libyan leader, Colonel Gaddafi, to release the two suspects for trial in the Netherlands. Libya had boycotted the sanctions on South Africa and President Mandela had not forgotten their loyalty. They made strange bedfellows. Mandela had won world support and Gaddafi, world hatred.

The trial had eventually taken place, and much of this was down to Nelson Mandela's mediation with the Libyan leader. The group wanted to thank the former South African president for stepping in and finding a solution to the deadlock. I had asked if I could tag along, and the Lockerbie group were more than happy to put me and my children on the guest list.

I wore a black dress for the event, a symbol of my widowhood. Theo was casual but passable; my daughter, on the other hand, refused to take off her baseball cap littered with logos, and proudly insisted on bringing the project she had done in Black History Month the previous year. Along with the hours of research my daughter had done for the project she had read Nelson Mandela's autobiography, *Long Walk to Freedom*.

'Do you think he will sign my project?' Tallena had asked. She was awarded an A star for it and she was just in Year 7.

'I'm sure he will darling. And your hat too, if you want him to.' We laughed together at the joke, knowing Tallena wouldn't take her hat off for anybody. Not even Nelson Mandela.

We had arrived at South Africa House in Trafalgar Square on a sunny July afternoon in an optimistic frame of mind. The atmosphere was buoyant with expectation. There were press and security present and a small crowd of onlookers who had heard that the South African president would be there. The meeting with the Lockerbie families was completely closed. There would be no photographers and no press. It was a rare private interview between a statesman and ordinary folk who had an extraordinary story. I felt it was a privilege to be included in the session.

South Africa House had arranged the meeting room with a table at the top where Nelson Mandela would sit flanked on either side by his wife, Graça Machel, and the South African commissioner. A program had been set of forty-five minutes followed by questions, then an opportunity if people wanted to have their photo taken with the ex-president, followed by afternoon tea. There was a window of two hours before his press conference in another room of the Consulate.

As I sat in the room, waiting for the entrance of the African leader, I struggled to ground myself in this place, in this moment. How had a small-town girl like me come to be in the presence of one of the icons of the twentieth century? I hoped very much to have a moment to speak to him. Clutched in my hands was a gift for the great man.

A friend of mine, Yo's husband was an artist and he had been commissioned to create a statue of Mandela. The position of the artwork was causing great debate: with the Consulate facing onto Trafalgar Square, it seemed the most logical place to site the iconic statue; but some British people were up in arms, declaring Trafalgar Square was exclusively for British dignitaries. Several times I had been to my friend's studio and seen the famous statue in the making. It was such a privilege to see the development taking place.

One day, just before my visit to South Africa House, Yo mentioned, 'We've been invited to a function to celebrate Nelson

Mandela's birthday next week. They're hoping to announce where they'll put the statue. Mandela is supposed to be there, so I hope they're diplomatic about it.'

Perfect, I thought; I would bring a gift for the former president; something he could remember me by. I hoped I would have an opportunity to hand him my painting of a baobab tree from my days in Africa.

Gazing around the room, I wondered whether there were secret police or bodyguards planted in the room. I scrutinized the faces, trying not to be obvious. A few people caught me looking at them and gave a cheery wave. Smiling back, I estimated I knew most of the faces from over my years of attending the Lockerbie meetings. These people had always included me and cared for me and I loved them. I was the only outsider there apart from a man who had lost his sister in the UTA disaster.

The audience chatted among themselves for a few minutes, waiting for the guest of honor. Suddenly, chatter dimmed to murmurs and hushed to silence. You could have heard a pin drop when the women, adorned in colorful native costumes, and Nelson, in his trademark casual shirt, appeared like apparitions in front of us. Instinctively, the audience rose and applauded. Waiting graciously for the clapping to stop, he bowed gracefully to the families and gestured for his wife and the commissioner to take their seats before he sat down himself. The audience followed suit.

Taking hold of the microphone, Dr. Jim Swire introduced himself and then gave a vote of thanks to the man who had made the Lockerbie trial possible. His speech was eloquent and humbling. Jim had a knack of delivery, which is why, I supposed, the families were grateful that he was the front man for the press. He indicated to the crowd that after President Mandela's delivery to them they would have an opportunity to put questions to him.

President Mandela was an advocate for prison reform and there was no one who could deny that he had earned the right to do so, after spending twenty-seven years in a cell. He had done something for the Lockerbie families; now he was requesting something in return. The families listened attentively, knowing the agenda, but there were not many, if any, that supported him at that moment in his pursuit to have convicted terrorist al-Megrahi returned to Libya to fulfill his sentence. Everyone in the room knew he would not be put into jail, but under house arrest, which was effectively freedom. It was an awkward moment and the Lockerbie relatives knew it would be brought up in the press conference later; they preferred to leave the issue until then, when they wouldn't be present and wouldn't need to comment on it. Wanting only to concentrate on the positive aura of the meeting, the crowd respectfully waited until he had finished.

During question time, a black man whom I recognized from an earlier meeting took the microphone that was being passed around and raised the issue of identity cards in Britain, then hotly under debate as an issue of freedom. Nelson Mandela gave a harrowing account of being beaten many times because he refused to carry an ID card. 'It was not the same as what we went through in apartheid. We could be shot, beaten or sent to prison because we were black in our own country. There is no comparison. Everybody will be required to carry an ID card if they are brought in, but then only black people were forced to carry an identity card and you could not even cross a street without it.' The words had the desired effect. It brought home the injustice and inhumane way in which all black people were treated in apartheid times. The somber moment lingered.

Before the question time came to a close I grabbed my moment. Taking the mike, I spoke directly to the panel at the front. I introduced myself and explained that I wasn't a Lockerbie victim but felt part of the group nonetheless because the Lockerbie families had always helped me. 'We share a connection in Libya,' I said. 'My husband was killed in unexplained circumstances in an air disaster in Libya. I have written a short letter if you have time to read it later. Also, I have a small gift, one of my paintings, because I know it's your birthday next week. I would be very happy if you were to accept it.' With that I stepped forward and walked up to the podium and handed one of the most famous men in the world my painting.

Surprise and gratitude covered the president's face. It was a perfect ending to the close of questions. We were invited to have our photos taken with Nelson, and he hugged each of the people present, myself included, and took the time to look through Tallena's project and sign it for her. He beamed as we all sang 'Happy Birthday' to him.

Still gleaming from the photo shoot and the opportunity to present the painting, I turned around while in line to get my afternoon tea and found myself face to face with Graça Machel, Nelson Mandela's third wife.

'Thank you for thinking of my husband,' she said to me gently. 'It means a great deal to me. I know how you must feel,' she went on. 'I too lost my husband in a plane crash under very mysterious circumstances.' Graça Machel had been married to the president of Mozambique when the UN plane he was travelling on had crashed.

What an astounding woman, I thought. She had married two African presidents in her lifetime and yet had the compassion to seek me out and thank me for my humble gift.

'The pain never goes away, but life can be good again,' Graça Machel said. She looked at her husband across the room and it was apparent that she truly loved him.

Out of such terrible tragedies, both mine and Lockerbie, this incredible afternoon had evolved. The framed photo of me and my children with Dr. Jim Swire and Nelson, as I now called him, would sit on my kitchen wall for years to come.

'Wow,' people would exclaim when they saw it, 'have you met

Nelson Mandela?'

'No,' I'd bait them. 'It's just taken at a wax works.'

I held on to that afternoon; in particular the words of a kind and graceful lady who looked right into my tortured soul and uttered a few simple but heartfelt words that made me feel a little less alone.

Back at home, it wasn't long before my own tragedy was fresh in my mind once more.

'We have the crash report, Mrs. Prazak,' a man from the Foreign Office told me calmly when I answered the phone one afternoon. Stunned, I covered the mouthpiece and asked the builders working in my house to put down their tools, then asked the man on the phone to repeat himself. Had I misheard? All these years later, they had information for me? I hardly dared hope.

'The crash report, Mrs. Prazak, from your husband's, um, accident. Exceptionally, we've had the forty-two page document translated for you, because of the long wait. You should receive it by the end of the week.'

It was like finally reaching the peak of a mountain I had climbed for nine years, always struggling with the next step. But instead of elation at reaching the top of the summit, I was soon tumbling back down, crashing from rock to rock. The white A4 (8 x 10) envelope looked innocuous enough, but its contents were devastating. The report was of another plane disaster that had happened off the coast of Sirte: a private jet belonging to one of the oil firms had plunged into the sea, killing three British citizens on board. I even recalled speaking to one of the widows through the Disaster Action program.

The builders that were fixing the kitchen stopped what they were doing when they heard me screaming and hurried out to survey me on my perch on the stairs and ask whether I was alright. While the builders put the kettle on I took some deep breaths and then picked up the phone.

'Hello, Mrs. Prazak,' said the Foreign Office man dryly. 'Did you receive the crash report?'

'Yes, I did, and it's the *wrong one*,' I said.

'We had forty-two pages translated from Arabic for you,' the man said uselessly.

'Well, you should have checked that it was the right plane crash, the one that my husband died in. It's obvious you cannot do your job,' I said furiously.

'Just a minute, Mrs. Prazak,' said the man defensively, 'the document was translated in Libya.'

'So the British Embassy staff there are idiots too and can't read or they'd have realized they asked for the wrong plane crash. This plane went down in the sea seven years after my husband's plane crash. I will tell you what it's like,' I went on. 'It's like receiving the crash report for the TWA plane that went down in the Hudson and you're waiting for the crash report for the Twin Towers. Do you see what you've done?'

The man attempted to interrupt my tirade: 'This would have happened in Tripoli, Mrs. Prazak. I am sorry...'

I was not letting anyone off the hook. 'Who put it in the envelope? This was posted from London. Couldn't you even check the document before you sent it out?' I was crying again now. 'This is a horrible, horrible thing you have done to me. My husband is dead, *dead*, and this kind of mistake is pure cruelty.'

The man's attitude changed. It was completely their mistake. In the forty-two pages of wrong translation no one in the Embassy in Tripoli had checked to see the flights had corresponded and no one at the Foreign Office in London had picked up on the mistake. He swallowed his pride and apologized genuinely. 'I am very sorry, Mrs. Prazak. I'll look into it to see what happened.'

I didn't bother with goodbye; the tears wouldn't allow it.

'I've made you a cup of tea, love,' John, the builder, said. 'It seems you had some bad news.'

Taking the cup in my trembling hand, I sipped the sweet tea politely.

John seemed to think for a moment, then he said softly, 'We didn't know you lost your husband, love. I lost my wife to cancer. It's hard to lose someone you love.' The builders had been in my house for the past few weeks and I knew he had mentioned his wife having a baby soon. I smiled kindly at his effort to comfort me, but my confusion must have been evident.

'It's my second wife having the baby,' he explained. 'My wife and I had five children together, and she died, and now this will be my sixth child but my new wife's first.'

'Oh, I see,' I said. 'Thank you for your kindness.'

John had shared his private grief with me when he didn't need to, as a way to reach out to me and make me feel less alone.

My meeting with Mandela's wife, and now my kind builder's words, had brought me to a new and valuable realization: you never know someone else's story. The person beside you could have been through so much. Though my grief and pain were an ever-constant, aching burden, I came to see that they weren't mine alone to carry.

Chapter 12

Moscow, 2008

Snow was scattered on the hard ground. Several fresh flurries had fallen since early morning. I stopped at the top of the steps to the metro, Bitzevsky Park, and surveyed the scene. The path, partly hidden by the snow, led to my destination, a short distance away. What was stopping me from beginning my journey, my new adventure? The wind stirred, and first it was hard to make out the shapes on the path ahead. I walked a few steps, and the blurs solidified: a pack of dogs, frozen, looking straight at me. The determination to arrive on time, if not decidedly early, for my new job was foremost. My mind flew back to Botswana, to the half-starved dogs – kept by fellow teachers as deterrents for petty thieves – that would bark as I walked across the school compound. The advice others had given me then rang true now: keep walking, and show no fear. Moving slowly, I edged myself past, my gaze fixed on the ground, avoiding eye contact. The chill of the morning air touched my exposed skin and I repositioned my woolen hat to keep any warmth in. With the dogs behind me – a quick glance over my shoulder confirmed they had no interest in me now – I refocused my mind back on the landmarks that had been pointed out to me the previous day on my orientation visit, when the deputy head, a friendly Welsh chap, had guided me from the metro, past the chemist and through the underpass to the school.

Pleased with myself that I had still managed to arrive early, having navigated a metro system whose signs meant little to me, I reached up and rang the school buzzer. A few seconds later a guard appeared from a hut just inside the school's premises. The school itself was uninspiring, in a poor condition. A former Soviet kindergarten, it was fully enclosed by a towering wire fence with no real grounds, no playground or sports field. The road outside the school was nicknamed 'Millionaires' Row' because the cars that dropped the children off were top of the range, driven by drivers or bodyguards, never parents: this was an exclusive private school patronized by the children of wealthy and powerful men and women; some, it was rumored, in the mafia. The snow lay over a meter high and only the pathway to the entrance of the school was shoveled for access. Where did the students go at break and lunchtime? I wondered.

In my new classroom I carefully wrote MRS PRAZAKOVA on the board. It was a long time since I had penned the full length of my married name. But this was Russia where it was natural to use the female ending for my Slavic name. I waited nervously for my students to arrive. Today was the start of the new term, and I had no idea what to expect. But whatever came my way, I was determined to throw myself into my work. What else was I to do? Theo and Tallena were many miles away in London. I was alone.

When the agency had called to ask whether I would consider going to Moscow to teach, I had looked around at my surroundings: a freezing basement in south-west London. I had spent the past four months there trapped in a Dickensian nightmare: a Scrooge for a boss who forced an Oliver-Twist-esque plea from me for heaters to bring up the sub-zero temperature. I was up to my eyeballs in debt, and living on credit cards. Now an art teacher in Moscow had suffered a massive heart attack, and they desperately needed a replacement to take the Year 11 students through their exams. The contract was for two terms only. At twenty and nineteen, Theo and Tallena were old enough to leave for a while, I thought; it would do them good to have a little independence. Relishing the thought of living in Moscow, a place I'd longed to visit – the art galleries! – I excitedly signed the contract. It was just like a paid holiday to me. The work was secondary to the experience of living and working in the former Soviet Union, the new Russia, the new federation. I toyed with the idea that it could be a new era for me also.

The school day went by in a flash: there were no issues with the classes, and the students had worked well, only too glad to have an art teacher again after an absence of four months. On my return journey I walked confidently past the dogs, which, colleagues had explained to me in the staffroom, were harmless; an oddity of the Russian winter, homeless beasts that sheltered in the Moscow metro system, taking refuge from the harshness of nature. On the train ride home I saw two men hurry to be the first to grab an empty seat, and I smiled, remembering how my daughter and I would do the same on the Shanghai metro when we had lived there three years before; etiquette and logic did not exist in the popular Chinese game of seat conquest.

Back at my new abode, a tiny one-bedroom apartment in a soulless block that was reminiscent of the council estate I lived on in London, I phoned home to check on the children – well, not so much children any more. I had last seen them at Heathrow two days before when I had cajoled them into coming to the airport to share a pizza and savor a few extra moments of companionship and motherhood I desperately wanted to fit in.

They had grown so in the last years, since I had brought my young family back from Botswana despondent and dissatisfied: the new life I craved hadn't materialized. Happily, the Lord had not answered my prayers to make a fresh start and sell up and move to foreign lands: I had rejected an offer of five thousand pounds less than the asking price on our house in London, and had taken in tenants rather than sell. So we had a home to come back to, which helped in our readjustment to city life. After years of bunk beds, the children were delighted to have their own rooms again. They were approaching the end of their childhood and on the verge of adolescence; they needed space.

I got a job teaching at a Catholic school in inner London, where I stayed from 2000 to 2005. It was hard: many of the students had behavioral problems. But it was rewarding when their artwork showed promise. I was proud of my achievements at the school, but each year it got harder. The students became more unruly, the violence increased. I found myself breaking up more and more fights, devoting more and more energy to controlling the classes rather than teaching them. It saddened me greatly that such students didn't care that they were wasting their classmates' precious years of learning.

Then violence spilled over into our personal lives; this time it was my son who bore the brunt. Theo was badly beaten twice between the ages of fourteen and sixteen, and both times he ended up in hospital from the attacks. The first time it was a boy at school. The attacker was taken to court, found guilty and then simply discharged: not even a fine, let alone community service or a harsher sentence for beating my son. The second time, seven youths attacked Theo, who was on his own, when he went to the corner shop to buy a drink. A passerby witnessed the attack and went to his rescue. The local gang had been targeting our house for weeks, mindlessly creating havoc and trying to scare us by breaking windows, ramming my front gate with a concrete bollard and climbing on my roof. The next-door neighbor had put barbed wire around his fence in an attempt to stop them. The area of London we lived in no longer felt safe, and the police did nothing to help ('They'll grow out it,' one police officer told me.)

I decided drastic action was needed to protect us: I took up a position as head of art, teaching in Shanghai, China. There the children did their A levels at a private school, but the contract was only for two years. When I returned home, the only job I could find was working for the Royal Mail.

Now, Tallena had begun a new university course, while Theo drifted along, not really focusing on his life or his abilities. I realized he needed to manage on his own, otherwise I was guilty of doing everything for him, from cooking his dinner to buying his cigarettes. It was time he learned how to operate a washing machine with the added extra of taking the clothes out to dry. The self-learning process was put into place. I would get a tenant to take my room and the money I got for rent would be given straight to the children to do their own food shopping. It was an ideal situation for them: Tallena would be able to save without having to pay for rent or food, and Theo would learn to cook and clean and make some attempt to look after himself. And after twenty years of childrearing, sixteen of them alone, I would build my own life again.

My colleagues at the school were welcoming. No doubt turning up in week one armed with a large box of extra special biscuits from London sweetened them up. It was my birthday, and I received various invitations. I didn't want to overstretch myself so early into my new adventure, and settled for a quiet drink with one colleague. Cole had a quiet manner and there was something about him that interested me. And he was good-looking, and it was a long time since I had been out with anyone good-looking. It had been a long time since I had been out with anyone at all. It wasn't a date; I knew that and preferred that. It was a quick celebratory drink with a new colleague, and it was preferable to being alone on my birthday in a strange city. We passed a pleasant couple of hours at a bar. Cole was surprised when I gulped my beer down a little too quickly. 'I only drink the first one that quickly,' I told him, smiling at his disapproval.

We talked about our lives and our children. Cole was divorced with a one child and had lived several years in Moscow. He colored in his past, but I could tell he was holding back. I talked about my children and my life in London. If Cole had guessed I was also divorced, I didn't correct him. I guarded my widowhood no matter how many beers I had. I liked him and decided he was pleasant and easy to chat to. It wasn't often I clicked so well with someone. For so long, since my husband's death, my children had been the center of my life. Now, I had to admit, I needed some direction of my own. My life had been spent seeking answers that never came. I hadn't let go of the questions, I never would; but I needed more than them now.

As the days went on, I fell into a comfortable routine. I acclimatized to the icy weather; I got over my childlike excitement when it snowed. Apart from the odd prima donna, the students were a pleasure to teach. I drank coffee in the staffroom, and got to know my colleagues. Many were expats and, like me, had no family over there. They welcomed me into their little community.

A couple of weeks into my new position I looked out of the window of my classroom to see a dark and foreboding sky belch out vast quantities of snow. Visibility was minimal. There was no rush to leave the school building: all the students had left and there were lessons to prepare for the next day, plus there was still plenty to do in the art room to make it more habitable. I decided I would keep busy and wait out the storm. But when I went to the staffroom to make a coffee I found most of the staff donning coats and scarves and hats and gloves.

They were surprised to see me working late.

'We're going for a drink in a minute, Fliss, would you like to come?' Cole asked.

'Don't stay here on your own, Felicity,' someone else advised. 'You might get locked in with this blizzard, or worse, if you're on your own and fall, you could be buried for hours under the snow and no one would know.'

Looking at the clock edging its way to five thirty p.m., I said, 'Just give me five minutes to get sorted.' I hurried back to my classroom and grabbed my hat, coat and scarf from the coat rack. Then I turned the light off and closed my classroom door, saying quietly, 'Thank you, Lord.'

We went together to a nearby bar. I really couldn't remember the last time I had sat around a table of ten or more people and enjoyed myself so much. No one was in a hurry to leave the raucous crowd hemmed in for the night by the conditions outside. It was a peculiar feeling on such a cold blustery night to feel so warm inside. The crowd was comfortable to be with. They told stories and joked and no one was the center of ridicule or judgment. It was a different world to what I had known. I had found a place to belong behind the former Iron Curtain.

Chapter 13

After the first four weeks in Moscow it was necessary to renew my visa by returning to London. This fell conveniently on the Russian Orthodox Easter, allowing me a week in London with my family. I was glad of the opportunity to check how my children were coping in my absence. It didn't matter how many times I had told them I had left Australia at the age of seventeen and travelled around the world on money I had earned myself, my children were not going to easily give up the comforts of home and having everything done for them. I hoped that by leaving them they would gain their independence at home.

Theo and Tallena seemed to have coped for a month on their own, if I ignored all the washing Theo had left around. But back in London there was the usual fight for my affection. I couldn't remember a time when the children didn't fight. As the years had gone by they had become more and more physical and threatening, and I had implored them both to grow out of it. I had learned to stand in the middle of fights at school, but I didn't expect to have to do it at home also. People assured me it was natural, normal even, and demonstrated a healthy family life. All siblings did it, they tried to reassure me. But in my family there was none of the 'wait till your father gets home' that so many of my friends fell back on.

There was no question that they would destroy each other while I was gone. The demonstrations of puerile behavior were for my benefit, designed to make me choose which one needed the telling off and which one was the victim. Either way I would lose and upset both children in the process. But without me there, they were best friends and allies, able to encourage and help each other. I didn't have reason to worry about them fighting while I was abroad. It was a show put on for me, and I hated every performance.

There was the usual stocking up of groceries before I left. And there was the new, American-style fridge freezer to put them in: a huge silver monster that stored more than ample food for a month so at least I knew they wouldn't starve for the first few weeks I was gone. I liked to set small goals for my teaching assignments. I was still very much in debt but had calculated that after three months this would be fully paid off, and the offer on the fridge was too good to pass up. It was my dream to have one of the American refrigerators, so I had treated myself.

'Where are you going to put it, Mum?' Tallena asked when the monstrously huge silver apparatus arrived. 'It's too big for the kitchen.'

'We'll put it by the wall for now,' I answered.

'But the breakfast bench is in the way,' Tallena pointed out.

'We can take that off the wall.' I was not going to be defeated.

'Do you want me to ask Danny to do the breakfast bench?' Tallena volunteered.

Danny had been her best friend since starting secondary school. Since Year 7 they had been inseparable. Hardly a month went by without her form teacher or head of year calling home about some mischief that the pair had got into; the fire alarm incident had involved a particularly grueling interview with the headteacher. I was secretly glad my daughter had such spirit. Tallena was bright, as was Danny. Theo, a year older, struggled all the time. He was bright in other ways, but not academically. The loss of his father had damaged him. I worried about him the most; he seemed to be drifting, unable to stick with a job, and he was becoming more and more reclusive as the months went on.

With promises to call soon, and book flights for Tallena to come visit in May for her birthday, I headed back to Moscow. Fleeing the nest wasn't easy. Total freedom wasn't obtainable; there was always a niggling worry in the back of my mind. But the best I could give my children at the moment, I was convinced, was not to be there to do everything for them. I was enjoying Russia, and the children were coping admirably.

Touching down at the airport in Moscow with a three-month visa in my hand, I felt that release of freedom again. My happy little routine in Moscow resumed, and I'd even adopted a new pet, rescued from the basement of the school: a pregnant cat. I continued to socialize with my colleagues, and though I protected my privacy carefully, I got to know rather too much about their personal lives at times.

Cole's relationship with a student, a fifteen-year-old boy, was the subject of some debate behind his back in the staffroom. The boy, Stephen, had showered Cole – who, it emerged, was gay – with gifts, which he had accepted, and had taken him to a concert.

'Fliss, it was all innocent. Nothing happened,' he said to me over a drink one night.

'But you can't go out with a student, Cole, no matter how innocent, and you should have given the gifts back. But hindsight is a fine thing.' I was speaking from experience. I'd had two encounters since my husband had died, after ten long years alone. The first I accepted, because I thought I had cared deeply for the man and that alone had evoked feelings in me that I thought would never surface again. But the other encounter I regretted bitterly. It was at a low point in my life when I thought I would never get out of the empty bottomless pit I had fallen into. The relationship lasted only a few weeks before I came to my senses. There was no way to undo the damage, but I didn't need to stay in the pit because of it. I climbed out of the mire and fought hard to salvage my life again. My success was that I was in Moscow, alive again.

'You have got to let it go, Cole. I can see you can't forget him, but he's only fifteen. You need to meet someone else.'

He smiled, then confided, 'I have met someone, on the Internet.'

'What! Here in Moscow? How did you do that in Russian?' I

was amazed at his skills.

'There are sites in English. Men are looking for women as well,' he explained.

The whole conversation was too heavy for me. I pondered how much I needed to know of people's personal lives. Weary of the night's revelations, I sighed at my empty glass. My own secrets stayed locked away, and now I would have to look at Cole in a different light. I would have preferred to remain in the dark.

Still, with personal entanglement came a varied social life, which was doing me the world of good. Now, with the bare tree outside my window sprouting leaves and the snow that had lain over the icy pavements and hard ground disappearing, spring was settling in, and soon it would be time for Tallena to visit. The exams went well, and an exhibition I organized of the students' work was appreciated. And there was still much to look forward to in the six weeks I had left of my short contract.

I called home to the children one evening to share the good news of the exhibition, but there was no answer. I left it another half hour, but the phone just rang out. I had expected them to be home at this time: late evening in Moscow, early evening in London. Dialing my mother's number this time, I knew I had to choose my words carefully. My mother had a tendency to overreact to situations, and I didn't want to set any alarm bells ringing.

'Hi, Mum,' I said when she picked up the phone. It wouldn't do to ask about the children straightaway; I had to gauge the moment to slip it in. Finally, after filling her in on tidbits of information, I casually dropped in, 'Have the kids been to see you today?'

'Tallena came round earlier; she was going to stay with her friend tonight,' my mother informed me.

'That's right, I'd forgotten that.' In all the turmoil of events it had slipped my mind. That's why she hadn't answered the phone. 'What about Theo, has he been around to see you too?'

'No, and I'm a bit worried about him, darling.' My mother paused.

Here we go again, I thought; she always thought the worst.

'Some boys kicked down your door yesterday and Theo had to chase them out of the house,' my mother imparted in a serious tone. 'Theo tried to fix it, but he hasn't got any money to buy tools.'

The conversation had taken an unexpected turn. 'What are you talking about, Mum? What boys? And what's wrong with the gate?'

'Some lads were near your house, about seven of them, planning to steal a motorbike. Theo could hear everything and asked them to move away. One of them had a dog and tried to set it on him.' My mother was panting now. 'Do you want me to call the police?'

Knowing my mother's tendency to overdramatize most events, I forced myself to calm down and reassure her. 'I'm sure he's just out somewhere. Perhaps he's at the shops,' I said, trying to smooth over my mother's anxiety. 'I'll get him to call you, when he comes in.' I rang off, telling myself my mother was always like this.

I tried ringing home a few more times, but finally the phone card ran out.

The next morning, even though it was a Saturday, I didn't linger in the morning and went in early to school and asked to use the phone to call home. It was only seven a.m. UK time when I first dialed my number. It rang and rang, but my children were never up by then, and I knew they wouldn't get up to answer the phone. Haphazardly, I fumbled about in the art room, watching the clock tick by to a more reasonable hour of the weekend to disturb my mother. Finally, at eight o'clock, without caring anymore whether I was interrupting her slumber, I dialed my mother's number.

'Hi, Mum,' I began cheerfully enough, 'did you get hold of

Theo okay last night?'

I fully expected my mother to reply in the affirmative. My mood changed abruptly when she replied, 'I've reported him missing to the police.'

'What!' I exclaimed.

'They took me seriously and put him down as a missing person.'

None of this was what I wanted to hear. My whole family hated the police. My children had been continually stopped and searched. All the police had ever done was harass us, even when we were broken into.

'Those louts probably got hold of him again, curse the lot of them,' my mother snarled.

'I'm sure he's okay,' I told my mother.

I dialed my sister's number, bracing myself for my sister's reprimand at phoning so early on a Saturday morning.

'I've been trying to reach you,' Elaine told me anxiously, 'the police have been on the phone to Peter all night.'

'Why have the police been on the phone? Has something happened?'

'After Mum reported Theo missing to the police last night they checked the local hospitals.'

I dreaded the rest of the story, I was afraid she was going to say that my mother had been phoning the police constantly. 'I wish Mum hadn't done that...' I began.

My sister cut me off. 'Well, it's just as well she did, because they located him in hospital. He's been beaten up. He needs surgery.'

My son was hurt and I was thousands of miles away.

Chapter 14

In my shock, my response to the devastating news imparted by my sister was a little inane. 'How did they get your number?' I was sure that Theo hadn't given it to them; he didn't sound like he was in any condition to give out information.

'Mum gave our phone number as next of kin when she reported him missing.'

I swallowed my anger as best I could. *I* was next of kin, I was his mother. I should have known. 'Which hospital is he in?' I demanded.

My sister had no idea, and neither did the police when I rang them because the officer who had called Elaine had finished his shift. So I started calling the hospitals myself, and finally Chelsea and Westminster confirmed that my son was there.

'Yes, we have a Theodore Prazak who was badly beaten last night,' the admissions lady said. 'Who are you?'

'I'm his mother,' I said wearily.

'I'm sorry, it's says here someone called Peter is his next of kin, so I can't tell you anything else.'

'I AM HIS NEXT OF KIN. I AM HIS MOTHER AND I AM RINGING FROM MOSCOW,' I said loudly, clearly enunciating each word. 'I need you to put me through to the ward where my son is now. I am not asking you. I am not saying please. Just *do it.*'

The woman put me straight through and I asked for the matron who, after a similar struggle on the next of kin issue, finally conceded to let me speak to Theo.

'Theo, darling, how are you?' I asked my son, open to expect the worst.

'Hi, Mum.' His words were slurred. 'I'm a bit sore, my jaw is broken. I have to have surgery to have it wired back together.'

'I'll come home,' I told him. 'Oh, darling, I'm so sorry.' I didn't know what to say to ease the discomfort that was evident in his speech.

'I'll be alright, Mum, don't worry about coming home.' Theo sounded very grown up for his twenty years but to me he was still my little boy.

I sent him my love and prayers and hung up. I knew it would be several hours until I would hear the results of the surgery; hours of worry and guilt that I wasn't there to be with my son, to protect him.

I decided to ring the airline with which I was booked to return to the UK in a few weeks, and see whether I could change my ticket for either that evening or Sunday. It wasn't possible as the flights were full; the earliest flight out was Tuesday. I tried the other airlines, though this would mean buying a new ticket, but there was no joy there either. I took stock of the situation. There were six weeks to go until the end of my contract and visa, and even though it would be unprofessional to let the school down, I needed to be there for my son, that was my priority. Would it even be worth my coming back? I would have to set cover work for my classes, but for how long? One or two weeks? There was no way of knowing.

Tallena would be disappointed that she wouldn't get her trip to Moscow, and I grimaced when I thought of the money I had paid for it all, including the very expensive visa. And the trip to St. Petersburg had already been arranged. The headway I thought I was making in my finances would dissolve, but money was nothing compared to the safety and health of my children.

One thing I couldn't put off was informing the headmaster. He was sympathetic, but explained that leaving Russia at short notice was not straightforward. My registration papers would have to be stamped by the local police to enable me to fly. It was no use asking for this to be done until I knew what flight I was on.

I killed the hours while Theo was in surgery cleaning out my art room. I didn't mind the laborious work, it held the tears at bay. Finally, as the evening approached, I could wait no longer and rang my sister. The news was good: the surgery had gone well, and my son was now the proud owner of a titanium plate holding his jaw together. I explained that the earliest flight was Tuesday, and Elaine suggested that she go and visit Theo and assess whether I needed to come. I decided that if she told me to come, I would do so immediately; but even if she said there was no need to fly over, I would consider it.

It was after seven o'clock when I left the school. I bought a phone card on the way home, so I could call the hospital. Theo could barely talk, so I left him to rest. Then I rang the police and told them what hospital Theo was in and what operation he had needed. 'This lout needs to be caught! He had a knife and it could have been far worse,' I told the policeman at the other end. I didn't know if he took anything down I said, but at least I got it off my mind.

Sunday morning was tortuously slow, then finally it was an acceptable hour, with the time difference, to call the UK.

'Hello, darling. How are you?' I asked my injured son lovingly.

'Hello, Mummy, I miss you,' Theo answered with some difficulty; in his pain and fear he was childlike again, needing his mother's love to make everything better. 'You don't need to come home. I'm okay.'

I wasn't convinced by his groggy attempt at reassurance. But when Tallena called later, having visited him, she assured me that though Theo's face was swollen and he could only drink through a straw, he was going to be fine. My sister confirmed the news a couple of days later when she visited, smuggling him in a burger and chips. The danger was past; my son would have a small scar but would recover otherwise unscathed from his attack.

Theo was discharged after five days in hospital, and Tallena flew out to Moscow the same day for her visit. I had staggered through the week half in a daze, and was struggling to see how I could unwind and enjoy the time with my daughter.

'How is Theo?' I asked her as soon as she came into the arrivals hall.

'He's alright, Mum, really. He is much better, and we fixed the door properly.'

I knew I needed to let go of my tension, so I said, 'Goodo, welcome to Moscow.'

We had twelve days together ahead, with her nineteenth birthday in the middle. Our destination for the weekend was St. Petersburg, and Tallena was excited to be travelling there on the overnight sleeper train. I was less enthralled, especially when a drunkard reeking of cheap whiskey decided to share our compartment; but eventually, after recruiting the guard, who I'm sure was KGB, to help, we were left alone to sleep.

The next morning dawned in St. Petersburg. We checked into our hotel, filling in the registration forms for the police; it was how things were done in the former USSR, and we had to abide by the rules. Then we went out to explore the colorful city, on foot, on a tourist bus, then on a boat cruising through the canal ways. Tallena allowed me one hour at the famous Hermitage Museum, and then, to feed her fascination with the true crimes that she read of in books, she begged me to visit a famous prison she had read of in a guide book. Kresty Prison was notorious for its overcrowding, and the solution adopted was that the cells were rotated so one shift of people slept at night, and a second shift slept during the day.

We took the metro to the stop listed in the guide book, but struggled to locate the prison and then find out where to go for a tour. Finally, we were directed to a reception area that had several glass windows and a machine from which you took a number and then lined up.

'Do you think we're in the right place, Mum? It doesn't really look like a tourist crowd.'

The people around us looked Russian, not like tourists. They were all carrying bags of some sort which, I belatedly realized, contained food for the inmates.

'We're not in the right place,' I said, turning to my daughter. 'These people are visiting their relatives or friends.' The realization came that we were intruding in people's private lives. Whatever shame or guilt these people suffered, they were trying to bring their loved ones what little they could to help their wretched existence.

Grabbing my daughter's hand, I pulled her away. Neither of us spoke for a while; it was hard to deal with the reality of what we had just seen. Finally Tallena broke the silence and said, 'That was horrible, Mum.'

So we gave up trying to find the organized tour of the prison and spent the rest of the weekend soaking up the beauty of the city instead.

Back in Moscow, I had to work during the day, but we travelled into town and explored the famous landmarks, fitting in as much sightseeing as we could.

'What's a Kremlin, Mum?' Tallena asked when I said we would go and see Red Square. I looked at my daughter and saw a new generation that had not been indoctrinated in the war of East and West. The Cold War had long since frozen over and Russia was emerging as a superpower again because of the power that oil brings to a nation. As if to underline my thoughts the city was preparing for the May Day parade, a display of military precision and armory with air force maneuvers in the skies.

On the day of the parade the staffroom at work was buzzing with talk. A young Australian teacher told us how he had wandered into Red Square the previous evening.

'Struth,' Johno said, 'I didn't know if I'd had too much vodka and was seeing things. There were armored tanks and army trucks, soldiers marching everywhere and everything you could think of, and then I started taking photos of the missiles.'

'You did what?' everyone chorused. 'It's a wonder you weren't arrested.'

'I was. I spent the night in one of their military barracks, near Red Square, and they just released me at five this morning. I came straight to school; I didn't have time to go home, or sleep.' Johno had his camera out by now and was showing us the military preview before the television cameras got it. 'I didn't know I was in a restricted area; you can usually walk straight across Red Square to the metro.'

'They are scud missiles you have taken there, no wonder you were arrested,' an ex-army man who had retrained in teaching told him. 'It's a wonder they didn't take the camera from you.'

Everyone wanted to know the details of the arrest. 'How did they see you there?'

Johno smiled. 'I asked one of the officers to take a picture of me in front of the tanks.'

'You did what?' The staff, enthralled, had completely forgotten the classes they should be heading to.

'They deleted all my pictures but I took out the memory card and put it in my shoe,' Johno said, clearly pleased by his 007 tactic.

'How come they let you go?' someone asked just as the head came in to see why no one was at lessons.

'They emptied my wallet.'

'How much did you lose?'

'Two thousand rubles.'

'Never carry money on you,' said the ex-army teacher. 'Just have enough so you don't get a beating.'

It was a jolly story, but it spoke volumes of life in Moscow at the time.

The tension of the previous week had past. My time with Tallena had soothed away the drama of Theo's attack.

'I'm going to miss you, darling,' I told my daughter on the eve of her departure. 'Moscow won't be the same without you.' I kissed her goodnight and then headed to bed. Before falling asleep I prayed as I did every night: 'Thank you, Lord, for all good things and for my children. Protect them with your love.'

Chapter 15

Once Tallena returned to the UK it continued to play on my mind that I hadn't rushed back to be at my son's bedside after the attack. I phoned home most nights. Tallena had set up Skype on my laptop so the call costs were minimal. As long as I heard their voices each night, I could relax and know they were safe. There were just four weeks to go until I returned home.

There was a buzz in the air when I walked into the staffroom on Monday morning. Written boldly on the cover board were the words *Champions League tickets available for tonight, see Michael.*

'Who's the joker that wrote that?' I scoffed. The tickets for the Chelsea v. Manchester match were exchanging hands for thousands of euros; in fact, one of my students had boasted that her dad had got box seats for four costing over ten thousand pounds. It was a huge event, a gold mine for touts, and you had to be careful that you didn't end up with the black market tickets that were bogus.

Then Michael arrived with the exciting news that he had ten tickets and was selling them at cost price. The teachers couldn't believe their luck and they were snapped up quickly, with one left to go. One hundred and thirty-five pounds was a lot of money, and the seats were in the Manchester end, but how could I turn down this a once-in-a-lifetime opportunity to see the team I supported, the team that was local to my Battersea home?

It was a night to remember. Russian police were everywhere, mounted on horses and lining the streets in their Cossack coats and furry hats. It was a mission just to get on the metro. To minimize clashes, the police had divided the city: the rival fans flew into airports on opposite sides of the city, and used different train lines. On our line, Manchester fans were everywhere, repeating: 'Reds are going to Moscow!' without pause. The atmosphere was electric.

We got to the stadium and shuffled through the crowd to our seats. Hearing the Chelsea supporters at the other end of the stadium, I dared not let slip even one Blues chant, not among the Reds. I texted Tallena: *At the Champions League match, in with the Reds*. She texted back: *Traitor*. It was a good match. Manchester won, and I couldn't begrudge them that, and I got to see the finale show put on at the end for the Champions. It was a further two hour wait before the police would give the okay that all the Chelsea fans had cleared out and we could leave the stadium. Thankfully the metro was running still, a concession to the game, and I fell into my bed at four a.m.

Life had settled down into normality again and the weather started to improve so I no longer needed to don six layers just to venture outside. There was a three-day holiday coming up tagged on to a weekend, and I thought about popping back to the UK, but I would be home soon enough. My contract ended at the end of June, a week before school finished; the three-month visa would be up and the school couldn't take the risk of overrunning the visa. It was just best to sit it out, and save the money.

'Danny's done the kitchen, Mum,' Tallena told me one evening via Skype. 'He's moved the kitchen bench and taken out the old freezer. I offered him money, but he wouldn't take it.'

Danny would have done a good job, I was sure of it. 'Well, maybe you could get a Chinese takeaway meal or two and share it when he comes around,' I suggested, knowing Danny always loved joining in with the family meal.

I remembered some years ago when we went to a restaurant and invited Danny to come along. 'Do you know, Mum,' Tallena informed me after the meal, 'that was the first time Danny had ever eaten at a restaurant.' Had I spoilt my children too much? Since Victor's death, I lived for the moment, and I appreciated little things, like Danny not wanting to take any money for helping, or taking him for his first meal at a restaurant.

'That Danny. What are we going to do with him?' I said to my daughter as we said goodbye.

There is no way to prepare yourself for tragedy; I knew that too well. I had been lulled into a false sense of security now that Theo's attack, although serious, had passed and we were back to the routine of our lives again. So when I gathered my patience and rang my mother for a long, rambling chat the next morning, the words Mum uttered came as a horrible shock.

'Oh, Felicity,' my mother's trembling voice began. I knew at once that something was very wrong. 'Have you heard from Tallena?'

'I spoke to her last night,' I said slowly, not sure where this was going. 'What's wrong, Mum?'

'It's terrible,' my mother said, barely able to get the words out. 'Danny's been killed.'

As it had that dark December day fifteen years before, the phone slipped from my grasp and bounced momentarily up and down on the twisted cord until it came to rest on the floor. I could hear my mother's voice crying out, 'Oh, daring,' as I fell on my knees and uttered in hopelessness 'no, no' so many times that the ulcerous word wrenched me in two.

The handset of the phone drifted in limbo for a few minutes. I was unable to pick it up or stop rocking to and fro. I wished I had never made the call. I wished I had heard wrongly, or misunderstood.

Finally, I gathered myself sufficiently to resume the conversation.

'What happened? How did it happen?'

I could barely talk; I desperately wanted to seek out my daughter, to tell her I loved her. To tell her I loved Danny. I closed my eyes tightly as if to shut out all other thoughts and said to the empty room, 'I meant protect Danny too, Lord. Protect Danny too.'

My mother was still on the phone, but was making no sense. Then Theo came on the line, distraught. He had gone around to his grandmother's for support. All he could tell me was that Danny was dead, and he didn't know any details.

Tallena's phone went straight to voicemail. Redialing the number every five minutes didn't help. Danny, just nineteen, with his wide, cheeky grin, was part of our lives. He was family. It was after midnight when I finally got to talk to my daughter. Hysterical, she related that Danny had been hit by a drunk driver who went through the red light on the pelican crossing he was using to safely cross the street. He was barely two hundred yards from his house, doing an errand for his mother before coming down to see Tallena at my place. 'Mum, he was thrown over a hundred feet by the car and his head was split open,' Tallena sobbed. 'The air ambulance was at the scene by the time I got there, but it was already too late.' Tallena was still there, at the roadside where he had died. Along with Danny's family, she couldn't bring herself to leave.

I tried to reason with my daughter. 'Go home and try to get some sleep, darling.'

'I can't leave here, Mum. I don't want to go home yet.'

Once again my child was in trouble, in pain, and I was too far away. Was the devil stalking my family? Why so much senseless violence and destruction all around?

That night I cried. I cried for my daughter, going through torrents of emotion that she was too young to experience when her father died but lay buried in her very essence and came pouring out of her now as she grieved for her best friend. I cried for Danny, whom we all loved, and for the family who had lost him. I cried for Victor, who should have been here. There was no end to the tears. It seemed that the monstrous night would never end. I tossed and turned, drifting into sleep for short periods only to wake up to realize the terrible pain that the day had brought.

This time going home was not an option; it was a necessity. Thankfully, the headteacher was understanding, and two days later I was scooping my devastated children into my arms.

The week that followed was turbulent and chaotic. It was also full of love. It would be impossible to have known Danny and not remember all the wonderful, unforgettable times he had enriched our lives.

'Remember the time Danny turned into a cat?' I said to lift the black cloud of sadness. 'He fell asleep on the sofa at night and the cat was where he had been the next morning.'

Theo joined in: 'What about that time he drank too much vodka and we couldn't lift him from the decking?'

'Or the time he came and did the garden for me, and painted the living room for nothing, just because he wanted to do a good turn?' I said.

But Tallena's grief was thick, impenetrable.

Danny's family invited us to view the body at the funeral home. 'It's going to be very hard,' I told my daughter, trying to prepare her for the worst. 'Are you sure you want to go?' But nothing could stop Tallena seeing her best friend. Every night she had gone back to the scene where he had been killed. There were dozens of flowers placed there now. I worried about her nightly vigil, but I knew she needed to grieve in her own ways. When a friend criticized my decision to let Tallena mourn in this way, I retorted, 'Did your child have to wait seven years to see where their father is buried?' I had turned my cheek too many times in the past to keep back real sentiment when someone openly offended me; I wasn't going to offer my daughter's cheek as well.

At the funeral home the next day Tallena and I were ushered into a room where Danny's young body was laid out. He had been dressed in clean clothes and a hat that belonged to Tallena. Rolling up the sleeve on the corpse in front of them, Tallena looked for the tattoo Danny had on the inside of his arm. It was still visible; there was no question it was Danny's body, but his spirit was no longer there. Then Tallena shocked me by lifting the baseball cap from his head to expose Danny's skull, cracked in several places.

'I hate him, Mum,' Tallena told me coldly.

I hoped she meant the killer, not God.

It was hard to leave my family, even though I would only be away for two weeks this time, winding up my time in Moscow. I would have liked to have stayed, but another teacher had taken a leave of absence to do a master's degree and was returning in the summer to take over my job. Realizing I had left it rather late, when I got back to Moscow I phoned the agency who had sent me out to Russia to ask if they had any positions available for the next school year.

'We only have one position,' said the agency worker apologetically, and he explained the details and location of the posting.

I took a moment to think, then replied, 'Yes. I can do Libya.'

God has a plan, I told myself. I knew my time had come.

Chapter 16

Tripoli, Libya, 2008

I arrived in Libya in the humid heat of August, full of anticipation, looking forward to exploring the city that would be my
home for the next three years: Tripoli. I was suntanned, relaxed
and optimistic thanks to a holiday that summer with the children
in Greece, where the scorching hot sun had melted away the fog
of despair hanging over us since Danny's death. My new post as
head of art at an international school promised responsibility
and challenge; and the access the job granted to Libya would, I
hope, open up opportunities in my quest to discover the cause of
my husband's death.

The first weeks, as usual, were a blur of settling into a new
school, a new home and a new city. I got to know my students –
mainly Libyan nationals – and straightened up the art
department. I bought rugs, baskets, cushions and lamps to
transform my bare apartment into a colorful, warm, inviting
home, and took in a couple of kittens for company, though
feeding them cost a fortune: Gaddafi deemed pets to be a luxury,
so there was a one hundred percent tax on imported food. The
challenge in kitting out the house was getting around the
sprawling city without a car. Taxis – unbelievably cheap – were
the preferred method of transport for most Westerners heading
to the main shopping thoroughfare, hidden behind abandoned
buildings and hastily erected fences and running along the coast,
overlooking a coastline marred by sewage.

I grew to know, and like, many of my colleagues, but to my
dismay relations with my new boss, the headteacher, Carl, were
soon strained. He had started off by violating the privacy I
guarded closely by announcing, in the first staff meeting to fifty
people in the room, that I had a history with Libya and that staff
should speak to me to find out more. I had kept my eyes focused

on the floor to hide the contempt I felt. In my own time, I would decide with whom I wanted to share my life story; and that wouldn't happen until I felt I could completely trust someone. But it wasn't long before more fissures appeared in our relationship when I felt unable to sit quietly when angered.

It did not sit well with me that I had not been paid for the induction week, during which I had organized classrooms, met parents and prepared for teaching.

'I've never had anyone ask to be paid for this week's work before,' Carl said to me indignantly when I handed him my written complaint. Begrudgingly, he took the letter from me and shoved it onto a towering pile of papers.

'Since I've written a letter I would like an answer in writing,' I said nervously as I made my way out, holding open the door for the next person on their way in with a complaint.

When it became clear payment would not be forthcoming, I changed tactics and requested some time off in lieu: two days in December during the Muslim holiday of Eid, when the school would be closed, to attend a big family reunion in London in honor of my mother's ninetieth birthday. Carl said he would see what he could do, but as the weeks crept by still I had no answer.

When I pressed him on the subject, his response was, 'I don't see why you should get time off in lieu. I don't get paid for a lot of the time I have to be here in the holidays, and I don't get extra time off for that.'

'With all due respect, Carl,' I said as politely as possibly, 'you get three times the salary I get. That's part of the territory.'

Incensed with my counterattack, Carl stopped what he was doing on the computer and shook his head silently.

The next time I put in the same request a month later, I had added another day. 'I would also like to go to my husband's grave on the national day, when the Libyans go.' Carl knew the basics of my past; still, his grunt was noncommittal.

Unfortunately, I was in his power: I could not leave the

country without his cooperation. Libya was not a country you could leave when you wanted to, and what type of visa you had made all the difference. I had not encountered the problem on my other visits to Libya, because all the visas and transport were always arranged for me, but this time I had residency in Libya, which meant in order to leave the country I needed an exit-entry visa. Arrangement of these could take three days, or three months if you were unlucky enough to upset the boss. Stories abounded in the staffroom of teachers stranded in Libya for the holidays, and one teacher had tried to leave from two weeks before his wife was due to give birth in the UK, but didn't make it back until his son was five weeks old. The school held the passports and arranged the teachers' visas, leaving them trapped.

With no answer to my request forthcoming from Carl, I decided to go ahead and arrange my flights. The obvious answer was to approach the Libyan *Arab* Airlines whose chairman had promised me free flights years before. But I soon found that the company had changed hands. The planes were the same, the head office building was the same, even the manager I went to see was the same, but the result was very different.

'We're not Libyan Arab Airlines now, Mrs. Prazak,' said the manager benignly to me as he gazed out at the view of Tripoli Harbor from his executive office in the high-rise headquarters, 'we're Libyan Airlines.'

'But it's still the same company, surely,' I reasoned with him. 'The chairman promised me that my family and I could come and go to Libya anytime we liked and they would take care of everything.'

'Do you have this in writing, madam?' the manager asked politely.

'I didn't realize the word of the chairman of Libyan Arab Airlines was not worth anything when I met him. I trusted he would keep his word, and you still have a responsibility to me, even if you have changed names. You inherited their debts.'

'I'll see what I can do,' the manager said, clearly uncomfortable with delivering an outright no in the face of my outrage.

The airline through which my husband had lost his life treated his widow as if she was his baggage they had to dispose of. Follow up e-mails and calls proved fruitless; then I recalled the Libyan Arab Airlines customer relations man who had once been so kind to me and the children: Mohammed. I knew he no longer worked for the airline, but he had authority that no one would question. And as well as his influence with the airline, I was keen to speak to him about another, more important matter: the outcome of the closed trial between Libyan Arab Airlines and the Libyan military that had brought down my husband's plane. I knew of the trial, which had taken place many years after Victor's death, but the results were classified. I had been trying to learn what I could of the proceedings; I had even appealed to the father of one of my students, who was the head of the air force, but to no avail. And the British government were unlikely to succeed where I had failed. They still hadn't even managed to get a copy of the correct crash report, despite my continual protests: 'A British citizen is killed in horrendous circumstances and you don't ask any questions about the trial!' Mohammed, then, was my last chance for answers.

I rang him on my mobile one morning before school, standing in the fresh air in the school courtyard. 'Mohammed, would I be able to come in and see you?' I asked after his secretary put me through.

'Of course, Mrs. Prazak, anything I can do to help, anything you need, just ask me.'

No time like the present, I decided. There were no classes today, just workshops, and I didn't need to attend the morning's workshop which was focused on year groups below the age range I taught. 'I'll try to come this morning,' I said.

As it turned out, the headteacher wouldn't allow me to take

the morning off – though I had carefully chosen a day when I had no lessons to teach. I was told I could go at lunchtime, which didn't leave me long for my meeting.

'You can't expect to just hop out of school with no notice. You should have told me about this in advance,' explained Carl.

'I didn't know whether this man could see me today, so there was no point in asking before,' I tried to explain, though I knew my words were wasted. 'Besides, even when I do ask you in advance, you don't answer me.' I was not just talking about the innumerable times I had asked for permission to go home to the UK at Eid: my request to see my husband's grave had also been overlooked. 'You said you would look into me going to the grave; have you done anything about it? It's an ideal time for me to go right now with these workshops because it means I don't have to get anyone to cover my lessons. I've only seen his grave twice in my life and I want to tell my children I went to visit it. I've been here nearly three months and never had a chance to see it yet.' I thought I might as well get everything off my chest. There were only two weeks to go before I went back to the UK and my children were sure to ask me about the grave.

'I'll ring the Embassy and see what I can do.' It was the automated response he gave all the time.

In the back of a taxi bound for Mohammed's office, anxiety set my stomach churning. This was a momentous day for me: sixteen years after Victor's death, would I finally get some answers? Since coming to Tripoli, I had learned that the plane crash was not even confirmed in Libya. A fellow teacher at the school, a Libyan called Adel, knew of it because he was from Benghazi from where most of the Libyans on board were travelling, and he had known people on board that ill-fated flight. Other staff had heard rumors. A technician said to me one day, 'You are a strong woman. We heard something about a crash, but we didn't know if it was true.' It was a harrowing portrayal of censorship that a closed country could get away with in 1992, but the Internet had changed much of that.

At Mohammed's office I sipped coffee silently as I waited. Finally, the door opened. It could have been Omar Sharif walking into the room, I would not have recognized him. The solid-framed man with a hearty smile I had met eight years ago was now very tanned and very lean. I wanted to ask about his health; the transformation was incredible and all I could think was, had he suffered some terrible illness that had reduced his size in half?

'You look like a movie star, Mohammed. I wouldn't have known you.' I intended the remark to be a compliment.

'Mrs. Prazak, how nice to see you!' Mohammed's rustic voice was unmistakable. 'So you are in Tripoli!' Gaddafi had recently snubbed Condoleezza Rice, the US Secretary of State, by refusing to shake hands with her because it was customary for men not to touch women during Ramadan, but to Mohammed I was an old friend and he wholeheartedly gripped my hand in his.

After another coffee and some polite small talk, I broached the subject I had waited so long to hear about. 'What happened at the trial, Mohammed?' I asked, my tone serious now.

'It was a closed trial, you know that, Mrs. Prazak,' Mohammed stated, as if to say he was giving me privileged information. 'But, off the record, I can tell you that the co-pilot of the fighter plane was found to be responsible, that part of the blame was ascribed to the malfunctioning guidance system, and that Libyan Arab Airlines was absolved from blame.'

I asked what happened to the pilot – the air traffic controller and pilots had been held in jail for years until the trial – but Mohammed neatly avoided the question. I didn't take much in after that. It was like hearing a verdict of guilty on a murder trial, which essentially it was. The only one left in the courtroom now was me; everyone else had gone.

I wasn't satisfied with Mohammed's response. Victor's death wasn't down to one man alone. But there was no suggestion that I could take the matter further, now the 'truth' was recorded in the Libyan court system. Not for the first time, I found myself wishing that the flight manifest had included American citizens. Not that I wished such tragedy on Americans of course, but I knew that then I would have had the might of the CIA on my side. Just look at Lockerbie and how American officials were on the scene before dawn broke. There wasn't a chance in hell that the CIA would have been as complacent as the British government in finding out what happened to their own citizens.

The meeting had come to an end; I was mindful that my boss would be waiting for me to turn up at the afternoon session at school. Before we said our goodbyes, I explained to Mohammed my issue with the airline refusing me free flights. One phone call later, problem solved. Gratefully, I shook hands with one of the most influential men I had ever met: no doubt a ruthless man professionally, but to me, a gentle and kind friend.

Back at school, I expected a reprimand for my tardy return, but instead when I reached Carl's office I walked into a row between a teacher and the head. Teaching in Libya was not without its limits. The teacher, Lola, had been hauled in over a complaint that she had used the word 'dictatorship' to describe Libya. In fact, she had been teaching the history of Nazi Germany at the time, and had used the comparison to help the students understand world political structures. She had carefully avoided mentioning Gaddafi.

The next morning, all members of staff were called to a briefing. 'Now, when I get a student coming to me complaining that teachers are calling Libya a dictatorship, I have to tread very carefully because some of these students are very well connected,' Carl explained. He made it clear that no political statements were to be made at any time concerning our host country, and he insinuated that we were being watched. He closed the briefing with a reminder for the women of suitable dress. I had been a little taken aback when I was told off for wearing shorts to the swimming pool on the school grounds; but had been careful to cover my legs from that point on. But Minnie, a voluptuous young reception teacher, on the other hand, was totally indignant at the interference that a top she had worn out shopping, on her own time, was unsuitable attire. 'I'm a forty-two, double-D bust size,' she said. 'Doesn't matter what top I wear, they're going to stick out.'

I did my best to conceal my smile.

Chapter 17

Finding Victor's grave once more became a personal pilgrimage for me. After all, I had agreed to the post in Libya in part to feel closer to my husband. But I had no idea how to get to the cemetery. I knew the name of the place, Al Sabt, from the death certificate, and that it was about fifty kilometers south of Tripoli. But I had been driven there in a bullet-proof Embassy car the first time I had come, and now I was hopelessly lost.

Sandra, a colleague who had become a good friend and in whom I had confided some of the details of my past, suggested I ask one of the regular taxi drivers, Sharif. Like many of the taxi drivers who picked up from the school, Sharif was retired from his profession. I assumed he was ex-secret police – most taxi drivers were; it would certainly explain his ability to smuggle in contraband wine from Tunisia. But when I asked him during a taxi ride one day, I was surprised to discover his previous employer had been none other than Libyan Arab Airlines.

Gold teeth flashing as he spoke in heavily-accented English, he told me of his part in another air disaster – the crash that had happened at Tripoli Airport; the one that had plunged me into needless panic because Victor was travelling that day and then selfish relief when he walked through the door unharmed. It was someone else's husband dead, someone else's tragedy, I had thought. Such things didn't happen to me, to my family.

'I was the maintenance technician on duty that day,' Sharif disclosed. 'I told them to keep circling until I could repair the satellite, but they didn't listen to me and attempted to land.'

I knew how the story ended, with fatalities strewn over the runway and the plane in pieces.

'It was foggy and they missed the approach to the runway,' Sharif explained. 'They said they were running low on fuel, but I couldn't get to the dish in time.'

'It must have been very hard for you,' I said, not knowing what else to say. 'My husband was travelling from Tripoli that day as well but he was okay. That time.' It seemed a silly statement to make, but I didn't know how else to put it.

'Yes, I remember the other accident,' Sharif said quietly. 'It came down before the airport.'

'I know, I've been there, but I don't know how to get there now,' I said.

Sharif was silent for a while and didn't offer any guidance. Uncomfortable, I decided not to probe further.

Still, I was no closer to locating the gravesite, until Sandra suggested an exploratory road trip. The map we had was sketchy to say the least, and after two hours of driving in what we hoped was the right direction we stumbled upon parts of the Great Man-Made River Project and knew we had gone wrong. We asked a number of local people, but their English was minimal and they would simply point in the direction of the airport, assuming that was our destination.

I gazed intently out of the window, hoping something would jog my memory. 'I'm sorry,' I said as we diverted onto a dirt road narrowly fenced in on one side by barbed wire. 'I remember the inside a bit and the parking area outside, but it was eight years ago. We came off a main road onto a dirt road, but I don't think it was this rough. I don't think we're going to find it. If you want to go back now I don't mind. I'm so grateful you tried.'

We stopped for refreshments, and asked again in a last ditch attempt at the shop if this was Al Sabt. Finally the shop owner understood where we wanted to go, but could not understand why any Westerner would want to see one of their cemeteries. We had been mispronouncing the name, the shopkeeper explained, and Al Sabt was where the plane had come down, not the burial site. The man gave us directions, and, thanking him, we set off again. Finally, we were driving alongside the high wall enclosing the cemetery. I noticed a mosque built onto the outside which I hadn't remembered at all; a new addition.

We stepped out of the vehicle and walked towards the gate, dusty, hot and tired. Still, my pace increased as we approached.

'Should we ask someone if we can go in?' Lou said who had also accompanied us.

I thought, *No one asked me if they could bury my husband here and I'm not asking some maintenance person for permission to see my husband's resting place.* 'No, we don't need to,' I said authoritatively, pushing the gate open. It swung back and I automatically went to head to the far left corner where I remembered the mass grave being.

I raced towards the monument that depicted the loss of life. But something was wrong. The walk was too long; I should have reached it by now. Mounds of earth that had not been there before obscured my view. Then I mounted the last mound, and was horror-struck. Where there should have been a huge, soulless slab of concrete there lay new graves instead.

'No,' I said out loud, though my friend was too far away to hear, having lingered near the gateway to respect my privacy. 'No, it can't be!'

What had happened? Where was the grave? How could they have desecrated it like this? Where were the bodies? *Where was Victor's body?*

Frantically, I began searching the rest of the cemetery for the obliterated grave. I remembered the lime-green roof and white-washed walls of the small mosque in the center from my earlier visits, but even the trees I remembered sitting under, reading a Bible passage, seemed different now.

Sandra, seeing her friend marching around the graveyard, came over to me. 'It's starting to get dark,' she said gently.

'I can't find the grave,' I spluttered, tears rolling down my face. Where I had expected to find solace, I had been confronted by loss and violation.

We looked together, but Victor's grave was absent, gone.

'Come on, love,' Sandra said at last, breaking the silence that had engulfed us. 'Let's go home. We can't find anything more out now. You'll be able to ring the Embassy tomorrow and ask them if they know anything.'

Back home, my mood was bleak. The Embassy officer I spoke to was, as usual, clueless, and though Mohammed promised to find out what he could, he had no immediate answer as to the distressing absence of Victor's grave.

Finally, I was coaxed from my gloom by Sandra, who encouraged me to join the staff for their trip to the Oasis Bar. Once a month the Embassy bar held an evening for the staff of the three major international schools in Tripoli, and it was a popular event, not only because the converted villa of the Oasis Bar was attractive and comfortable, but because it was the one chance to purchase alcohol legally. The staff on the bus put on by the school had one thing in mind: drink as much as they could because they wouldn't get another chance for a month, other than homebrew or Sharif's overpriced wine. It seemed a suitable distraction from my brooding.

But sitting in the peaceful setting of the Oasis, surrounding by the palm trees and bougainvillea that added shocks of color to the garden, I couldn't even bring myself to drink my wine. It had been a mistake to come: the jovial atmosphere was an irritant, not a mood enhancer. I got up from the table and went inside to the bar area. Last month I had been drinking tequila shots lined up along the bar with the other new recruits, then we had danced the night away, oblivious to the fact we were in Libya, a former terrorist state. Now I asked for a bottle of wine – with the cork left in – and some cans of beer and handed over the tokens that were taken as payment there. I would share the beer now and take the wine home so that I could sit and drink a toast to Victor, alone.

As I was paying I spotted the Ambassador walking in, and, leaving my order for the moment, I hurried over to intercept him before he became involved in speaking to someone else. He assured me he had heard of my dismal visit to the cemetery, and was looking into the matter. But he wondered whether I had got the right place? I couldn't see how I had been in the wrong cemetery: we had been right in Al Sabt, and it was the only one we could find. I thanked him for his help in advance, and returned to the bar where I was presented with my beers and the bottle of wine, open.

'You opened the bottle,' I said to the barman.

'I have to open it, madam,' the barman answered.

'I don't want to drink it yet; I just want to have the beer now, so can I get the cork please?' I asked politely.

The manageress, who was standing nearby, was having none of it. 'You are not allowed to take the wine off the premises!' she said loudly.

'I don't remember saying I was going to take it off the premises,' I said. I had hoped to take the wine out, but that was looking unlikely.

Finally, I gave up convincing the unpleasant manageress to give me a cork, or if not, refund my money, and took the drinks to a table to share with my colleagues. I put four of the beers on the floor by my bag, knowing it would be a free for all if I left all the alcohol on the table. It was when I was moving to another table that, for ease of carrying, I put the beers in my bag.

The manageress, who had been watching me like a hawk, charged over and started shouting at me so everyone in the near vicinity could hear. 'I want to see inside your bag! Show me your bag!' The woman was enraged. I refused to submit to her stop and search attempt; what was this, gangland? A heated argument ensued, and a hush fell over the courtyard as people stopped their chatter to watch. Over the other side of the garden I could see Carl, sitting with the Ambassador and his wife, glaring at me as if I had just committed murder.

Finally accepting she had met her match in fighting this little lady from Battersea, the manageress stormed off in high dudgeon to tell tales to Carl, and it wasn't long before he came over to stick his oar in. After the day I'd had, I wasn't about to take yet another misplaced scolding, and I exploded. 'Carl, I'm not taking alcohol off the premises. I am still here, aren't I? What's going on here? No one has caught me doing this. I'm not taking this, not after the week I've had. The British Government allows my husband to be buried in a mass grave without my permission. They ignore requests for an inquest. They give me the wrong crash report after nine years, and this week I find out my husband's grave is possibly desecrated and obliterated and no one bothered to tell me. Not the Libyans and not the Embassy. And now, because I ask for a cork to be left in a bottle of wine, I'm persecuted. I have not done anything wrong.'

Carl looked shocked by my outburst. I was pretty taken aback myself. 'Alright, sit down and have a quiet drink until we go.'

I did as I was told, sitting quietly until the end of the evening, fuming. As I was preparing to leave, I came upon the vindictive manageress and another lady in conversation.

'You did the right thing, Angela,' the lady was saying to the manageress.

'What do you mean she did the right thing?' I blurted out, all sense of decorum gone in my fury. I couldn't believe my ears. 'That woman has done nothing but cause trouble for me. Angela here has gone up to my boss and accused me of all sorts of things. She's even told the Ambassador that I've stolen drink. It's unbelievable. I paid for everything I brought! You show me where it says anywhere in this building that you can't take drink off the premises. And I haven't even left the building.' I looked at the lady, my expression hard. 'Who are you anyway?' I demanded.

'I am the wife of the vice consul,' she said without giving her name.

'And I'm Felicity Prazak. Make sure you remember my name. You will hear it again.' And I stalked away.

Back at my table, my friends were preparing to leave. I eyed the tableful of booze before me. 'Seems a shame to just leave it,' I remarked, feeling dangerously rebellious.

Quick as a flash, one can of beer got lost in Minnie's forty-two-double-D cleavage, another disappeared into Lola's handbag and the last two were slipped into Ryan's trouser pockets. Together, we walked towards the exit, past the security guard and into the night. Minutes later, in the car of the Irish couple who were driving us home, I produced my still-full wine glass, expertly hidden under my jacket, and took a sip.

'I had to have a trophy for the night, I need to remember this,' I said to my colleagues' amusement.

The next morning, lucidity and calm returned, and I reflected that while I still maintained I was in the right, perhaps I had been a little too vehement in my criticism of Angela. I decided I would write her a letter of apology; not as an acceptance of responsibility, but because, after all, she had just been doing her job.

Then my friend Gina, a fellow teacher, called me to come over to her apartment at once, and the e-mail she showed me blew any idea of an apology out of the water. The Embassy had sent a round robin e-mail to all sorts of expatriate groups in Tripoli, from the Hash House Harriers to the British Women's Group, the Society of Saint George and the Scottish Caledonian Society to some darts team I'd never heard of. The e-mail contained a warning based on a grossly twisted version of events at the Oasis Bar; though I wasn't named, I was clearly the 'person in question'.

'How dare they say such things?' I blurted out to Gina. 'Look what it says here: "When we identify the person, there will be consequences." I told the silly cow my name!'

'What about this bit?' Gina couldn't help herself from laughing. '"If anyone is so drunk they should get a buddy to drive them home."'

'I hardly even had one glass of wine!' I protested. 'And what's this nonsense about the person in question desecrating the mosque at the corner of the main road! I admit I was rude to the bar manager, whoever she was,' I said, 'but nothing else. They're attributing someone else's misdemeanors to me.'

Rage tore at me and my immediate reaction was to confront the Embassy over their lies. I found myself wondering whether this was a plan to make me look bad in case I was going to make an international noise about my husband's grave being ransacked.

The sensible course of action seemed to be to see Carl in the first instance. He was surprisingly understanding, but told me I was banned from the Oasis for three months for my rudeness to the manageress. I accepted the ban, but was clear I was not about to take the blame for anything more.

And that would have been the end of the matter, no doubt, had someone not leaked the e-mail to the UK's *Sunday Observer*, which printed a story that 'The British Embassy in Libya has been forced to issue a stern letter to its diplomats and employees regarding use of the Oasis Club', thus removing me from the frame and pinning the blame on the Embassy's own staff. The Ambassador was furious, believing the publicity could damage the delicate relationship between the Libyans and the British. I was intrigued; were British journalists now taking more of an interest in events in Tripoli? Over the years I had been contacted a few times by journalists, but the stories had never got to press – capped due to lack of interest by an editor, or perhaps, I sometimes wondered, by the British government looking to gag me. The Oasis fiasco had provided a glimmer of hope that the tide was turning; perhaps in the future a journalist would take an interest in Libya past and present, and help me in my search for answers. In fact, I called the *Sunday Observer* journalist, Oliver Marre ready to tell my side of the story, but when it came to giving him details, I uncharacteristically backed down. 'Don't spend your time and energy on the little issues, because then no one will take any notice when the bigger ones come along,' I said to myself.

My time would come.

Chapter 18

I had tried several churches in Tripoli before settling on the Anglican Church. I couldn't help feeling I had been partly persuaded by my mother's late conversion in life from Catholicism, which she felt had strangled her, to the Anglican Church at the ripe old age of eighty-eight. The new Anglican priest and his wife, who arrived a few weeks after I began attending, brought new energy. Matthew, the vicar, delivered captivating sermons, and his wife Elizabeth kept in his shadow but seemed a pleasant and kind woman who offered her services at the school on a voluntary basis. And my friendship with the couple blossomed when they came to help at the prop-making after-school club I was running in aid of the amateur dramatics society.

Then, one afternoon, Carl delivered the terrible news that Matthew had been found dead in the church that morning, apparently of a massive heart attack. I immediately wanted to rush to Elizabeth, but was assured she was with friends. I left a few messages over the day, offering any help she may need, or company. That evening I attended the church home group, hoping to see my friend and offer some comfort. Bible study was abandoned and a time of prayer was dedicated to Elizabeth. People offered their condolences as best they could, and to each Elizabeth said, 'The Lord giveth and the Lord taketh away.'

The next day Carl brought the staff together to impart the sad news, though we all knew by now. Afterwards, Sandra asked me, 'Did you find out when the funeral is, or what's happening? What about the body? Are they flying it home, to the UK?'

'Elizabeth was in such a state of shock last night at the prayer meeting,' I said. 'She just kept saying the Lord giveth and the Lord taketh away and the body was just like a glove and the glove had been removed and the body was dead. She said it didn't matter where he was buried; he was gone.'

'I see,' said Sandra.

'She's wrong,' I said bleakly. 'It really does matter where he is buried.'

Having accompanied me on my search for Victor's grave, Sandra, more than anyone, knew where I was coming from.

'Well, you're the one who would know. Talk to her,' she urged.

That afternoon I went to the church to find Elizabeth; I had to try to help.

'I am going in to the Church to be with her this afternoon, straight after school. The Indian community is coming in to give their condolences to her.'

'Whatever we can do to help, let us know,' Lola called out again as she left the room. Members of the Indian religious community were there, giving their condolences, and so I sat a few pews back to wait my turn. 'The Lord giveth and the Lord taketh away,' Elizabeth repeated. She was still in shock, but her simplistic view on life didn't sit well with me. Matthew had been so good for the Church, he had brought it back to life, and out of the blue he had been struck down. None of it made any sense to me.

I spotted a young man sitting nearby who looked the image of a younger Matthew. There was no mistaking that he was Elizabeth's son. After a few minutes I went up and introduced myself. We chatted for a while, and I was relieved when John explained that he had convinced his mother to bring his father home.

Finally, there was a break in the well-wishers surrounding Elizabeth and I took the opportunity to go over and ask if I could get her anything.

She replied simply, 'There is nothing I want.' I fully understood her grief.

'John said you're going to take Matthew home now,' I said to

Elizabeth. 'I am so pleased to hear that.'

Elizabeth said they had to go in the morning to formally identify the body at the morgue. 'It's so they can officially seal the casket to release it to fly home.'

The Indian priest sat nearby, who was listening to our conversation, thought he was helping when he said, 'I have organized for the other denominations to view the body tonight at ten p.m. so we can pray for his soul.'

'What do you mean?' I asked, intrigued.

'The Catholic Church will send a priest and so will the Greek Orthodox and the Coptic Christians together with the Nigerian Church leaders. Altogether there will be the five churches in Tripoli merging together to pray for his soul.' I barely had time to compute what he had said before he casually delivered a chilling final comment: 'We did it for the British victims that came down in the sea.'

'What victims?' I demanded at once, heart pounding.

'The three British men who died in the plane crash a few years ago. They were in the morgue and the Ambassador had to come to agree to release the bodies,' the Indian clergyman explained.

'Are you sure?' I quizzed him.

'Yes, I'm telling you, we all got together and prayed for their souls and the Embassy arranged the release of the bodies and the flight back to England.' The Indian pastor was adamant in his recall of the incident. 'Yes, yes, the plane had come down in the sea and there was no one else to pray for them.'

Outwardly, I smiled; inwardly, I crumbled. I was beside myself. These men had been flown home? It was procedure to fly them home? Why not Victor? Why not Victor? Sixteen years after the disaster, what else was I going to find out accidentally, by chance? My head was swimming with the new information, but I had to focus on Elizabeth.

'We will do the same tonight,' the priest was saying. 'You should be there at ten o'clock, Elizabeth, and John also.'

'How long do you stay there?' I asked.

'We can be there a number of hours and other people come in too,' the priest said.

I wondered whether Elizabeth and her son actually wanted to be in a small room in the morgue with the body of their loved one surrounded by a handful of strangers worshipping in their own style. I remembered Tallena and I viewing Danny's body; I didn't think we could have got through that with an audience.

'Are you sure you want to see his body laid out like that, Elizabeth?' I asked with concern.

'It appears I have to go,' Elizabeth said.

'You don't have to do anything you don't want to do,' I told her adamantly.

The priest chose that moment to tell Elizabeth not to cry, that her husband was in a better place. I was repulsed by the authority in his tone, and said loudly, 'You cry all you want to, Elizabeth, as often and as long as you want to, and don't let anyone stop you. Tears are prayers, remember that. And every tear you shed is for the love of your husband and your great loss. You are allowed to cry any time you want to.' I glared at the Indian priest and he walked away, leaving us two women alone with our tissues and our heartache.

Gently, I guided Elizabeth into the souk, and together with John we sat and drank peppermint tea. I suggested a thanksgiving service in the next few days, and offered to take charge of arrangements. As we discussed readings and refreshments, I firmly ignored the part of me that was crying out after the priest's careless words; I didn't mention my own despair to either Elizabeth or John as we sat sipping our tea and watching the sun set over Tripoli.

The day of the service dawned, and I was up already. I let out my kittens and made some tea. A nudging headache tickled the back of my head and I decided to take some painkillers before it got out of hand. It would have been better to eat, but I wasn't in the mood. The preceding days had been hectic to say the least, and I was determined to finish the arrangements this morning in time for the service. The chief job was moving the food I had ordered from the canteen to Carl's car for transportation. The problem, I soon discovered, was that there were a lot of trays, and only me to carry them the considerable distance from the canteen, down two flights of stairs, and across the grounds to the playground. I estimated it would take five trips, and as I did not have the keys to Carl's car, I would have to leave the food on the ground; not ideal.

I scouted around for some help, but the school was deserted. Eventually, I plucked up the courage to knock on Carl's door.

'I'm just on Skype to my children,' he told me matter-of-factly. 'I can't help you at the moment.' He closed the door in my face.

Thankfully, a colleague, Bert, bumped into me on my first trip, sniffing and struggling with trays, and at once offered to help.

'Oh good, you've done it all. I was just coming,' Carl said for Bert's benefit when he arrived at his car, knowing he had left all the work to me. 'Are you ready to go?'

'I just have to go back and get my bag,' I said. I hadn't wanted to leave it unattended by the car; it was a risk in itself that the sandwiches would still be there for each journey.

'Well, hurry up, I can't wait all day. The service starts in half an hour,' Carl said, annoyed.

Bert caught up with me as I hurried back for my bag, and I felt somewhat vindicated when he said, 'He could have helped you. He's a real bastard for how he's treated you.' Bert's words would stay with me for the rest of my time in Libya.

Finally, we made it to the service, trays of food intact, and I could relax: I had done all I could. I sat with the school crowd that had come, two rows behind the grieving family, and the ushers handed out the order of service sheets I had given them on the way in. The service began and I closed my eyes, letting the hymns swelling around the chamber flow into my heart. Sadness surrounded me and I felt very deeply for Elizabeth who despite all her devotion to God in accepting that her husband was gone must have been crying inside at her loss.

The vicar who held the service did an admirable job. Trying to color in Matthew's life, he said, 'Matthew's very first job as an engineer was at a desalination plant in Libya. All those years ago, and the Lord returned him here. It finished where it started.' His words flowed into a monologue of events and acclamations but I heard nothing after that sentence: 'It finished where it started.' These words had come to me before, when I had heard of the job in Libya, and now I was hearing them again. It was some solace that God had chosen me to be with Elizabeth and help her all I could in her hour of need. There was no one that would understand her loss more than me.

After the service, I caught sight of the British Ambassador and his wife and I went over to them to greet them.

'I hear you've done a lot of the organizing for this, Felicity,' said the Ambassador. 'You've done a very good job.'

'Thank you,' I said calmly, then added, 'you never know when life experiences will help someone else.'

'I'm sorry about what happened the other week,' the Ambassador said. He was referring to the letter following the Oasis Bar incident which had been put into circulation and then sent to the press. 'It was out of my hands. I let the manager take care of the events.' He paused, waiting for a reaction from me, then said apologetically, 'Do you want me to do something about it?'

'You know I was banned for three months,' I said. 'I can accept that because maybe I was short with the manageress. But I didn't do anything wrong, and I certainly didn't go anywhere near the mosque or any of that other business that was circulated around Tripoli.'

The Ambassador could gauge that I was a victim of circumstances. Keen to make amends, he said the words I had been waiting to hear: 'Do you still want to visit the grave? I can arrange a car to take you on Sunday, if that is agreeable.'

'Yes please,' I said at once. I didn't ask how it came to be that he could now offer this – that the location of the gravesite seemed to be known. 'But I'll have to ask Carl,' I said. Sunday in Libya is a school day but, pushed into a corner, Carl had no option but to agree with the Ambassador's request.

Sunday arrived, and I arose with a mixture of trepidation at the coming journey and relief that I would finally know the truth of what had happened to Victor's grave. After taking part in Matthew's farewell, I needed to honor my own husband. It had taken three months – well, eight years and three months – and now it was time to return.

True to his word, the Ambassador sent a car to pick me up at nine o'clock. I asked the driver to set his odometer to zero so as to know the exact distance from Tripoli, and then I tried to note down on paper the route we took, though it was hard – there were few landmarks in the arid landscape. I sat silently; my mind was full, and besides, I tried hard not to get into conversations with drivers. The minute you spoke to one he might turn around to chat and show you a picture of his third child on his mobile phone, hands completely off the steering wheel, the car swerving all about the road with other drivers blowing their horns and mouthing obscenities. But this was an Embassy car not a local taxi.

After an hour, we pulled up at a cemetery that seemed familiar.

'What's that over there?' I asked, pointing at a new monument that had been erected directly outside the cemetery gate. There was a chain rope around it, and I was familiar with the style.

'It's to commemorate a battle with the Italians,' the driver told me.

It definitely hadn't been there when I had come in 1993 or later, with the children, and nor had it been there when I had come a few weeks before. Was this a different cemetery – the right one? An excited pace quickened my step as I creaked open the huge gates. Walking quickly, I moved over the earth and tumbleweeds that drifted about with the breeze, and immediately saw it: the mass grave. It was more rundown than I remembered, decayed by age and blistering heat, the grass growing through cracks in the concrete.

Tears were a familiar friend and they reappeared, overwhelming me, more with relief than grief this time. My husband's resting place was still there and the worry that had built up at seeing the wrong grave sank into limbo. It was an unkempt, forsaken, untended ground, yet I was pleased to see it; pleased that this holy ground, as I considered it, had not been desecrated.

As I stood before my husband's grave, I thought back to the memorial service I had held at the church in London. Calling it a thanksgiving service had seemed so apt at the time. I'd had everything to be thankful for: a husband I adored, and even though he was gone, there was no mistaking my pride in having been his wife. And our two children, though young and fatherless, had known their father's love. Yes, the thanksgiving service had been healing and proper. But what had been lacking was a blessing or a service at the gravesite. And the idea emerged that perhaps it was not too late. Perhaps it was never too late to commemorate a life and pray for a soul that has passed. Perhaps, like Matthew, I could see Victor bound for eternity to the Lord.

It was a calm and serene woman who walked back to the car that day. 'Thank you for waiting for me,' I said to the driver, although I knew he had no choice. Peace was holding me together now; at last I had been with my husband again.

As we drove away I looked back at the tall iron gates, closed once more, behind which my beloved slept. I could not possibly have imagined then that I would return to the grave so soon.

Chapter 19

The weeks moved on, and soon we were into December. With still no response from the headteacher on my request for two days off, I booked a flight via Libyan Airlines for Wednesday 3rd December. I was packed and ready to leave in good time that day, but then the phone went: Carl instructed me to meet him immediately. I did so reluctantly; if I was to make the plane, I had to be ready to dash off to the waiting taxi.

'You aren't going anywhere today,' he said bluntly.

'What? But you didn't let me know yesterday that I couldn't go. You asked me to have cover work ready.'

He shook his head. 'We had a meeting this morning. You'll have to wait till Friday to go.'

'But the next Libyan Airlines flight isn't until Saturday, and the party's on Friday; I'll miss it,' I attempted to explain.

'Then you'll have to fly BA. The British Airways flight is thirteen hundred dinars,' Carl told me matter-of-factly.

I was incensed. 'Let me understand this: you want me to pay over six hundred pounds for a ticket to London when I don't have any money and I have a free ticket with Libyan Airways? Even Afriqiyah Airways are only 700 dinars.'

Carl was unaffected. 'Go Afriqiyah Airways then. I'll tell accounts to advance you the money, and get a driver to collect the ticket.'

There was no arguing. Now I would get a Friday flight, which fell during the Eid holiday, so I would not need any time off school. The flight with Afriqiyah Airways would cost me three hundred and fifty pounds, and I would not be getting my time off in lieu. I conceded that I would still make the party in the evening for my mother's birthday; but not on my terms. Carl had won this battle, but why did it have to be a struggle at all? Seeking the truth of my husband's death was enough of a fight for me.

Twitching nervously, I waited in Tripoli Airport for my flight home. On the drive to the airport the taxi driver, Sharif, retold his account of the crash at the airport; just what I needed before taking to the skies. On arrival Sharif had unloaded my small bag and gleamed his gold teeth at me, and I had handed him twenty dinars and waited expectantly for the five dinars change that was not forthcoming; Sharif gave a disgruntled look when he realized he would receive no tip that day.

The flight was delayed over two hours at Tripoli International Airport, and I only just made it to my mother's party in time. The family reunion went well; it was lovely to see the children and my mother was radiantly happy, which made the struggle in getting home worthwhile. My current place of domicile was a source of fascination to my family. 'Why would you want to go back there after what happened to you?' a cousin asked me. It was hard to explain the pull Libya had in my life: I had exhausted all avenues and felt that being in the country where the tragedy had happened was my last option. The stigma of the pariah state had not left most people's minds; Libya was still regarded as a terrorist nation by most of the world. But I was finding it a pleasant enough place to live, but for the problems with my boss.

Packing for my return journey to Tripoli four days later took a lot of concerted effort because I was determined to smuggle across some home comforts courtesy of the local supermarket. Along with the many boxes of cat food I balanced out in my suitcases, I thought I would try my luck with a couple of wine boxes. People took wine kits in all the time – it was generally accepted that the Westerns enjoyed their brew and nothing was said; I had tried this myself, but had ended up with a concoction that tasted a lot like raspberry cordial and lacked any kick – and I hoped the wine boxes would be mistaken for kits. Surely all that would happen if it went horribly wrong was they would take them from me? By the same rationalization, I decided to empty out the contents of a ginger ale bottle and substitute them with whiskey, and I added to my stash some ham – forbidden food in a Muslim country – and packs of chocolate. I buried the contraband under lacy knickers and women's magazines in the cases, in the hope of putting off a security official during a search, but in the event I glided through security and customs. It was bold, some would say foolish, but I was giddy with the thought of rebellion. A strange kind of retribution for my husband's death.

'People were wondering if you would come back or not,' Sandra said to me at the school briefing the day after my return to Libya.

'I was always coming back,' I said, trying not to let my surprise show.

'What with the Oasis affair and the trouble you had over using your ticket, we weren't sure you hadn't had enough.'

'Takes more than insinuation and lies to make me quit,' I said with determination. 'I haven't even begun yet to seek the justice that I'm owed.' I thought of the children I taught, many of them sons and daughters of important people in Libya, and of my hope of gaining access to those in positions of power in the country. Then, changing the subject quickly, I said lightly, 'Who can keep away from this place? What would I do for entertainment?'

We had one week left at the school before the Christmas break, and the staff party was provoking discussion. A list had been put up in the staffroom for staff to put down their names to indicate whether they were going to bring a savory dish or a dessert. Carl and his wife Wendy would supply the turkey, which would be a massive bird to satisfy sixty staff and some spouses, and Wendy would cook her special Christmas pudding.

The staff were divided between those who didn't mind bringing and sharing and those who wanted a more traditional Christmas dinner provided for them. But in the previous international schools I had worked at, Christmas dinner was something of an institution, a chance for the management to treat the staff as a thank you for all their hard work. The catering staff would lay on the turkey with chestnut stuffing and sausages wrapped in bacon accompanied by cranberry sauce, roasted vegetables and the obligatory sprouts. The head would then take everyone down the local boozer where we would while away the afternoon becoming increasingly merry as we swapped tales of our students over the previous term.

I took it upon myself to explain to Carl that the staff morale was in need of such a boost. 'I've never worked anywhere where we didn't get a proper Christmas dinner, even in China,' I told him.

'Felicity, I have a hard enough time getting any money out of the company for expenses for entertainment. No one else is complaining about having to bring their own food. Only you,' he pointed out.

'Actually, I'm not even going to the party – I have another engagement – but I'm the only one who will tell you. It doesn't mean the others don't think the same.' I wondered if Carl had experience at international schools where it was the norm to throw functions for the staff at hotels and other venues that they would not normally get the opportunity to visit. I thought of some the places I had been in my teaching career; even in Botswana no expense was spared in organizing braais and safari drives to keep the Western staff happy.

Coming out of Carl's office felt like walking dejectedly off a battlefield. I didn't mind being the spokesperson for the others but it wasn't even my battle and I had to be careful that he wouldn't turn around and stop my exit visa to leave for Christmas in a few days.

As it was, I was delighted to be excused from attending the Christmas function so that I could go to an event organized by one of the Embassies. The staff do was held in the basement of one of the villas, away from prying eyes of Libyan neighbors who might frown upon the smell of liquor rising up to their balconies. On my return from the Embassy event I called in late at the school do. On entering and seeing the dark environment, droning, noisy music and flashing lights I regretted my decision to pop by, but I decided to enter into the spirit of the event and was soon dancing and enjoying myself. It was moments like these that I saw a different Libya: away from the young men heckling from their cars as I drove down the road, the red tape of the bureaucrats, the need to cover my body from top to toe, even in the oppressive heat.

Keeping within the festive mood, I decided to hold a party for the invited few. Nothing tastes as good as forbidden fruit, and we washed down our ham sandwiches with intoxicating ginger ale and wine from the boxes. The drinks party was a huge success: the twenty or so people on the guest list didn't stop talking about it to the rest of the staff. 'Way better than the staff do, Felicity, well done' was the verdict. Buzzing, I was determined to replenish my forbidden supplies on my next run home and to outdo my Christmas bash the next summer (and indeed I would do so, but little did I know then that the gathering would be aptly named my deportation party).

Term ended on the 18th of December, and a crowd of us headed to the airport to take the British Airways flight back to London; some were going on to explore Europe, but I was looking forward to snuggling up at home for Christmas.

As I queued with my friend Gina, we looked around worriedly at the throngs in the airport.

'I heard them say they're overbooked,' Gina said. 'We should be alright, we were quite early?' she stated a little nervously. The thought of being bumped off the flight was horrifying.

'Look, there's the Ambassador and his wife,' I said excitedly, pointing to a much shorter queue beside us. 'They're on the same flight as us.'

'Yeah, but wouldn't you know it, they're travelling first class.' Nudging a little closer, we were able to overhear the young Libyan man on the first class check-in desk talk to the Ambassador and his wife.

'Dignitaries or not sir,' he was saying, 'you do not have a first class ticket and will have to join the queue for economy.' The check-in assistant pointed to the long line at the back and promptly called out, 'Next,' before the Ambassador could engage in any more conversation.

Gina and I stifled our inappropriate giggles and Gina said, 'I bet your friend at the Observer would like to hear that story.'

But I wasn't interested in running to the paper with such gossip. The Ambassador, after all, had always been very polite and helpful to me. I had e-mailed to thank him for the use of his car and inform him that I had found the right grave this time, but I couldn't resist adding that I was a little surprised that I'd had to go on my own, and then the clanger: what was being done about my case? And in the meantime I had written an angry e-mail to the British foreign secretary demanding to know what was being done about investigating the death of my husband, a British citizen; and I had copied the Ambassador in on that correspondence. On the plane the Ambassador got up to stretch his legs and walked past me and Gina. He stopped to greet us and exchanged small talk, and though he didn't mention my e-mails, his conversation with me was a sign of acknowledgement.

My time home seemed to pass in a heartbeat. Pain from the death of Danny was raw and it had overshadowed Christmas. Tallena had started another course at a different university, but neither the course nor the time was right. Theo was drifting along, unable to find a direction in life. I despaired at my failure in raising the children on my own. I could not protect my daughter from her grief in losing her best friend, and I could not create in my son a sense of purpose and ambition. There was no doubt in my mind that my son would have benefited from his father's easygoing approach to life. He would have taught his son about motorcycles and car engines and how to fix just about anything. When Theo was just a boy my heart would break when I saw him rub his chin the same funny little way as his father had and turn his bicycle upside down to examine the cogs spinning and turning.

I didn't know how to help my children any more. I had done all I could but it wasn't enough. Our family had been left to struggle and do the best we could, but years of striving to make ends meet had left the children dependent on me and I needed them to take the next step and become independent. The Libyan military's blunder, or contrived attack, had imprisoned us in a time capsule: we were trapped, neglected and forgotten, and could not move forward.

During the Christmas holiday we were invited to attend a memorial service to commemorate the twenty-year anniversary of the Lockerbie bombing. The security at Heathrow was prominent, with armed police outside the chapel directing the traffic to keep moving, and as we came down the swirling staircase to the basement of the chapel we were greeted by armed officers. I worried for a moment about the police presence. Were they just being extra cautious, or was there any threat of a terrorist attack today? Certainly we would be trapped if a bomb went off in the chapel: the only escape route seemed to be the staircase we had just descended. I nodded hello to familiar faces and agreed to catch up at the hotel reception afterwards. It dawned on me that this would be the perfect hostage situation. All of these families had each just received the last tranche of their ten million dollar settlement from Gaddafi. This room was full of multi-millionaires. If there had been a threat, the police had taken it very seriously.

Taking our seats in the third row, I noticed the BBC camera on us and decided not to tell my children, who would have objected to the intrusion. My attention was focused on the plaque that Jim

Swire had made for the tenth anniversary, listing those who had lost their lives. Thoughtfully, he had added Victor's name.

The service was beautiful. Even staff of the dissolved Pan Am came and recounted their memories of the horrific night when, having just finished their shift, they heard the terrible news on the radio and rushed back to Heathrow, working through the night to do what they could. These members still met regularly to support each other, and I thought they were the forgotten victims of the disaster. The lilting tones of the violin and the soprano singer filled the small chapel, and tears rolled down people's faces, releasing again their suffering and their grief. I felt privileged to be a part of moments like these. I prayed for the Lockerbie families who had lost their precious loved ones twenty years ago that day, and I prayed for my son and daughter sitting either side of me who had lost their father in equally dire circumstances sixteen years before.

After the service some two hundred people were milling about and several coaches had been laid on to move us to the hotel where the reception was to be held. I spotted Jim and John Mosey talking to a news reporter. The two had worked tirelessly for the past twenty years to find the truth of what happened, and neither believed they had ever been told it. I knew the Rev. John Mosey had opened at least two orphanages in the Third World, and he was keen to open one in Libya. What a truly giving man of God, I thought, and again my eyes swelled up with the privilege of knowing such men.

The service had been so beautiful that I saw people's faces radiating when we entered the reception. The mood was light and the heaviness of the service was replaced with a near joyous banter. People milled about, smiling and chatting to other people there that they may not have seen for the past ten years, since the last memorial, but the common bond they shared brought their conversations alive.

My children had eaten their sandwiches and drunk their

refreshment and were eager now to get back to their own lives. I wanted to stay, but it was late now. We hurried home, arriving just in time to see the service televised. The cameras had settled on Theo and Tallena and me more than once. Perhaps they thought they were delivering a poignant close-up of a Lockerbie widow twenty years on and her fatherless children, now young adults. They were nearly right.

Chapter 20

Christmas gave a new lease of life. The teachers' batteries had been recharged; the break into civilization had restored spirits and sanity. Even Tripoli seemed more energetic, forging ahead in regenerating its metropolis. Skyscraper buildings were popping up all over the capital, cranes swinging in the air as they lifted concrete blocks to build the latest complex, and even more foreign workers flooded in for the construction sites. Oil was not the only industry revived after the sanctions were lifted. New foods could be seen filling the shop shelves, and it was best to buy up large quantities if you found a favorite food because there was no telling when they would appear again. I even discovered one or two Western-style coffee shops by the seafront, which helped relieve the tediousness of something to do.

Usually, I spent my time when I wasn't at school sitting on my veranda with a non-alcoholic beer, basking in the sunshine and catching the breeze that filtered around the corner. A neighbor, Vee, and I had made it our mission to develop the small communal garden. I got one of my taxi drivers, Haj, to put a tap on the pipeline and bought a hose to water the flowers I planted. It was amazing how the plants grew in the sand. Along with the vibrant geraniums in ceramic pots I added shocks of color with native shrubs. It looked glorious in the winter months, during which the weather was more like spring in the UK, the smell of the plants mingling together with the jasmine and lemon blossoms.

'If only we could keep it like this, duck,' Vee smiled at me. 'It would be our own little haven. It's a shame we can't do something about the guards coming in all the time to use the outside kitchen and toilet.'

The villa had an outside building that housed a toilet used by the school guards. They often left food scattered in the kitchen, encouraging the rats, and the smell from the toilet – a hole in the ground – pervaded the garden; not to mention the encroachment it was on our privacy to have a constant procession of men traipsing through to use the facilities.

'They either leave the door open and the smell comes out, or they bang it shut, making the loudest noise they can. The number of times I've been woken up on the weekend with the guards using that toilet I can't tell you,' I confided in Vee. 'And I'm sure they just come in to have a nose about and see who's at my place.'

'But they shouldn't even be using that toilet, this is our private space. There are toilets at school for them to use,' Vee said. 'Something needs to be done about it,' Vee said, 'but it doesn't matter how many times Carl tells them, they still come in here to our villa.'

Even Haj the taxi driver I had found couldn't believe the affront of the guards using the toilet by my back door. He was appalled by the conduct of the younger Libyan men. 'You are a lone woman; they are not to come into your garden.' Determined to deal with the problem, I decided to enlist Haj's help in building a wall, to block the path of the guards. But he had a better idea: put a padlock on the toilet door.

We didn't have long to wait before one of the guards came to snoop at us women on the pretense of using the toilet. Shaking his head at the younger guard, the Libyan driver, in his Friday mosque clothes, waved his finger and spoke to him assertively in Arabic.

'He won't be coming here again, Felicity,' Haj said to me as the guard stalked off. 'It's not right and they know it's not right.'

What had been lost in those years of sanctions in Libya, I wondered to myself. The middle-aged men were gentlemen, but the younger men had less decorum. Perhaps, like me, they felt the need to rebel.

Saturdays were usually the hardest day to fill in, and with my garden freshly tidied and privacy secured, I looked at my well-stocked freezer and decided to take out the pork chops I had smuggled over and invite some colleagues for a barbecue. To my delight Elizabeth had returned to Tripoli, having spent two months rattling around an empty house struggling to find a comfortable fit in her new garment of widowhood, and she was first on my list to invite.

She looked pleasantly surprised to see me when she opened the door, and accepted my invitation. 'But first,' she said, 'tell me what you have done about the Art House and doing your exhibition?'

I had been promised an exhibition at the Art House, the main gallery in Tripoli, years ago, when Mohammed had seen some of my work during my visit to the city with the children to see Victor's grave, and introduced me to the director of the gallery. But when I went to see the director, Mr. Jana, a pleasant man approaching sixty and with a reasonable command of English, while he remembered me from my earlier visit, he was noncommittal on exhibiting my work. The gallery was fully booked this year, he said, and anyway, they mainly promoted Libyan artists. He suggested I get a group of foreign artists together; that perhaps we could do an exhibition on how foreigners view Libya. I was not impressed; with Mohammed's influence years before, this man had all but promised me a sole exhibition. And I knew my work was powerful. I had exhibited at the National Gallery in Gaborone when I worked in Botswana and in other prestigious venues, such as the Palace of Westminster in London. At the inaugural opening of the Pump House Gallery in Battersea Park newspaper photographers had got their money shot when the then minister for the arts, David Mellor, stood in front of my satire of the snakes and ladders game of the housing market. I had been selected to do a three women group show for the Egyptian Embassy for UNESCO, who were promoting the rebuilding of the Great Library at Alexandra. And my curriculum vitae even extended to the Louvre in Paris, where my work had hung for one week as part of the Maltese Biennale.

And since coming to Libya, I had found all manner of inspiration for my artwork; for when you looked in the right places, this was a beautiful country. I had been captivated by the world-renowned ruins at Leptis Magna. The Libyans viewed them with near-contempt, saying they were Italian and they hated anything to do with Italian rule, but for me the buildings and mosaics surrounded by lush greenery and the azure of the Mediterranean were awe-inspiring. Better still were the places off the beaten track I visited with the Archaeological Society – ruins out in the desert. I never went anywhere without my sketchbook.

'I didn't hear back from the other artists I e-mailed, so I don't have any proposal for the gallery,' I said. Dispirited, I had put the exhibition at the bottom of my list of things to do in Libya.

'Why don't we go and see them again and jolly them along a bit?' Elizabeth suggested.

'What, today? I wasn't thinking of it,' I said, thinking of the potato salad I wanted to make and the dessert I would have to prepare.

'There's no time like the present.' Elizabeth smiled.

'You know, you're right,' I said. If I waited for people to get back to me, it wouldn't happen.

And an hour later Elizabeth and I were sitting in the courtyard of the gallery drinking coffee with the director, and hearing the golden words, 'Please come to the exhibition and meet the curator of the gallery. I will introduce you to him and you can discuss a plan for your work.'

A couple of weeks later, I was having a meal with friends after church when my attention was drawn to the phone conversation of the man sitting beside me. The Turkish restaurant was noisy, and consequently Jess was talking loudly, and I thought he had mistakenly put his phone on loudspeaker as I could hear every word being spoken.

'Yes, yes, I can hear you alright, Ambassador. I have a pen ready here to take down the details.' Jess was the lay preacher at the church and it was natural for him to be in touch with dignitaries, but I knew the Ambassador worshipped at the Catholic Church so I wondered what they could be discussing.

Not wanting to pry, I made sure my eyes avoided the pad he had out but I couldn't help overhearing the gist of the conversation.

'You need twenty people from the church for the cocktails and ten for the meal with His Grace,' Jess said, making sure his instructions were clear. 'And when can we expect His Grace to arrive?' Jess queried.

I stopped chewing, stunned. There was only one man I knew of whose title was 'His Grace'. Was it some kind of code they were speaking to outwit any surveillance, or was the Archbishop of Canterbury, His Grace Doctor Rowan Williams, the head of the Church of England, actually coming to Libya? Straining to hear with the clash of the dishes being served on the tables and the din of the conversation, I thought I heard the Ambassador say, 'Next week then,' as the two men were ending their conversation.

Curiosity stirred, I waited for Jess to divulge the information to the group. But all he said was, 'Well, that was an interesting call.'

I sat in silence for the rest of the meal, contemplating the phone call. I had heard a rumor that the Archbishop was coming to Libya, but I had dismissed it as nonsense. What would be his purpose in coming? I vaguely remembered talk in the papers about the Archbishop and the introduction of sharia law in Britain, and decided I would need to go to the school and check the newspapers online the next day. I hoped the Internet would be working; it was often down in Libya.

The next morning I was at school early. Overnight I had deliberated on the fact that the Archbishop may be coming over, and how I could gain an audience with him if that were the case. I hoped Jess would have considered me for the list for the pre-dinner cocktails, if not dinner also. He knew the basics of my story. But wanting to be on the guest list, I decided, was not the same as getting on to it, so I decided to make myself known to the Archbishop of Canterbury myself.

There was no doubt I loved the ex-pat life where you were invited to Embassy functions; it was nice to put on a pretty frock and a lick of makeup to feel you were worth a second glance. But I had another agenda for wanting to greet and shake hands with the head of the Church of England. If anyone could organize a blessing for my husband at the gravesite, he could. And if he needed permission from the Islamic Call Society, it wouldn't be prudent of them to refuse His Grace. There was obviously motive for him coming to Libya, and as long I could approach him with my request, surely he could consider it? I had to believe he would.

I clapped my hands together when the Internet launched at last. Going from link to link on the different search engines, I found the confirmation that Dr. Williams was indeed coming to Tripoli in a week, and I managed to find an e-mail address for his secretary. I explained my situation, and my desire for a Christian blessing, and ended with the words: *To rebuild the bridges that people talk about, they must first repair the damage they have inflicted on others.*

The next day Elizabeth accidentally let slip that she had been invited to the dinner the Ambassador was hosting for His Grace. I could fully understand why Elizabeth had been invited: she was the surviving wife of the vicar who had just died. As soon as she told me, she burst into tears.

'What's wrong, Elizabeth?' I asked, concerned.

'It's not me, they wanted to see, it's Matthew. And he's dead.'

'Oh, Elizabeth,' I said, putting my arm around her shoulder, 'of course they want to see you too.'

'It's you who should be meeting His Grace, it's you they

haven't done anything for,' she said through her tears.

It wasn't the moment to say 'I know'; I kept my sadness to myself. I didn't mention the e-mail to the Archbishop, to which I had received no reply yet.

When the day of the reception for the Archbishop arrived, it was clear to me that several members of staff at the school were attending the event. James and Emma diplomatically said they had another engagement on Thursday evening, but were silent when I asked what it was, and Rob Kernel and his wife were finishing work early that day to run some errand. Blane Copperfield's wife sometimes sang in the church choir, but she wasn't a regular churchgoer like me, yet she boasted in the staffroom at lunchtime about the big-wig cocktail party she was going to that night.

It hurt that I had been omitted from the list, but I tried not to let my disappointment show. I wondered whether Carl had said something to Jess to make him leave me off the list. As soon as the thought entered my mind my phone rang in class. It was Carl, unusually summoning me mid-class to his office. Mystified, I headed to his office. Was I to receive a late invitation to the do via my boss?

'Take a seat,' Carl indicated to me. My alarm bells were ringing now: he had always left me standing before. He closed the screen on his laptop, which again was a first while talking to me, and turned to me, putting his hands in a prayer-like pose, and said, 'Now, the Ambassador has asked me to talk to you.'

Now I was worried. 'The Ambassador?'

'Yes, the Ambassador has asked me to talk to you about the trip of the Archbishop of Canterbury.'

I sat in the chair quietly, seething inside. As far as I was concerned, I had e-mailed the Archbishop privately. It was not Carl's or the Ambassador's business what I had said to the Archbishop.

Carl continued with what sounded like a prepared speech.

'Now, the Archbishop's visit to Tripoli has no political agenda, and the Archbishop doesn't want to get involved with any political situation.'

Standing up, I went to leave. 'Then the Archbishop needs to tell me that himself,' I said.

'If you could just hear me out,' he said and motioned for me to sit down.

Reluctantly, I complied.

'The Archbishop's trip is about building bridges here.'

'Then they need to fix what is broken.' I was outraged. Carl must have seen the e-mail I had sent privately to the Archbishop; otherwise why would he refer to the bridges?

Then Carl delivered the first positive words of the meeting: 'You will get a chance to meet the Archbishop, Felicity, he's very sympathetic to your case. He's doing the service on Friday at church and there will be a lunch afterwards, so he's made time for you to meet him then.'

I had no choice but to pass on my thanks to the Ambassador for arranging the meeting, and leave Carl's office as quickly as I could so he wouldn't see my tears. I had just been slapped on one side of the face and kissed on the other; I didn't know where I was. My private mail had been kicked around the diplomatic circuit until they had decided what to do with me. I didn't like being kept out of the way at the function that evening. And how was a service at Victor's grave political? I had been promised time to talk to the Archbishop, but I knew all too well what the lunches were like at church, and I doubted I would get the chance to open up as I wanted to. It was frustrating, to say the least, to be within reach of a man who could help fulfil my dearest wish to see my husband at peace, but be denied a proper audience. All I could do was follow instructions, and hope the Archbishop would reach out to me.

Chapter 21

Knowing I had been promised an audience with the Archbishop helped me focus the next morning, but it didn't stop me changing my clothes for the fourth time as if I were a teenager on my first date. 'It's not right, girls,' I said to my cats. 'It's too black and dour.' Holding up another more colorful top, I looked at the cats rubbing up against my legs and asked, 'What do you think of this one? Does it lift up my face a bit? Does it say widow who needs help but isn't helpless?' The cats seemed to agree with me, which was good, as if I didn't leave soon I would be all flustered and rushing at the last minute.

I was glad of the opportunity to sit in church and listen to the Egyptian Christians harmonize their songs in Arabic as I contemplated the forthcoming meeting. I prayed the right words would come to me when I was finally introduced to the Archbishop. The church began to fill up rather quickly and I was glad I had arrived early and was sitting near the front. The pews were filling up with familiar faces and people I had never seen before. I was pleasantly surprised when I caught sight of an American girl, Pam, I had once chatted to for nearly an hour at the Oasis, before my embarrassing banishment. Mouthing a silent hello to her, I made a mental note to find her after the service. There was still ten minutes to go before the service began and already the church was full.

It was a relatively large building that had been a Catholic church in the time the Italians had ruled Libya. Slowly it was being revamped and it had some redeeming features. An ancient altar had been uncovered in the renovations, surrounded by mosaics and Roman columns. The rather high ceiling allowed the light in from tall windows that had been covered over with wire mesh to stop the pigeon population getting in and nesting in the rafters. The church had been derelict and neglected for many years until it had been used as an art gallery, I had learned. It had been given to the Anglican Church just two years ago as a place of worship by the Islamic Call Society, whose position still mystified me.

My thoughts were suddenly interrupted by a charming voice saying, 'Hello, Felicity. How are you?' Looking up, I couldn't hide my surprise at seeing the Ambassador leaning into the row where I was sitting. He took my hand and kissed me on the cheek.

'I'm, I'm fine, Sir Vincent. How are you?' I stuttered back, not knowing what to say. He was a charming man with impeccable manners and I admired him in many ways.

Gently tugging on his wife, who was engaged in a conversation with someone near her, he said, 'Say hello to Felicity, darling.'

Lady Fean immediately stopped her conversation and planted an equally surprising kiss on my cheek. Very sweetly, she said, 'Hello, Felicity. We hope to see you after the service.'

Not knowing what else to say, I replied, 'I'll look forward to that.'

Snubbed one day and sought out the next, I thought to myself as the small talk ended and silence fell in the church to denote that the service was about to begin.

The procession coming down the aisle saw the twelve-strong choir, then lay priests and clergymen, followed by bishops who had flown in from around Northern Africa proceeding down before the Archbishop in all his splendor. His Grace brought an air of pageantry that delighted me. Who would have thought, I reflected, that I had decided to stay with the Anglican Church mostly because they had been so lovely to my mother in London and now in exchange I was about to meet the head of the Church of England. His Grace's voice carried throughout the church like none other, and the power within the man showed. Visiting Orthodox and Coptic Christians sat among the bishops; I could have been in Lambeth Palace or Westminster Abbey with so many holy men present. The sermon was moving and sincere and the choir did justice to the sound system that had been temporarily installed. Most touching was the Arabic choir and the words of 'Kyrie Eleison' I had come to recognize as meaning 'Lord have mercy'.

January was still a little chilly, and in the stillness of the church I had grown cold, so after the service I decided to stand in the sunshine of the courtyard. The entourage of priests was lined up by the central doorway, standing either side to greet the congregation as they filed out. I decided to take the side entrance to the courtyard to warm up, not wanting to pass the Archbishop at that moment. I judged he would be caught up for a while with greeting people and photo opportunities.

'Hello there,' a voice called out to me as I stood in the sunshine, adjusting my simple black cardigan. *Maybe I should have worn the blue one?* my head was saying to make me worry unnecessarily.

I turned to see the American girl and her companion coming towards me.

'Oh, hello, Pam. How lovely to see you,' I sang back. It was like meeting an old friend and conversation flowed easily.

'How did you hear about the Archbishop's visit to today's service?' I asked quizzically. As I understood it, only church members had been informed.

'The Embassy hears everything,' Pam said jokingly.

With a puzzled look, I asked 'What, your Embassy told your school?' I had assumed Pam was a teacher at the American school.

Pam laughed heartily at the case of mistaken identity. 'No,' she informed me. 'I work at the American Embassy. I'm a diplomat.'

I couldn't have looked more embarrassed. 'I'm sorry, I thought because you were at the Oasis on teachers' night that you were a teacher,' I said.

'Not for love or money!' Pam retorted and we both burst out laughing.

We chatted in the sun for a while and then I noticed the guest party heading back into the church.

'Are you staying for lunch?' I asked.

'Actually, I haven't been invited,' said Pam.

'Well, I'm inviting you and your friend to lunch, then, if you'd like to come.' I eyed the Archbishop disappearing back into church and didn't want to miss my chance for a meeting. 'Please excuse me, I have to dash.'

Inside the Archbishop was posing for several formal photos and I waited by the wall, hoping I would be able to catch him as he walked past. I was feeling a little dejected that I would then have to start explaining who I was.

Deep in deliberations, I heard a voice saying, 'Oh, Felicity, I've been looking for you. I want to introduce you to His Grace.' Looking over my shoulder, I saw the Ambassador approaching. He spoke softly to his aide, who then approached the aide of the Archbishop. Then His Grace began moving towards me.

Letting go of my anguish, I listened while the Ambassador introduced me.

'Thank you for meeting with me, Your Grace.' I dipped into my bag, brought out a brown envelope and handed it over. 'I know you are busy now but when you have time this briefly explains my situation, and I have put in one of my drawings of Libya as a souvenir for you.' I forged ahead, thinking I would only have a brief few minutes with the Archbishop. 'What I really want for my husband is a Christian blessing at the mass grave.' My voice choked up as I said the words, and even sixteen years hadn't mellowed the passion that stirred in my voice.

Looking straight into my eyes, he said, 'I'm going to arrange that for you.' He looked around momentarily and beckoned two bishops over. 'This is Bishop Bill Musk, he's in charge of the entire Diocese in Northern Africa, and this is Bishop Munier. They are going to arrange the service for you with my blessing. I am so sorry to learn of your very tragic loss.' His words were comforting and penetrated straight to my heart.

He had been holding an object that his aide had given him when he first came to approach, and now he took my hand kindly and said, 'This is for you.' And he placed a gift on the palm of my hand.

Through my tears I could barely manage a 'Thank you.' He motioned that he would see me later at lunch.

The two bishops stayed with me for a few minutes, and to my utter surprise they asked whether I would be able to go on Sunday for the service. 'I will be travelling back to Egypt on Sunday afternoon,' Bishop Bill said, 'and Bishop Munier will be heading to Tunisia, and the Ambassador has offered a car for Sunday morning.'

It dawned on me then that even though I hadn't been invited to the function I had certainly been discussed at some length, and the Ambassador had joined them in the talks about Sunday.

'Yes, yes, Sunday would be perfect.' Of course what I really wanted was for my children to be able to be there as well, but I had learned that with Libya you must take the offer when it's handed to you because it may not be there later.

'I don't know whether Carl will let me go again,' I said truthfully to the Ambassador who had come to join our group. I cheekily added, 'He's just over there, would you be able to ask him?' The Ambassador smiled a knowing smile; he knew that Carl wouldn't refuse him.

It was all arranged and Jess announced that the lunch was being served. Pam had come back inside with her friend, and I motioned for them to come and eat with me.

'I'm glad you decided to stay,' I said, smiling.

'I saw you talking to the Archbishop for a long time,' Pam said.

'I'll tell you about it one day,' I said to my new friend.

'I'll look forward to that,' Pam bounced back. To my surprise, some months later, when we two had cemented our friendship, Pam would share a similar story to mine, if not as close to home. There was a smile on my face when I left the church. After his meal the Archbishop had come to find me again and had chatted to me and the other women for nearly half an hour. I hadn't needed the setting of a lavish Embassy do. In the bowels of the neglected church in Tripoli the head of the Church of England had sought out my company by his own volition, not by what formality instructed him to do.

Coming to Libya had been the right decision, I knew now. Finally, after sixteen painful years, a Christian blessing could take place at the mass grave, a feat that would have been simply unachievable had I not been in Libya.

The next day, 1st February 2009, I handed a program I had made to the five people – the two bishops, Jess, the lay preacher, Pastor Hamdy and Elizabeth as my companion – who were to attend the very private service at the grave. I desperately wished my children could be with me, and the best I could do was include them in the program. I had printed a photograph of the young family when Victor was home and the children were toddlers. It was a beautiful picture, one of the very few of the four of us together. I included two other pictures: a scan of the beauti-fully-painted wooden cross that had been the Archbishop's gift to me, and a photo of the brass plaque I had made for Victor years before and never been able to mount on his grave. I included details of my beloved husband's life and death, and on the last page I thanked the people who had made the service possible: the Archbishop, the Ambassador, the two bishops, the clergymen from the church in Tripoli and Elizabeth, my friend who knew the pain of losing a husband. With reservations, I also thanked Carl for allowing me time off work to attend a ritual that most people take for granted: the funeral of their loved one.

As we drove out to the cemetery I reflected that I was glad of the privacy and calm, so different to the media frenzy surrounding the Lockerbie families, the television cameras and the newsmen and police guards that had intrusively dominated the twentieth anniversary memorial. The cold winter night of the 21st of December at Heathrow Airport just a few weeks ago seemed far removed from the stillness of the sultry dessert where just a few ambling goats in the rocky terrain could be heard bleating in the background.

The same driver who had taken me to the grave just a few weeks ago in December could not remember the way, and had to stop several times to ask directions. The unmarked dirt roads rambled off to nameless places. It was harsh countryside, baked dry by the merciless, blazing sun each summer, and even in the winter there was no greenery, just a few shrubs and nettles that pierced through the rocky ground to disturb the soil.

The cars arrived at the cemetery mid-morning, and we filed to the harsh slab of concrete, assembling in a semi-circle before the marble plaque written only in Arabic. I was pleased to see the two bishops dressed in their long robes and purple vestments and the dog collars of the lay priest: Christian symbolism in the heart of the desert. The sun blazed down on us, but little warmth was felt, and tumbleweeds rolled around aimlessly, pushed around by the breeze that made the torn green flag flap and disturb the silence that penetrated the somber moment.

Bishop Bill cleared his throat, and with years of experience behind him in conducting funerals, he knew how to choose the words that were sacred to me. Finally, after sixteen years, Victor's soul was committed to the Lord. Elizabeth had brought flowers and she laid them at the base of the plaque. I had etched the words that were engraved on the brass plaque I was forbidden to lay at the site sixteen years ago onto a board, and I found some rocks to secure it in an upright position. I knew as soon as we left it would be blown away or removed by a caretaker. But for the purpose of the committal, it was a focal point. Bishop Bill placed the program into his prayer book and I knew without asking that he had never performed such an unusual ceremony in his career as a priest.

There were no cameras rolling, no reporters capturing the tearful moments, but as if caught on a moving screen I imagined the sweeping panoramic portrayal of the lens fixing on a moment in time where we stood on holy ground. It had been a moving ceremony, heightened by the fact that it had taken sixteen years to achieve. Taking a last look at the surrounding area, I could never have imagined that the next time I returned to the gravesite it would be with the journalist of a national paper and the visit would make the front page of the world section.

Chapter 22

'Now I want to tell you about the dinner on Thursday night,' Elizabeth began carefully once the graveside service was behind us.

I was keen to hear about the reception for the Archbishop of Canterbury to which I had been denied an invitation in order, apparently, to avoid stirring up political issues.

'It was you who should have been there, Felicity,' Elizabeth announced.

I wanted to agree wholeheartedly with her but I just replied carefully, 'No one invited me. It's as if I don't exist.'

'Believe me, they know you do exist,' Elizabeth replied. 'I had a very interesting conversation with the vice consul and he wants you to get in touch with him.'

I gazed at Elizabeth, astonished. 'The vice consul wants me to get in touch with him?' Victor's committal ceremony had barely passed and here I was confronted with another issue.

'I happened to be sitting next to a very gallant young man at dinner who turned out to be the vice consul at the Embassy. He was saying that all the issues with Libya are mostly resolved now that the Lockerbie families have had the second tranche of their payments.'

I knew from attending the Lockerbie group meetings that Libya had reneged on paying the second payment of about three million dollars for each family for a couple of years, and at one point the families had doubted that they would receive it at all. I could have said to them, 'Well, I've never received anything from the Libyans. So I guess seven million dollars each, plus the money from the Pan Am insurers, isn't too bad a settlement, even without the final three million.' But I didn't think like that: the Lockerbie families were my friends and had been a source of great support to me; and I believed they deserved the money.

'It wasn't just the Lockerbie victims they paid,' I told Elizabeth wearily. 'Libya has compensated everyone from the UTA bombings; they received two payments because Chirac insisted they be compensated again once the amount of ten million dollars for each Lockerbie victim was announced. Just like the Americans, the French leader refused to do business with Libya until Gaddafi agreed to the second payment. Libya has also paid compensation over the La Belle Disco bombing that happened in Germany. And now the IRA victims are even wanting a slice and have the backing of the government. And what does the UK government do for me? Just brush my husband's death under the carpet. They don't have the guts to stand up to Gaddafi.'

Elizabeth gave a blank look at the mention of the IRA victims; it wasn't openly broadcast on the news at that point, but I had got wind of it. She was keen to get back to her story. 'Anyway, I said to him not all the cases are resolved. And I was about to mention you when the vice consul said to me, "I know who you're talking about, and I want you to ask Mrs. Prazak to get in touch with me so that we can help her. Please ask her to call me." And he gave me this card with his number on it.'

I was overwhelmed. It wasn't the Libyans I had to worry about spying on me and knowing all my movements, but it seemed the British Embassy was also keeping a beady eye on me: they read my private e-mail, and knew whom I was close to.

'I have his card in the apartment; I'll give it to you when we get back,' Elizabeth concluded, glad to be imparting good news.

I was suspicious more than happy. How did this man intend to help me when no one in the British government had done so for the past sixteen years?

Two weeks passed by as I focused on my school work. I didn't call the vice consul, because I knew the Embassy only opened during school hours and that Carl would not give me time off for any more personal business. 'You've had two days off now to go to the grave,' he had told me. 'I hope you won't be asking for any more personal time because you know what the answer will be.'

I tried not to pull a face. It was two half days I had taken off. Other members of staff had clocked up weeks in total of sick leave, and I had not taken a single day off for illness but had worked through chronic headaches brought on by stress. Yet, two half days to visit my husband's grave was construed as taking liberties.

When Elizabeth caught me in the hallway rushing to class one day she asked if I had met with the vice consul yet.

'Carl just won't let me have any more time off,' I said apologetically.

'You'll have to find a way to go, Felicity; I think it could be quite beneficial for you.'

'Surely they should contact me if they know anything new,' I said. But the thought of what the vice consul may have to tell me was niggling at me, so by the end of the week I telephoned him.

'Hello, Mrs. Prazak,' said the vice consul in reply to my nervous greeting. 'I've been waiting for you to call me. We'd like you to come into the Embassy and see what we can do to help you. When would you be able to come?'

It was all very mysterious. Why not just phone or e-mail me? But I decided I might as well go and see what they could offer.

Wednesday afternoon I didn't teach any classes, so I suggested a meeting then.

'I'm sorry, I'm in a meeting all day Wednesday. What about Thursday afternoon, say two p.m.?'

He couldn't have picked a worse time. Both my classes that afternoon were a handful on the last two lessons of the week, and it would not be straightforward organizing cover.

But I found myself replying, 'Yes, that will be fine, thank you.'

It was one week away and I knew I would have to find a way to go. It crossed my mind to lie and say I had a doctor's appointment. Several people had come up to me recently and asked whether I was okay. I hadn't been looking very well for a while. Then I had a brainwave: I would sidestep Carl and go directly to Roma, the head of secondary. Carl need never know.

Roma, happily, was perfectly accommodating, and even though I had permission to leave, when Thursday came I still felt like I was sneaking out of class when I left the school at lunchtime.

Haj drove me in his taxi to the Embassy, and agreed to wait. The pass was waiting at the security gate as the vice consul had stated, and a guard was called to take me to the main entrance of the large, sprawling villa. The grounds were immense and beautiful; I remembered them partly from the Queen's birthday celebrations I had attended years before while visiting Libya with the children. Surrounded by spring flowers, it was hard to believe we were in the city of Tripoli. In the villa security cameras watched as I was led up three flights of stairs and through steel doors that would not be out of place securing the vault of a bank.

'You don't have a lift then,' I chirped, out of breath, as a well-dressed gentleman in a pinstriped suit greeted me.

He laughed appropriately at my quip and introduced himself as the vice consul.

'I won't keep you a minute; I'm just on the phone in my office. Please do take a seat.'

I was left alone with the vice consul's aide, a rather dark-skinned man.

'Are you Libyan?' I asked him.

The man answered with an air of piety, 'No, I'm British.'

When the vice consul reappeared and formally introduced me to his aide I was startled to realize I recognized the man's name as one I had heard Carl mention in the staffroom from time to time; the two men were friends. Uneasily, I questioned my naïvety at coming here alone. I should have brought a witness to whatever it was that was about to take place.

The vice consul finished his call, and I was duly ushered into his large office. I attempted to make myself comfortable on an oversized sofa in the corner. The aide sat opposite. I didn't attempt to engage him in conversation again after my first blunder, but waited quietly for the vice consul to settle himself a respectable distance from me on the sofa.

'Sorry about that, Mrs. Prazak,' he offered. 'I trust you and my aide have been getting acquainted.' Before I could speak he said, 'Actually, we've met before.'

Looking over at the young man Elizabeth had described as gallant, I couldn't for the life of me remember meeting him anywhere. I said, 'I'm sorry but I don't remember meeting you.'

'It was at the Oasis,' the vice consul said.

'Oh my gosh,' I blurted out before I could stop myself. 'I wasn't rude to you, was I?' A memory flooding back: standing up to a pompous woman who declared, *I am the wife of the vice consul.*

The man laughed and told me good humoredly, 'No, no you weren't.'

By the way the vice consul had laughed I knew our brief meeting had been inoffensive, and a hazy recollection emerged in my mind of the event. It had been the school visit the month before the disastrous Oasis Bar trip, and the new teachers were letting their hair down. We had tequila shots lined up along the bar. Lola had bought the round, and I had insisted I didn't do shots, but Lola had paid no attention to my protest and had banged on the bar and counted down. Three, two, one and the newly arrived teachers in a dry Muslim country rammed the tequila down their throats, knowing it would be another month before they had freedom like this again. In my half-intoxicated state I said to the chap standing waiting at the bar in his pinstriped suit, 'I wouldn't stand here too long, you might get forced to forget you're in Libya.' We had joked for a few minutes and then he had moved on. The level-headed vice consul had been amused by the antics of the inebriated teachers; his wife, the next month, was not.

Remembering our first meeting diffused some of my tension. The vice consul firstly offered his condolences and reiterated his commitment to help me.

'After receiving your letter...' – I thought he must be referring to the one I had sent to the foreign secretary – '... we've asked our counterparts in the Libyan government for the crash report. We'll assist you in getting any information you request.'

'With all due respect, sir, I hope you do a better job than your predecessors who sent me the wrong crash report. Can you imagine the widow of a man who died in the Twin Towers receiving the TWA report of the plane that went down in the Hudson years before? Can you actually imagine how that woman would feel? Or what the press would have made of it?'

'I'm sorry that happened to you,' the vice consul said quite genuinely. 'What is it you think the British government should be doing for you? How can we help?'

It struck me as an odd question. I had pleaded my case dozens of times, and asked for the crash report and trial transcript at least once or twice a year.

'I want the crash report, I want the trial transcript and I want compensation,' I said, my voice choked with emotion. 'And you know my husband was buried without my permission and I have never had the body back, so...' I lingered for impact. 'So I want his body returned so that I can have an inquest. That's my right, and that's what you should be giving me.'

It was asking the mountain to go to Mohammed: impossible. But somehow I had to believe it was possible. Or at least that I could ask for the impossible knowing anything is possible with God. But I was dealing with man and asking him to do what was impossible in a Muslim world. Britain wanted lucrative oil deals with Libya; it didn't want ghosts to come alive from the dead.

The aide, who had been sitting silently up until now, spoke for the first time. 'That's not feasible, Mrs. Prazak.' He spoke with authority but I questioned him anyway.

'Why can't I have an inquest? I'm entitled to it, and it's the job of the British Embassy to organize it.' They couldn't argue with me. It is the right of the relative of any British subject killed abroad in suspicious circumstances to ask for an inquest. But they had no intention of granting me my rights.

'It is the British government that is at fault for allowing Victor to be buried in a mass grave without lodging a protest to the Libyan authorities.'

'We didn't have an Embassy here at the time of your husband's death,' the aide countered.

Had they actually checked their files? I wondered. I had sat downstairs in this very building six months after Victor was killed and the wife of the head of Mission had poured me a drink after I had been to the grave for the first time. Certainly, to get any alcohol into the country all those years ago they had the same diplomatic immunity and status they were now enjoying at the Oasis Bar.

'You had a Mission here, and I met the head of Mission sixteen years ago,' I stated for the record.

'Who was that?' the vice consul piped up, interested.

'I think his name was Mr. Brown,' I said hazily. 'His wife told me how they had to hide in the cellar when the Americans dropped their bombs on Tripoli in 1986. So there has always been a British Mission here, even though there were no diplomatic relations to speak of.'

The game of cat and mouse wasn't working for the two men: I was too quick with my answers.

'I came here because you told Elizabeth you wanted to help me and all I've had so far is fob offs and a grilling.' I had won the first round of what seemed like a fight in the boxing ring. I stood in my imaginary defense pose, lashing out before they could say anything. 'If it takes me another sixteen years to get to the truth, I will carry on as I have done, asking questions that the British government should be finding out the answers to instead of sweeping my husband's case under the carpet. And don't think I'll sit silently forever while you people fail me.'

The vice consul had gone quiet, deliberating on his next words, then he said, 'It's best not to get the press involved. They're only after selling newspapers.'

'I've actually found any press I've talked to have been very nice and quite genuine,' I contradicted him. 'And I've seen the Lockerbie people use the press to their own advantage,' I added. 'They've kept the disaster in people's minds by contacting the media or having some new evidence or theory brought to light; they've kept it in the public domain by bringing it up every three months for the past twenty years.' I knew he couldn't argue with that.

The vice consul looked alarmed that the meeting was veering away from an amicable exchange. He took the risk of asking a direct question.

'You mentioned compensation earlier, Mrs. Prazak. Do you have a figure in mind?' He was careful how he asked the question and I was sensitive enough to realize he wasn't being intrusive, but it was hard to answer all the same.

'How much do you think my pain is worth? How much do you think the loss of my children's father is worth, the effect it has had on them not having his love in their lives any more? Or me for that matter. How much compensation should I have received when they buried my husband without my permission in a country I can't even get into if I want to? How much trauma was I caused when you sent me the wrong crash report? I've had to bring up my two children on my own making ends meet every day, what is that worth?

'Ten million dollars, that's what the Lockerbie families got. Is my pain or loss any less than theirs? It's not more and it's not less. One person's life is not worth more than another person's life. And no one can deny that Libya did this to my family. Their military brought my husband's plane down; they can't deny that.

Yet they continue to ignore me and my family and our suffering. So I see no reason why I am not entitled to the same: ten million dollars.'

The figure didn't matter to me. One or two million dollars would have been recognition. It was the principle.

'There are certain things we can do as an Embassy, and other things we can't,' said the vice consul, who had sat unflinching through my monologue. 'We can't get involved with asking for compensation for you; that would be a civil case. Even in the case of the Lockerbie families and the UTA families that you've mentioned,' he said, 'they had legal representation to act for them. We can ask for the crash report for you and will continue to do that but I must stress that any financial matters should be done through a lawyer.'

'But I don't know how to go about getting a lawyer. I thought about it after Victor died, but how could I engage one? Gaddafi owned the airline and was the head of the military. Where would I find a lawyer to challenge Gaddafi? I thought perhaps I could approach the Libyans myself, so they would see the truth without a messy lawsuit, but it hasn't worked. And now, all these years later, I don't know how to proceed legally.' I wasn't sure whether being so candid with them was to my advantage, but above all I wanted to be truthful.

'We can help you there to a degree. We have a list of very good Libyan lawyers that we recommend. We've checked them out as much as we could,' the aide told me. 'I'll get it for you.'

Immediately the penny dropped. This was the point of the meeting. I had talked endlessly about my loss and pain but they weren't interested in that. They were interested in diffusing their role as an Embassy in the investigation of Victor's death, smoothing it over with a civil case.

'I don't know if I can do this. I don't even know if money means anything at all to me. It would never give me the life I lost.' I was confused now having talked for too long about painful matters.

'It could help your children,' the vice consul said sincerely. 'These things need to be done legally, Mrs. Prazak, and you need a lawyer for that. You're here in Libya now and you may find someone prepared to help.'

The aide handed me the list of lawyers and I put on my glasses to glance at the unfamiliar names. 'I don't know where to start,' I said, looking at the two columns of names. In total there were about twenty lawyers listed, some dealt with civil cases and some criminal. To me, it wasn't a civil issue but a criminal one. The MiG co-pilot had been found to be responsible, so the military were to blame. So why would I have to pursue this as a civil action?

Shaking my head, I just repeated, 'I don't know if I can do this.' I could see a long, messy legal battle ahead.

It had been an intense meeting and the vice consul could see that I was worn out. He wanted to end on a positive note.

'By the way, Mrs. Prazak, you know you are no longer banned from the Oasis.'

I couldn't help smiling. 'Thank you.'

Chapter 23

I spent the evening following my meeting with the vice consul at a dinner party, and inevitably my visit to the Embassy was a source of fascination among my friends. We sat on the balcony of Sandra's apartment, sipping fairly palatable homebrew, while I gave a brief account of the afternoon.

'They advised me to get a lawyer,' I finished.

'Who are you going to sue?' Emmet, Sandra's husband, asked bluntly.

'I don't know,' I said defensively. 'I don't even know if I'm going to get a lawyer.' I wasn't sure, after sixteen years, if I could live though all that pain again.

'But you've already had money from Libya, haven't you, Felicity,' said Emmet.

'No, actually I've never had a penny from Libya,' I said with sour distaste. 'The derisory amount of sixty thousand dollars, which was forty thousand pounds at the time, was from Libyan Arab Airlines, paid out from their insurance policy under a subsidiary of Lloyds. It wasn't Libyan money at all, and nowhere near the ten million dollars that the Libyans gave to Lockerbie, even though they maintained they didn't do it.'

'But they admitted responsibility, Felicity. Everyone knows they're guilty of the Lockerbie bombings,' Emmet said.

I was getting agitated with the tone of the conversation. 'Libya admitted responsibility, not guilt. It was the only option for it to get back into the Western world and start doing business with them again. Just look at what they paid the Lockerbie families, two hundred and seventy million dollars. Was it worth it? Just look at how Tripoli is forging ahead and reinventing itself. Look at all the lucrative oil deals coming their way. Do you think Libya is suffering because it paid out that money? No, it's thriving now, and it's only going to reap in more money. Oil is being discovered on a daily basis; they can hardly keep up with the number of new fields. They just discovered an ancient Roman settlement in the desert and they buried it because there's an oil field right by it ready to start production. And oil will buy them power. Whether Libya is responsible or guilty concerning Lockerbie isn't the issue. They can't deny what happened in their backyard: their military war plane brought down the passenger plane my husband was in. So who should I blame, the MiG, flown by the Libyan military, or the UN?' I was angry now.

Emmet lurched back on his chair and exclaimed, 'What you are saying, the UN were involved in the accident?'

'You don't know it was an accident,' I retorted. 'Have you read the crash report? Because I certainly haven't. Don't be like all the rest and make assumptions.'

'How can you now blame the UN?' Emmet was acting like this were an imaginary scenario in which he could play devil's advocate, and was missing the fact that he was toying with the feelings of a widow who had lost her husband so tragically.

'They put the sanctions on the civilian airline; didn't you know Libya was not allowed to buy any spare parts or maintenance equipment for its civilian fleet during the air embargo? Airlines need maintaining all the time. Who knows whether some critical equipment wasn't working?' But I did know, I thought: Mohammed had told me the crash report – the one that existed but which I had never seen – apportioned part of the blame to the malfunctioning guidance system. But Mohammed had told me this off the record, so my tongue was tied.

Seeing the growing tension between me and Emmet, another friend, Don, stepped in. 'What do you think the Embassy, or the British government, have to gain if you hire a lawyer?' he asked.

I looked over to him. 'That's a good question,' I said. 'They're not going to advise me to do something unless they get something out of it.' I was suddenly exhausted. 'Actually, I'm a bit tired. I might go,' I said, not wanting to share my grief any longer;

it was too personal and this latest development would take some time to fathom.

Emmet was like a dog with a bone. 'But why should you get more money, Felicity? What about the other victims, the Libyans who were killed.'

'What about the other victims? I said. 'I can't fight everyone else's battles. I can barely fight my own, and not one person has ever bothered to help me. If they had banded together to demand the truth, of course I'd have joined them. But as for the money, I can tell you, their compensation bought them a heck of a lot more in Benghazi than what I could get in London for sixty thousand dollars. Do you think that bought me a house in London? The payout they got could more than cover buying a villa or farm in Benghazi.'

Back at my apartment, I was relieved to be away from probing questions, and also worrying how much I had divulged. If it got back to Carl that I had been to the Embassy and was considering a court case against the State, I could just imagine his outrage.

The next morning I was watering my garden when Sandra stopped by to apologize for her husband's words the night before, which she put down to too much drink.

'You don't have to apologize, Sandra,' I said. 'Everyone is entitled to their opinion, and it's not as if I haven't heard it all before.'

'Yes, I know, but I don't know what got into him. I'm sorry if he upset you,' Sandra said.

I was tired of being accommodating and understanding. 'Just think, how would Emmet feel if it were him in my shoes? How would he feel if you were blown out of the sky? Do you think it would be nice if people criticized him for wanting to know the truth and wanting a decent and proper settlement for losing you? Just think, I had to retrain and re-educate myself in order to look after my two children. What part of this has been easy for me?'

'I know you've been though a lot, and just being here you're making strides, chipping away to find out more,' Sandra said, trying to encourage me and smooth over some of the damage her husband had done. 'Maybe we could go for a drive to that plant nursery you've been looking for later, after church. Give me a ring when you get back if you want to go.' Sandra offered kindly.

I muttered a quiet 'maybe' in reply.

To shake myself out of the gloom, I decided to go and see Mr. Jana, the director of the Art House, the next day. I had met Emad the curator briefly at the private view, and that had been a positive step, but I needed a date set for the exhibition. To my amazement Mr. Jana took out his calendar and penciled in the end of May for two weeks. 'We won't charge you for the hire of the gallery,' he said generously, 'just the framing we do. We'll leave it up to you to do the invitations and posters and bring some to the gallery for us to hand out, and if you want to do some refreshments, it's up to you.'

I was over the moon that a date had been set: I had just over three months to plan and execute my own show in Tripoli. Now I had a focus: I had to complete many of my unfinished drawings and do some large paintings to fill the space at the gallery. It was a pleasant area, not overly big, but it could accommodate numerous pieces of work, depending on how I wanted to hang them. I had found some discarded board that I knew would come in handy for large paintings, and I knew just where to start. I had drawn the skyline of Tripoli from the church roof when the pastor had asked me up there one day; all I had on me at the time was my Bible, so I had used two blank pages to sketch the building outlines, taking in the mosque, the abandoned synagogue and the cranes in action, changing the skyline as I drew.

I was full of inspiration and energy, and hurried home to commence the painting. But first, I wrote a short letter explaining who I was and what had happened to my husband and that I wanted to take action against the institution that was responsible for Victor's death. There was no way of knowing which lawyer would be interested in my case, so I sent the same letter in an e-mail to each of the lawyers on the list provided by the Embassy. Then I cleared my mind, and picked up my paintbrush.

It was certainly a challenge finding time to paint; my time was so taken up by teaching and what seemed to be endless meetings. The worst was when Carl addressed the whole school once a month. No one really knew why he called these meetings; the subject never touched on school issues. A particularly memorable one was all about Richard Branson's new book. The whole school sat through a book review chapter by chapter of the self-made millionaire who owned the Virgin Group. At one point in the meeting I had to nudge Lou the librarian, who had fallen asleep after the first hour. I would have left her alone to doze through chapters five to ten except Lou had started to snore and Don, sitting on the other side of Lou, looked over to me to do something. Perhaps he thought it was inappropriate to touch a female member of staff in Tripoli and that the few Libyan teachers in the room would not approve. Two hours later, as Sandra and I hurried out of the room, pushing past the other staff on a mission for air and sanity, I commented to her, 'Perhaps I should tell Carl all about Richard's team meetings.' I had worked for Branson when I first came to London, and instead of dreary meetings, the Virgin boss would put on barbecues and parties for his staff at his manor house in Oxfordshire. That was a lifetime ago, I thought, but it seemed I did have a knack for meeting important people.

But some of my students were far better connected than me. Out of the blue one day a Year 7 student, Jamila, stayed behind after class and asked whether I had any children. I didn't usually divulge much information about my personal life to students, but this plump little girl was very likeable and was a simple sort, classed by the school as having learning difficulties. And, interestingly, she was also Colonel Gaddafi's niece. Her mother was the leader's sister; her father, his right-hand man: Abdullah al-Senoussi.

'Yes, Jamila, I do,' I said. 'I have a son and a daughter back in England.'

'Why aren't your children with you?' Jamila wanted to know.

'They're grown up now, Jamila, but I would love them to come here,' I answered.

'I will speak to my parents; your children should be with you. They will arrange it.'

'Oh, Jamila, really?' I said carefully. I was starting to rethink the assumption that Jamila was backward; she seemed very sharp. 'You know one thing I would like also is to see the plane wreckage.'

Abdul, the prime minister's son, had also lingered behind, listening to the conversation. 'My father will take you to it,' he said.

I covered my surprise; these children knew of the crash, no explanation was needed.

'Oh, thank you, Abdul. Maybe if I wrote him a letter asking for it... would you give it to him?' I said.

The children capered off, and left me to my thoughts. I recalled a conversation I'd had with Sharif, the taxi driver, who had told me that last year Gaddafi had thrown a lavish birthday party for Jamila, his niece, that cost over one hundred thousand dinars. They had spent more on the party than I had been given for my husband's life, to bring two children up for the next twenty years or so. Jamila was the innocent party, but still, the imbalance sickened me.

My mind was racing. Maybe this was an avenue I could explore; it was a friendly way of doing things and the children were more than happy to help. Ethically, I wasn't sure where I stood. The two very well-connected Libyan children had offered their help, and I thought they had showed incredible compassion for me. But alarm bells were ringing and I needed to establish whether they could actually help me. I had tried to pass a message to the chief of the air force via a student previously, and that had amounted to nothing. Still, it wouldn't hurt to write a short letter, I decided. But I might as well have cast the letter to the wind; only in hindsight I saw it choose to protect me.

Chapter 24

While checking my e-mails, I found a reply from one of the lawyers I had e-mailed. Strangely, the lawyer cited a 'conflict of interest' as his reason for not being able to take on my case. I did not know whether this conflict was because they represented Libyan Arab Airlines, or because I wanted to sue the state. I e-mailed them back to ask for clarification, but they ignored the question. If the truth was that they were too scared to act for me, then most lawyers would be the same and that would explain the lack of response after two weeks of waiting. If it was because they acted for the defaulted LAA, then they would know there could be a lawsuit on the horizon. Either way, I was left with an uneasy feeling.

Then, a couple of days later, progress at last. I checked my e-mail again and found a reply from another law firm. They asked me to phone and make an appointment as soon as possible to discuss my case. I called immediately and arranged to see them at three p.m. the next day; they closed for the weekend then, but would stay open for me. *Boy, that's a development*, I thought.

I asked Haj, the taxi driver from our pool at the school, to pick me up at half past two. We were cutting it fine to arrive at three. But Haj was a whiz in the backstreets of Tripoli. He took me through an area I had never seen before. We went past the Tuesday Market, a massive expanse of fruit and vegetables brought in from the farms, and then past countless pens of sheep and lambs along the side of the road, some awaiting slaughter, some already dead, their decapitated heads hanging from the makeshift noose outside many shops. Blood soaked the pavements and the metallic scent filled the air and made my stomach heave. 'We're nearly there,' Haj said to me to take my mind off the gruesome sight. It might have been commonplace to him, but he was aware of the horror on my face.

A large villa loomed above me, nestled on a corner of a main road. It was an impressive building. This was not some backstreet law firm. With Haj waiting for me, I was buzzed through a security gate and then through the main entrance. A receptionist greeted me. Her English was limited but she knew why I was there and picked up the telephone and spoke in Arabic. A few minutes later a very tall, lean, distinguished gentleman with grey hair appeared and greeted me in perfect English. He dismissed the receptionist to go home and enjoy her weekend, and motioned that I join him in a conference room on the ground floor.

Introducing himself, Mr. Khalid El-Walid explained that this was just an informal meeting to speak to me, and he asked whether I could come again on Saturday when he would be able to give me an answer as to whether he was prepared to take the case. I agreed, relieved to discover the firm was open on a Saturday, so I would be able to come outside of school hours.

The lawyer wrote down some details as we spoke. The meeting lasted about forty minutes, and I found I felt relaxed with Mr. Khalid; my usually suspicious mind was completely at rest with his integrity and motives, whatever they were in taking on such a case.

Before he ended the informal meeting Mr. Khalid shook my hand and said sincerely, 'I am very sorry for your loss.'

'Thank you, Mr. Khalid,' I said warmly. 'I will see you at eleven on Saturday then.' I smiled back at him. Even if he decided he couldn't help me and bore bad news on Saturday, he would have taken the time to look into it and that's all I could ask.

Hope was growing in me. I felt like I was walking along a ledge, each step sending my body swaying with the wind, and I could tumble over in an effort to regain my balance. I needed to think about the latest development and know what it meant for my life and my children's lives.

I couldn't wait for Saturday to come around. The next day I opted not to go to church, but to spend the morning cleaning. My mind would not have been on the service, and I did not want to engage in small talk and risk it getting back to Carl that I was consulting a lawyer; it was to do with my private life, nothing to do with school, and I would tell him only if I wanted to. In the evening, I had plans to go to a Hash House Harriers walk and after-party with Pam, the American lady from the US Embassy I had befriended.

'How was church?' I asked as we drove in Pam's four-by-four.

'It was good,' Pam smiled back. 'You weren't there?'

'I'm avoiding Carl,' I volleyed back.

'Yeah, I heard some stories about him,' Pam said tactfully.

'Now do you have the map to find the place?' I asked.

'I think I know the way to this villa, it's by the Chinese Embassy and I've been to the house before. It's at Hans', one of the German diplomats,' Pam answered.

'Oh wow, that means real beer!' I said excitedly, knowing the diplomats had no problem in obtaining alcohol and were quite generous with it on occasions like this.

'I knew that would get you going,' Pam joked.

Pam knew the route to the villa. We pulled up outside next to several cars. There were ten or so people from school, and it made a comfortable network of people. The walk was across some farmland and took us past a paddock where Libyan men sat in their national costume that they wore to the mosque, smoking shisha and drinking mint tea. The ceremonial tea drinking fascinated me. They would pour the tea from a silver teapot that had been heating over hot coals into glasses from a height of about a foot. I had once tasted it with almonds in and was surprised how palatable it was. The men, mostly forty and over, were scattered around the field, some sitting on makeshift stools and some reclining under a Bedouin tent. It was a rare and rural sight that would never be put on for tourists, and I stopped to ask one of the men if I could take a photo on my phone. He refused and I respected his decision.

'That's a sight you don't see every day,' Pam remarked as we followed the trail, which was marked out in flour.

'I would've loved to have done a painting of that,' I sighed.

'Oh, you're an artist!' Pam exclaimed. 'Is that why you were talking to the Archbishop that time?'

Letting out a nervous laugh, I said, 'Oh no, that was for something completely different.' I had known Pam for three months, and had no reason to doubt her integrity, so I decided to confide my story.

Pam listened intently, then astonished me by saying, 'I have a similar story. I was working in the Peace Corps in Chad,' she said solemnly, 'and we had just finished our tour there. I decided to stay a few more days, but my best friend – I knew her from school and we'd joined the Peace Corps together – decided to try to get home straightaway and she took the UTA plane.'

Pam hadn't finished her sentence but I had interrupted unintentionally, putting my hand over my mouth and uttering, 'No!' I knew the details of the UTA flight that had left Chad and blown up over the desert because I had met a man through the Lockerbie group who had lost his sister in the crash. Libya was accused of the atrocity, and they were tried in absentia and found guilty without Libya being represented by any counsel. I knew that the families had received two payments for their loss, though it wouldn't be prudent to mention that now. What a strange and small world to discover that Pam had lost her best friend in a bombing connected to Libya.

'I am very sorry,' I said to Pam. 'It must be very hard for you being here, having lost your best friend.'

'And also for you,' Pam acknowledged.

'Actually, it gives me a chance to feel I'm near to my husband in many senses. Do you still see your friend's family?' I asked.

'They built a small school in Chad in the village where we

worked for the Peace Corps. I went back there one time, just because I had to go back for all memories of my friend, and I took some photos of the school and took them to her family. That's the only time I've seen them.'

'What an incredible thing to do,' I said. 'There are so many wonderful people in this world and they can give out of their pain and loss. She must have been a lovely friend.'

'Yes, yes, she was,' Pam replied, and I knew instantly why I had liked her right from the beginning.

We walked on in silence for a few more minutes, each having heard a facet of the other's life that wasn't shared with others often because they wouldn't understand. It cemented a bond between us.

The mention of the UTA disaster stayed with me even the next day at the office of the lawyer.

'We have looked into the plane disaster and tried to find out what we could in a short time,' said Mr. Khalid as we sat in the conference room. 'It appears to be as you said at the first meeting.' He was referring to my declaration that it was not just an accident. The lawyer looked at the widow and said, 'We are prepared to take on your case, on a continuances fee, because that's what you've stated.'

I felt my heart pumping, and I tried to look beyond his eyes, beyond the man I saw in front of me. I wanted to know what he knew. But I had to remain calm and collected.

'We need to go over some details and you must find the affidavit you signed to get the compensation from the airline, but it's not a problem, we can still do a lot of things before that,' he went on. 'The other major point, apart from the affidavit, is the prescripted time. The number of years has well past. It's nearly seventeen years now.' He stopped and waited for my response.

'There was nothing I could do. I was in tremendous grief and my children were very young. I had no way of approaching a lawyer in Libya, and no means to do so. There were sanctions on

Libya and there were no diplomatic relations.' My voice trembled; even after so long, I desperately wanted him to understand my anguish and the impossible situation I was in.

'If I'd had this case even four years up until the prescripted time,' Mr. Khalid said, 'there's no telling where we could have gone with it.' He stopped because he knew the shocking history of the disaster and he knew the widow had been duped.

'Even my lawyer in the UK wrote to me saying he had no idea of how to go about contacting a lawyer in Libya,' I said. 'And he's a good lawyer; he acted for some of the Lockerbie families. He was a high-profile man with all the right contacts.' I drew a breath. 'Even if I had been able to find a Libyan lawyer, and I am very sorry if this sounds rude, but I would have had no way of knowing whether he would act honestly for me or whether he was just in Gaddafi's pockets and too scared to act for me. How would I know?' It was a rhetorical question. I was trying to be careful that I didn't offend the gentleman before me. It didn't even cross my mind that this man would be bought off by Gaddafi.

'And how could I sue without knowing the results of the trial, which I have never been told officially? This is why prescriptive time should not come into it. The trial had not taken place for me to know who was guilty, so how would I know whom to sue?'

'But when was the trial?' the lawyer asked to put the time frame into perspective.

I considered the hopelessness of my case. A military warplane, more than likely carrying live missiles, brings down a passenger plane, and a high-caliber lawyer such as Mr. Khalid didn't even know a trial had taken place in his backyard. It was a closed trial; that's what Mohammed had said. Perhaps I could phone him for another meeting and ask the date the trial had taken place.

'All I know is that both military pilots and the air traffic controller were still in jail awaiting trial seven years after the disaster.'

'I understand what you're saying,' said Mr. Khalid patiently, 'but if would have been better for you to have started proceedings at least. Yes, Gaddafi is a dictator, but even he cannot defy Muslim law. Under Islamic law, he can be accountable for murder. And there is no prescripted time for murder.'

It was a statement that put my mind at rest, not least because it put to rest a silly preconceived notion that his office might have been bugged.

The topic of Lockerbie and UTA came up. I knew the Lockerbie families had received ten million dollars each, apart from what they already had from Pan Am insurers, which was decided according to merits. The higher the victim's earnings, the higher the settlement; there was a report in the paper of the widow of a high-powered executive receiving nineteen million dollars. Papers exaggerate everything, I had been told, when I had compared this to my derisory sum of sixty thousand dollars. And she didn't even have any children, I had stormed.

'And who knows how much the UTA families received,' I said to Mr. Khalid, 'but I know Chirac would not do business with Gaddafi until it was brought in line with the Lockerbie families after they received their payment.'

'I can tell you it was a lot more than sixty thousand dollars,' the lawyer said, and I realized he knew more than he was saying. I wanted to ask him whether he had represented the families of the UTA victims in any way. Was that why he was eager to take on my case? He was certainly a successful lawyer, I gauged from the building alone, and his style spelled success, but he was also careful in a regime where people could disappear for speaking too candidly. It wasn't the right time to ask any questions, but it seemed strange that only the day before I had found a connection to the UTA bombing while walking in a field in Libya.

Before I left the lawyer stressed that I must find the affidavit and he would do what he could in the meantime to research the case. I wasn't fazed by the request, although I hadn't seen the document since I had signed it some fifteen odd years ago. It would be in the attic, I told myself; all the papers are up there along with all the love letters I couldn't bear to read again. I explained to the lawyer that I would look for it at Easter when I went back to the UK (I had managed to talk Libyan Airlines into rescheduling the flight I'd been unable to take at Christmas).

'Come and see me as soon as you get back; we don't want to waste any more time.' The lawyer ended the meeting and we shook hands.

I walked out of his office with a spring in my step. To have the backing of a very prominent lawyer was a real breakthrough after all these years. I must be fate that I was in Libya, I decided. It was the Lord's plan.

Chapter 25

Every mountain has a cascading road down, and the roller-coaster plunge I took down from the summit of happiness the next day threatened to diminish the elation I had felt coming out of the lawyer's office. The tumble down occurred in Carl's office at lunchtime.

The school was trying to get International Baccalaureate accreditation, which meant sending the teachers for training during the summer holidays. I'd had the choice of Berlin or Manchester; no contest! Going to Berlin with some of my colleagues was something to look forward to, and it would mean signing up for a further two years in Libya so the school could ensure it recouped the investment, which I was happy to do. But my happiness at the forthcoming training lasted only until I was told that Carl had said I would have to defer the course until the following year. Trying to keep my cool, I had e-mailed and set up a meeting with the head.

A colleague was ahead of me in the queue when I got to Carl's office and I politely let her go into office before me, even though I had a fixed appointment. The wait of two or three minutes made me foot tap involuntarily; I knew this would be a hard battle to fight and the likelihood of me winning was zero. But I would make my protest at the risk of being called a moaner never-theless.

The strain on the teacher's face as she came out of Carl's office was enough to tell me things hadn't gone her way.

'He's in a foul mood,' she muttered under her breath before leaving.

It was not a good sign and I had to steel myself for the onslaught before entering the head's office.

'Hello, Carl,' I said politely, waiting for him to turn around from the computer screen and greet me. His eyes stayed fixed on the screen.

I tried the next tactic. 'You said to come at lunchtime today to talk about the IB course.'

'Look, Felicity,' Carl said without taking his eyes off the screen, 'I've decided you'll do the IB course next year.'

'But I need to do it now to fully understand it and be prepared to start it with what is my Year 10 at the moment. They will be the first to do the IB when it starts after next year.'

In an unexpected shift, Carl said, 'I don't even know if we're going to offer the IB for art.'

'What, you can't be serious?' To me, this was indicative of what the head thought of the art syllabus.

Carl was furious now. 'Look, Felicity, there are issues over your ability to teach at that level, at A level.'

He proceeded to remind me of complaints from some of my students, spoilt rich girls who had caused trouble for me when I'd deservedly given them low marks for their poor artwork and behavior in class.

'That's all nonsense, Carl, and you know it,' I said bluntly. 'I had a one hundred percent pass rate at A level at all my other schools. You just don't like me and that's why you won't send me.'

The bell had gone and I could hear the students rushing from the playground to their next lesson.

'You need to go to your class,' Carl snarled.

But, in tears now, I was in no fit state to teach, so I asked him to arrange cover. My first impulse was to go home and let the despair dissolve me. But instead, I went to see Roma, the head of secondary. Roma wasn't exactly a friend at school, but even she was confused by the aspersions cast on my teaching ability. She left me sniffling in her office and went to see Carl to try to ascertain the reason for his behavior. When she returned, her expression was grim.

'It wasn't easy to get the information out of him, but he did admit to me the real reason you aren't going to do the IB course – because of the morning you had off to see your friend,' Roma revealed. She was referring to the time I had gone to see Mohammed who had told me about the closed trial and the verdict of the court in apportioning blame to the co-pilot of the fighter plane.

'But I didn't have the morning off because he wouldn't let me,' I spluttered in disbelief. 'I went at lunchtime.'

Roma had another perspective of the situation, 'Yes, but I heard you say you were going to have the morning off from the workshops without permission.'

'Roma, I've done those workshops loads of times. And this was a meeting I really needed to have; I'd waited years for to find out who was responsible for my husband's death.'

'Yes, but not in school time, honey,' Roma said.

'So the real reason is because I wanted to find out answers about my husband's death,' I summed up. I looked at Roma and said, 'Thank you for finding all of that out. I understand what's against me now.'

It was hard not to be bitter about the whole episode. I hadn't left the school without permission to see Mohammed. I had done as Carl instructed me to do and gone at lunchtime, and now because of this I was the only one in the school not going to do professional training that I needed to do my job.

I had a mission to find the affidavit during my short holiday that would also be taken up with shopping and cleaning for the children, who managed to a degree without me but were glad to be children again and let their mother look after them.

It was a relief to go home at Easter and escape the oppressive atmosphere at the school. Three hours by plane, but I felt I was a lifetime away from Tripoli. The house was a complete tip when I walked in. Piles of dirty dishes sat on the work surfaces of the kitchen, the cats' food tray looked like it hadn't been cleaned in weeks and the air was thick with the stench of overflowing ashtrays. The lounge was even worse than the kitchen, and I closed the door as quickly as I'd opened it.

'Hello, Mum!' Theo cheerfully greeted me as he bounced down the stairs. I sighed, not knowing what to do. It was the first time I had come back to such a mess; they usually rallied around and cleaned up when they knew I was coming home. Tallena would direct Theo to his jobs, and reluctantly he would acquiesce to stop his sister nagging. My head was screaming at the mess, but instead of saying anything I hugged the children and started cleaning up. It took four hours before the kitchen was clean.

Theo sat by the computer all this time, not lifting a finger, and I was too perturbed to ask for help. I made myself a well-earned cup of tea and sat down to talk to my son.

'Theo, we need to do the lounge in a minute,' I said plainly.

'Leave it alone, Mum. You're only just home five minutes and you're moaning. Where's my presents? Did you get my cigarettes?' Theo demanded.

'You can have your cigarettes, Theo, but we need to clean the lounge first,' I said, hoping to coax him into doing his share.

'Don't tell me what to do. You can't tell me what to do any more!' Theo shouted.

'He's always like this; he won't do anything to help. He lives like a pig,' Tallena commented.

I was really concerned now. I knew my son was having problems, that he was drifting with no desire to get a job, that he was smoking weed.

'Get up and help Mum, Theo!' Tallena bellowed at her brother.

'You're both bitches, go to hell!' was Theo's response.

I couldn't believe I'd got entangled in such an unpleasant argument within minutes of arriving home. 'It's the dope talking, Theo, you're not being reasonable,' I said, heartbroken.

'That's right. You always blame the dope and not yourself.

You're to blame, Mother. You're a right bitch mother.'

I swallowed. 'Don't swear at me. Come on, we all have to get along and make the most of the time I'm home. I've only got six days.'

It was hard to take Theo's rudeness, but I knew he was angry and lost. For years he'd been exploding in fits of rage, swearing at me, punching the walls, leaving huge craters in the plaster, breaking furniture, kicking cupboard doors. Once he had picked up a knife and stabbed the breakfast bench and dishwasher, leaving dents in both. He had even attacked me, putting his hands around my throat. That time I had let the police arrest him, which far from serving as a wake-up call seemed to have fueled his anger. I did not press charges. 'Throw him out!' some friends would advise when I was near exhaustion with trying to coax my son onto a course or even sign on to get some dole money to keep him in cigarette money. It was hardline advice, and I knew I could never do it. 'He just wouldn't be able to cope on his own,' I said honestly.

And after the storm would come the calm, when, like today, after refusing to help me and swearing at me, he would apologize for his outburst or breaking my property or calling me names. He would often cry because of the shame, and I would hold him and pray that he would let go of the rage consuming him.

How much of Theo's anger was due to his father's death I couldn't tell. His young life had been full of trauma that no child should have to go through. I felt guilty that I had been unable to protect him from the pain, and I worried that he blamed me somehow.

The lawyer had insisted that I find the affidavit, so I left Theo tidying the lounge, contrite now, and climbed up to the loft to root through the treasure trove that lay hidden there. One suitcase contained my wedding dress and shoes, another the children's christening outfits. Beside Victor's love letters, tied up in bundles, every one of them placed lovingly back in its envelope, there was a box of newspaper clippings on Lockerbie and another one with ministerial letters in reply to my many requests for information: blue envelopes were from the Foreign Office and yellow ones from my member of Parliament; the names were all different but the message was the same: we won't help you. There was a box with important papers which held the deeds to my house, and I guessed that the sought-after document was in there. I put my hand in and pulled out three papers: the affidavit, an old newspaper clipping from the day after the tragedy showing Victor's face, and a love letter. Perhaps it was the last one I ever received because it wasn't with the others. As I glanced at the letter, still folded, my eyes caught one sentence: *My darling, I love you so much.* I couldn't bring myself to read any more, and tucked it away at the bottom of the box. I turned the light off, climbed down the ladder and closed the hatch, glad the Lord had led me to find what I needed without effort or worry.

Finding the document seemed to lift the tension in the air, and the rest of my visit at home passed pleasantly. As I packed my suitcase for my return to Tripoli, I couldn't help dreading the return to school. My problems with my boss were making my work life increasingly stressful. But at least this time I had another, better, reason to return to Libya: to make progress in pursuing justice for Victor, for us all. I hardly dared believe there may be some hope after all this time.

Chapter 26

The journey from London to Tripoli Airport was becoming a regular commute for me. I joined the long queues at the immigration counter – hundreds of Third World workers were lined up; cheap labor and brought in by the planeload – and I prepared myself for the twenty to thirty minute wait. Within seconds of turning my phone back on it rang.

'Hello, Carl. I have a doctor's note,' I said politely, predicting his impending strike.

I was returning to school a day late, on the Monday. Before I left we had been told this was a holiday, so I wasn't concerned about my tardy return, especially as I had a note from the doctor signing me off due to strep throat.

'I'm not concerned if you have a doctor's certificate,' Carl rallied. 'It's your lack of notice that's not acceptable.'

'Carl, I phoned the school several times yesterday and no one answered, and I sent you two e-mails. One to the school account and one to your personal e-mail.' It crossed my mind that perhaps the Internet was down as usual, but that wasn't my problem. He would get the e-mail when it was up and running again and he would see that I had done as I said.

'No one answered your call because it was a holiday yesterday,' Carl answered.

I knew I hadn't confused the days. Before I left Carl had stood up in front of the staff and announced that the holiday was Monday, today, not Sunday.

'You should have phoned today if you weren't going to be in today,' Carl said sternly. 'I had to ring your home to find out where you were.'

'What, you rang my house in London?' I queried. 'Well, my children would have told you I was travelling today.' And with that, I hung up. It wasn't that he had checked up on me that had bothered me, but that he would have been fully aware that I was travelling because my children would have told him, so there was no need for this grilling practically as soon as I'd touched down on the tarmac. The phone call had been unsettling, and I turned my phone off immediately. Whatever else he had to say could wait until tomorrow when I was back at school, I thought.

Saturday was the earliest I could see the lawyer to give him the affidavit. Although I did consider using more of my sick days – the UK doctor had signed me off for the week, and I did not feel well – I didn't want to stir Carl up further.

The lawyer was pleased to see the document when I handed him the affidavit. I felt it was a sign that he could begin his investigations in earnest, but he made no pretense it would go against me that I had signed it. I reiterated that I'd felt I had no choice but to sign it. Would it have been any different if I had found him sixteen years ago? How would I have possibly have funded the trip? It took Libyan Arab Airlines seven years to arrange my visit with the children to the grave. Even then it would have been too late. How could I, crumbling in early widowhood with two young toddlers not even school age, be expected to travel to Libya when no planes were flying there, set myself up in accommodation and look after my children while I searched for a lawyer, not knowing any Arabic? There wasn't even any British Embassy at the time to give me a list of lawyers. Did people actually think through what they expected me to do on my own?

Mr. Khalid moved on. 'We did some digging and found out we were involved in this case,' he said, 'but not in representing the airline or the victims. The law firm represented the farmer who lost his livelihood when the plane crashed into his field.'

On my journey in 2000, Mohammed had taken us to the field and told the story of the farmer who had lost his farm, not because the olive trees and crops wouldn't bear fruit again, but because no one would touch his fruits ever again because they were unclean. He was ruined, Mohammed had told me. He'd neglected to mention the compensation package that the farmer had received. Mr. Khalid looked down at the file on the farmer, all written in Arabic. I knew the settlement fee was written there, and I suspected it was a lot more than I had received for the loss of my husband.

'The good news is we can start moving on this because we have an avenue to explore.'

I realized the law firm's previous connection with the plane disaster was a positive thing. Maybe they could access documents from the courts more easily because they had been involved. I wasn't quite sure, but I felt the lawyer was committed to the case now and I thanked him and left it in his capable hands.

I had decided to lie low and just get through the next term, avoiding Carl as much as possible. What I had to put first was teaching my classes. Preparation for my exhibition kept me busy; my paintings were coming together. And as well as the artworks I had to arrange the mailing list, the posters, the media involvement and the private view.

I was impressed when the lawyer called me in for a meeting so soon after our last. He suggested that before going ahead with any legal procedures we try a friendly approach and write a letter to the Human Rights Commission in Tripoli, beseeching them to consider my plight and act compassionately towards me. I agreed that it was worth a try, though really I wanted to get my teeth into some more substantial litigation, especially given the second piece of information the lawyer had dug up:

'We've found out that a number of families did try to contest the compensation awarded, especially after they found out that one passenger was paid over three hundred thousand dollars.' Mr. Khalid put an affidavit on the table detailing a payout of three hundred thousand dollars to a Filipino family whose Libyan husband/father had died on the flight. 'Several Libyan families found out and went to court to try to get their settlement increased,' Mr. Khalid said, laying down copies of their affidavits as well. 'They won the first court case and they were hopeful that there was going to be another payment, but it was turned down by the high court because they too were not in the prescripted time. They persisted with the legal proceedings, demanding they at least make it up to three hundred thousand dollars for each of them then.'

I was barely able to contain myself. 'Well, good on them. At least they gave it a good shot,' I managed. I admired the Libyan families for their courage to fight the courts in Libya. It was one thing for me, as a foreigner, to instigate legal proceedings, but there were little or no rights for the Libyan people under such an intense regime.

'Not really,' said Mr. Khalid. 'A catastrophe like this and they ask for peanuts like three hundred thousand dollars? The sky was the limit; their lawyers didn't have guts and were playing it safe.'

I looked long and hard at him. He knew something that he was not telling me, and I needed to get to the bottom of it, but I knew that timing is everything so I agreed to the friendly approach as a first step. The lawyer advised me to wait three months for an answer, then we would take it from there. So we would take a break for the long, hot summer.

I decided to e-mail my lawyer in the UK, the one I had gone to for help right after Victor died, to tell him I now had proof another party had received far more compensation than me. His response was disappointing: as sorry as he was for my situation, he could do nothing to help; he believed the proof made no difference all these years later to pursuing a better settlement figure. My only hope was to sue under Islamic law unless I heard back from the Human Rights Committee. I would need to switch off and let the new Libyan lawyer do his job.

April had passed quickly and May was upon me. My

exhibition was to commence at the end of May, and preparations kept me out of mischief. Emad, the curator of the Art House, was a great help; I was astonished when I discovered that, like Mohammed, he had once worked for Libyan Arab Airlines. It was a small world in Libya.

The night of the show was spectacular. My paintings, newly framed – at my expense – were blasts of color juxtaposed with the white walls. Libyana News wanted to do an interview with me, and I tried to stand steady in my heels and long maroon gown as I spoke of the majesty of the Libyan dessert and its ruins, and that out of the great tragedy of losing my husband here I had found real beauty. I was poetic and did justice to my host country; I wondered whether they would leave in the mention of the plane crash. The guests arrived; among them, I was delighted to see, the British Ambassador and his wife. Emad introduced me to several Libyan artists, and the press took photographs of me together with the well-known artists and art critics. At the end of the private show I was astonished to find that several of my paintings had sold. Pam had reserved one, and surprisingly Carl had bought three Leptis scenes to go in the library at school.

The show was extended beyond the two weeks promised to four weeks. Two evenings a week and on Saturdays, my day off, I went to keep Emad company. Emad arranged for me to go to the final show at the art college in Sabratha the following next week. Nothing could have prepared me for the poverty that struck me as I walked into the decaying gallery near one of the treasures of the Roman Empire, the ruins of Sabratha. We were greeted with mint tea and three of the students, young women, accompanied us around the gallery, explaining the folklore behind the paintings. Nothing was provided by the college, I discovered, apart from the space to paint; the students had to find their own way to finance their paints and materials, often without their families' support. I asked what they would go on to do. 'Sometimes we just have to get married and we can't carry on with our passion for art,' they told me. 'But sometimes we find a way after we have brought up our children.' It was a sobering experience for me and an insight into Libyan society. I hoped one day these women would be free to become the artists they truly were. I had pushed for my chance to show my work at the Art House, and I hoped one day those women or the ones who followed them would be warriors too. They asked me to come back as a visiting lecturer, and I would have gladly given my time for free, but it was not to be for, although I did not know it then, my days in Libya were numbered.

With only two weeks left to go before term ended and I returned to the UK, I was invited to attend the Queen's birthday celebrations at the British Embassy. The British Ambassador had bought one of my paintings and sent his driver over with the money, so I was happy to have the chance to hand it to him in person.

I made my way to the party. In the Embassy gardens hundreds of guests milled about, sipping cocktails supplied by waiters circulating among the throngs. I spotted the Ambassador chatting to Carl, went over, and handed him the picture, the press' cameras flashing.

'We really love your painting, Felicity,' the Ambassador said warmly.

'I look at my paintings like a prayer,' I told him, 'giving something back to God what He gave me. And as difficult as it has been for me here sometimes,' I added, aware of Carl's gaze on me, 'I have really enjoyed this year and being in Libya.'

As was expected at such events, I circulated among the crowd, greeting old friends. When I headed to the bar to replenish my drink I was surprised to find I recognized the barman as the aide who had been in the vice consul's office when he had advised me to engage a Libyan lawyer. *What is a high-powered diplomat doing serving drinks at the bar when normally they engage West African staff to do that?* I wondered.

I took my drink to the other side of the garden to chat to a parent from the school, but I noticed that a large, well-built security guard in plain clothes had stopped at the same time I had. Chatting to the parent, I stole a look over my shoulder and noticed the guard's eyes on me. I walked on, testing, and sure enough the security guard was following me. I stood for a couple of minutes without moving to see if he would carry on or stop and watch me. I was on my third drink by now and had some Dutch courage, so I introduced myself to two Arabic-looking men nearby. It wasn't an usual thing to do; the point of the garden party was networking, and exchanging phone numbers. As luck would have it, one of the men was a reporter with the Associated Press. I deliberately stayed talking to the men for over ten minutes, and before moving on I asked for the reporter's card. That would put the cat among the pigeons.

I couldn't resist going to the bar for another drink, and challenging the aide directly. 'Anees, you're watching me, aren't you?'

His response was adamantly in the negative.

'Alright then, I'll have a beer, please,' I said, and he poured a glass. I gave him a knowing look. The can was still half full and I had a glass all but full of froth. 'Thank you,' I said. 'I'll be going now to talk to my friend from the American Embassy. I can see you have other people to serve.' I knew the man had no intention of serving more drinks. He was no barman.

Pam was amused when I recounted my undercover operation to catch them spying on me. Pointing up at the bar, she said, 'Look, he's still looking at you and not serving anyone at all. You should be honored they have your security so much in mind; you're a celebrity after all.' Pam was referring to the recent coverage of my exhibition in the papers and on the television and radio.

'I think they are more worried what I'll say to Miliband than the papers,' I said referring to the scathing letter I had written to the foreign minister about Victor's death.

The next day I retold the spying incident at break time. The staff were divided between those who believed me and those who thought I had a wild imagination.

'Oh, Felicity, who would want to follow you?' one teacher said a little rudely. 'Unless it's about what you did at the Oasis? They might have thought you were stealing drink again.'

I soon put the teacher right on that score. Then, to make my position clear, I spoke very precisely when I said, 'The reason why they were following me is because I am suing Gaddafi.'

'I believe you, Felicity,' my colleague Adel said quietly to me later. He was a Libyan from Benghazi who had lost friends on flight 1103. 'The British will be watching you like a hawk to see if this case comes to trial, because then there will be a lot of bereaved families supporting you. But be careful what you say at school. There are spies all around here,' he warned. Then he added kindly, 'You are a remarkable woman to make a stand for what you believe in.'

I gave Adel a smile of gratitude. It took courage for a Libyan to speak his mind like that. Very few at school saw the real Libya; where family members disappeared and no questions could be asked. The more I talked to Libyan people who would open up about their suffering, the more I realized it wasn't only the West that thought Gaddafi's rule was seriously flawed.

Chapter 27

Back in the UK for the summer, the media was buzzing with the hype of the talk of the release of the convicted terrorist al-Megrahi. The Libyan had been found guilty of conspiring to bomb Pan Am flight 103 in a court of law. After spending just seven years in a Scottish prison, there was talk of releasing him on compassionate grounds to return to die in Libya. The world was stunned, but I had known of the release since the previous year when it had been brought to my attention at a Lockerbie meeting. 'Apparently, al-Megrahi is suffering from terminal cancer,' Dr. Jim Swire had announced to the group. Jim had visited al-Megrahi personally at Greenock Prison and had come away convinced that this was not a scam, and that the convicted terrorist was dying of prostate cancer.

The news was a blow to the British families, many of whom were skeptical as to the Libyan's guilt. They had hoped that al-Megrahi's impending appeal would bring new evidence to light and take them one step closer to knowing why their loved ones had been so brutally murdered. But if al-Megrahi was released on compassionate grounds, then the appeal would not go ahead.

The billboards in Tripoli and all over Libya had already started to change before I left Libya at the end of June. The huge portrait of Gaddafi, mostly in military garb, was lowered, and a new one raised in its place, depicting an ageing Gaddafi and the words *Forty years in power*. It would take months to change all the billboards of Gaddafi, which cropped up haphazardly all over Libya and dominated the Tripoli skyline. It would be an occasion to be in Tripoli on the anniversary of the leader's fortieth year in power. A big cleanup campaign had begun to rid the city of its garbage image and the countryside of the plastic bags that littered the land everywhere.

A streamlined Tripoli was needed to impress the West when

the cameras loomed in on the leader on the first of September in Green Square watching his powerful military might be paraded in front of the dignitaries and for all the world to see. Libya was now in a powerful position. It was opening up to the West, and huge oil deposits were found on a near-daily basis. They were in a position to buy as many arms as they wanted and Britain was keen to sell them. And while the Scottish government tried to convince the public the convicted bomber was to be released on humanitarian grounds, everyone knew the color of oil.

The first few days of the controversy I listened and watched with some interest, trying to predict the movements of the press. Justice seemed to be dangling on a string, swaying from side to side, with the papers bouncing article upon article about Libya and its changed pariah status. There was hardly a day in August 2009 when the media did not carry a story about Libya and what it owed to the West. Now that it had the renewed status of one of the richest nations that was not in a war zone, the West wanted to be allies with the former rogue state. Huge oil deals dangled in the balance. If Britain didn't play its cards right the lucrative oil deals would go elsewhere and the collapsed Russian economy could not supply Britain with all its oil needs for much longer.

'What about Victor?' a voice in my head said repeatedly amid all the chaos that the press unleashed throughout the build-up to the anniversary of Gaddafi's anniversary in power. It was hard to pick up a paper or turn the television on and not scream back at it that all the truth needed to be told. There was no question that Libya was responsible for my husband's death: their military warplane had brought down the passenger plane.

Timing was everything. If the timing was right, people were interested in my case. I knew Libya would stay at the center of attention until Gaddafi's big day in September, so I decided to circulate a brief description of my case to the media.

I was out shopping with Tallena a few days before my return to Libya for the autumn term when the first call came through.

'This is the editor at the news desk,' said a man, giving a name which, in the noisy shop, I wasn't able to catch. 'Am I talking to Mrs. Prazak?' the man asked.

'Yes, you are,' I said.

The editor got straight to the point. 'I'm with the *Express*. We'd like to do a story on you. Are you home?'

'Actually, no, I'm shopping at the minute and it's a little bit hard to hear you,' I stuttering, nervous at the urgency of his call.

'When will you be home?' the editor persisted.

Looking at the time on my phone I saw it was approaching midday. I could have been back home in twenty minutes, but I decided to tell him two o'clock so I would have time to tidy the house before a journalist walked in on the morning chaos I had left behind.

'Alright, I'll have a reporter at your home for two p.m. I want to get this in tomorrow's paper.' The editor took down my address and hung up.

I was somewhat stunned, but delighted at the interest. With talk of al-Megrahi's release the public would associate my case as being unresolved as a criminal was set free. There had to be some equality to balance out the generosity that was being demonstrated to the Libyans, and it was time something good happened in our lives.

Then my phone rang again.

'Hello, Mrs. Prazak?' the enquiring voice at the other end asked. Again, I didn't catch the name of the person, but I assumed this was a reporter briefed by the editor I'd just spoken to.

'Can you talk at the minute?' the voice queried.

'Well, actually two o'clock is better for me,' I said and added, 'like I said.'

The voice at the other end picked up on the comment immediately. 'Has someone else rung you, Mrs. Prazak?' he asked, and I realized I was speaking to a different paper entirely.

'Who am I speaking to please?' I asked.

'It's Dipesh Gadher here, Mrs. Prazak, from *The Sunday Times*,' the man answered politely.

'I'm sorry,' I said, 'I thought you were the *Express*.'

'Mrs. Prazak, have you agreed to do a story with the *Express*? I am the deputy editor of *The Sunday Times* and we are really interested in your story.'

I related the fact that the *Express* reporter was coming at two p.m. to my house.

'But you haven't signed anything?' the deputy editor probed. 'We really want this story, Mrs. Prazak,' the man said.

I was now in a muddle, and to make matters worse, a shop assistant was trying to get my attention to finish a transaction. 'I'm really, really sorry but I'm just right in the middle of something,' I told the editor. 'Could you possibly phone me back in half an hour or twenty minutes?' I said, rethinking the timeline.

Fifteen minutes later the phone rang.

'Hello, Mrs. Prazak?' a female voice asked. 'We need to send a photographer around to you as well. Are you back home yet?'

I explained that I had just missed a bus and didn't know how long I would have to wait for the next one.

'Do you think you will be home by one p.m.?' the woman pushed. 'It's just we have a photographer in the area and it would be good to get it out of the way before the journalist comes at two.'

Realizing I was speaking to the *Daily Express*, I uttered an 'alright' and took a note of her name. The caller's details were withheld and I didn't think to ask for her number. It was nearly half twelve and I was cutting it fine to get back in half an hour if another bus didn't come along quickly.

As soon as I hung up my phone beeped to tell me there was a voice message. Dipesh from *The Sunday Times* had rung while I was on the phone to the *Express*. He left his number and asked me to call him.

Before I took another step the phone rang again.

'Mrs. Prazak, it's Dipesh Gadher here again. How are you?' he asked.

The truthful answer was, *Rushed off my feet, flustered by the calls and confused*, but I simply said, 'Fine, thank you.'

'I've spoken to my boss and we really want to do an exclusive on your story,' he told me.

'But I've said I will do the interview with the *Express*,' I said. 'A photographer and a journalist are coming today and I already said I would do it.' I didn't like to give my word and then back down. It was a shame he hadn't rung before the *Express*, but I felt I had to go through with it. 'Can't you both run the story?' I asked, knowing the papers often carried various version of the same feature. Then, trying my luck, I added, 'Would they be prepared to pay me?'

'Sadly not, I'm afraid. We don't pay for articles,' said Dipesh. 'But it's quite common for our sister paper, *The Times*, to run the article on a Monday as well, and not to be critical about another paper, but we are one of the most respected newspapers in the country.' Dipesh was trying his best to persuade me. '*The Express*, on the other hand, is well-known for its conspiracy theories, and if you want to be credible then an article in our paper would be taken more seriously.'

This line of thought was inducing me to think about who would see the article in a national newspaper on a Sunday if I agreed to do it.

'You only have to look at the series of Diana conspiracy theories that they print to know they're not taken that seriously,' Dipesh pointed out.

I nearly interrupted him then to comment that I believed there might be some substance to what they printed, but I knew that was not the issue at that moment.

'We plan on doing a really big spread on you and highlighting your case. I believe the British public will look at this as a humanitarian case and raise awareness for you,' Dipesh explained.

'How many words do you think you will print?' I said, weighing up the situation.

'I want to get one of my best journalists and she'll do about a thousand.'

'Alright,' I said. I could imagine Dipesh punching the air at such an easy switchover. 'I don't like backing out when I've already agreed to the *Express* article, but I think you're right that your readership will help me more.'

'Can you call me after you've put them off? I'm sorry to have to ask you to do this, but we do appreciate it,' Dipesh said.

I didn't even have the number for the *Express*. I would have to look it up as soon as I got home and hope I had enough time to put them off. It was a fidgety wait for the next bus. I filled Tallena in on the latest events.

'They never help us, Mum, I don't know why you bother!' was Tallena's response to the developments of the morning. 'And I don't want my photograph taken either. No one ever helps us!' Tallena was adamant that it was all a waste of time. We'd had journalists come to interview us before over the years, but it usually ended up nowhere, or at best as a small piece in the paper or magazine; just a sad story that created no support.

'That's not true, Tallena,' I told my daughter gently. 'Even though it took seven years before you were allowed to see Daddy's grave, people did help us to do that. The Ambassador in particular, and Libyan Arab Airlines was very good to us.'

Back at home I found the number for the *Express* and asked to be put through the news desk. I was unable to speak to anyone about the story and so left a message saying that I was very sorry but I wouldn't be able to do the interview until Monday now. *The Sunday Times* didn't mind me speaking to anyone then, after their story had appeared first. Then I did my best to convince Theo and Tallena to agree to a photo shoot for *The Sunday Times*.

'It means a lot to me to have us all in the photo,' I reasoned.

'I don't want my photo in the paper,' Theo protested.

A pounding noise came from my gate and I looked up, startled. It must be the *Express* photographer. I thought I would pretend not to be in but the knocking persisted.

'Mum, you have to answer the door!' Tallena told me.

Knowing Tallena was right, I caved in and pulled the gate open.

The photographer's face was instantly relieved.

'I'm really sorry,' I said, 'but I phoned the paper half an hour ago and left a message I couldn't do this today.'

'Why not?' the photographer demanded. I had learned the art of sidestepping direct questions I didn't want to answer and told him again I was sorry but suggested he call the news desk who could confirm I had postponed the interview until Monday. The disgruntled photographer left in a mood; I couldn't blame him. Half an hour later the *Express* journalist arrived, demanding ten minutes of my time on the doorstep, and was similarly unimpressed when I sent him away. Once he left, the editor at the *Express* called me, and I explained myself for a third time.

'Have you had another offer from another paper?' he blurted out. 'Which one?'

'I'm sorry,' was my reply, 'but unless you are able to make it financially worthwhile for me I cannot do the interview until Monday.'

It was the best approach to getting the editor off my back. He wasn't interested in buying my story.

Dipesh phoned a few minutes later and I told him the coast was clear for his reporter to do the interview. I worried whether I had made the right choice, but the only way I could judge would be by seeing the article on Sunday. My stomach fluttered with anticipation. This was my big chance!

Chapter 28

Telling my story to the journalist later that evening took a lot longer than the ten minutes the *Express* had wanted at the door. For two and a half hours I recounted the events as they had happened from the moment I had turned on the television at lunchtime on the 22nd of December 1992 and seen the breaking news carrying the images of the wreckage of the plane crash. The journalist looked up from time to time and wrote copious notes in shorthand in a pocket-sized notepad. Sometimes she would stop me to clarify some point or ask for the correct spelling of unusual words. I had thought the interview would be more probing, bordering on intrusive, to get to the nitty-gritty of the court case I was thinking of launching.

'What do you hope to get out of being in Libya?' the journalist asked after I had told my story. I took a few moments to think about how I would answer the question. I wanted to make it clear that I been sought out to do this job in Libya; I hadn't gone begging for a job as a way to get into the country to take action against it. 'Primarily, I went there to do my job,' I said, 'and I think I do it very well. However, now that I am there I see it as my last chance to be able to do anything at all. I have never got anywhere with discovering the truth about my husband's death, and now that I am there I at least have a chance to do that through this lawyer,' I said

'What about monetary compensation, are you looking for that?' the journalist asked.

I was tired of having to defend my need for compensation. 'People tell you money doesn't mean anything, or no matter how much you get, it will never bring back the person you've lost. When they tell you money doesn't matter, they're talking a lot of rot. Of course it matters. They haven't had to manage on the little that I got. Do you know, not even counting anything for me, I received a thousand pounds a year for each child until they were adults? Do you think you can bring a child up in this country on a thousand pounds a year? Do you think you can feed them, clothe them, put a roof over their head and pay all the bills on one thousand pounds a year? Yes, money does matter. It's only when you don't have it that you know that.' The realism was hard hitting for the journalist. I thought much of what I had said would be omitted from the article.

I evaded her probing questions of what I thought of al-Megrahi's controversial release from prison. But when the journalist continued to press me, I looked directly at her and said, 'Megrahi will go home to a hero's welcome.'

The journalist disagreed.

'I am telling you,' I said firmly. 'Megrahi will go home to a hero's welcome. Make no mistake of that.' He would fly back Afriqiyah Airways, and I knew the man that would arrange it: Mohammed, who was now in a senior position in that airline.

The journalist contradicted me again, saying, 'They're not even sure that he will go home now, and the Libyans have promised that they will keep it very low-key if he does.'

I wondered if she had any recollection of Fhimah – the other Libyan arrested in connection with the Lockerbie bombing but found not guilty – being released, and the scenes of jubilation in the streets of Tripoli the moment he stepped off the plane. I wanted to shake the woman to make her understand that no one in Libya believed they were responsible for the bombing of Pan Am. I knew the Libyan mentality and I knew they would party all night.

As the reporter was leaving she thanked me for my time and wished me all the best, then let me know the photographer would be coming in the morning.

'That might be a problem,' I said, all too aware my children would put up resistance to the event.

'Do you want me to have a word?' She knew a family photo

would be a focal point to the story and it was important to have both children in the shot. The journalist was persuasive, and even my demonstrative daughter couldn't think of any argument to disagree with the logic the journalist laid down. Tallena mellowed and agreed to do the shoot, and Theo followed suit, and the next day they sat beside me and posed for the photos.

It was an apprehensive wait until the dawn on Sunday. Saturday drifted past with more developments on the media scene. A well-known figure from Radio 4 contacted me after receiving my e-mail that had been passed on from a television station. I had never thought of contacting the radio stations myself; perhaps this could be a new avenue to pursue. He rang twice that day to discuss the interview he wanted to do with me early on Sunday morning. I agreed to do it, even though I worried that they would ask questions that were out of my league. I was happy, looking forward to Sunday: everything was finally coming together; God had parted the clouds and made an opening for me to tell my story.

The elation lasted until the phone rang. Again. The fact that the phone was ringing late on Saturday evening told me the news wasn't good.

'Mrs. Prazak?' Dipesh asked.

'Hello, Dipesh,' I said warily. 'Is everything alright?'

'I am very sorry, Felicity,' he began.

I decided to cut in to save him embarrassment of delivering his message. 'They've axed the story,' I said without emotion. 'It sounds like there is a gag on my story.'

'Not at all,' Dipesh assured me. 'Another story came in relating to the Lockerbie case. I am really sorry. I know you turned down the *Express* because I persuaded you to. Maybe you could get back to them?'

But I knew I had burnt my bridges there. 'Oh well, thank you for your interest,' I said.

'It's not all bad news, Mrs. Prazak,' Dipesh ventured. 'The full story is in the online version of the paper. If you have access to the Internet you can read it from tonight, and there's still a small piece in the paper.'

'A small piece?' I echoed. He explained they had printed a hundred words next to the half-page story on al-Megrahi and the other breaking news that had stolen my space.

Dipesh apologized once more, and then said goodbye. I was sitting, dejected, when the phone rang again.

'Mrs. Prazak? I'm ringing from Radio 4. Unfortunately, we won't be doing the interview tomorrow morning with you.'

'Why not?' I asked bluntly. I had accepted the news gracefully from Dipesh, but this now reeked of conspiracy to silence me.

'I am afraid I'm just here to pass on the message. I'm very sorry.'

Sunday dawned and I rose early but decided not to rush to the newsagent's. I would have my coffee and dwell on the morning that would have been if they had printed my story in full. There were just six days until I went back to Libya, and I doubted I had the strength to approach the papers again. I had given it my best shot. When I finally bought *The Sunday Times*, it was only on the third attempt of carefully scouring through every article that I caught sight of the small article entitled 'Widow moves to Libya in a last-ditch attempt to find answers to her husband's death'. I grimaced at the headline.

'Mum, there are two different messages on Facebook about you,' Theo called. He was on the laptop; I had asked him to look for the online version of the story. 'They're trying to contact you via me.'

The first was another radio station who had seen the article and was interested in doing a piece with me. They left their contact details and asked me to ring them. The second was more interesting: a freelance journalist who thought the story needed more coverage. Perhaps I had given up too easily. I phoned both but got voicemail.

Theo called me over again, having found the article, strangely, in the world news section. Reading the article didn't lift my spirits. The journalist was no doubt renowned in her field, but I didn't like the angle. I wanted something hard-hitting focusing on the struggle for justice and the impending court case. This was more a timeline of events. 'Perhaps it would have been better with the pictures?' offered Tallena, who also recognized the words didn't carry the punch we wanted. Images speak a thousand words, but there not one accompanied the online version.

On Monday I did a phone interview with the freelance journalist, but kept the story as brief as possible. The journalist listened attentively and said he would see what he could do, but later rang to say because the story had appeared online it had really been told. I remained optimistic about the radio station lead for a day or two, but they later rang and said the story had moved on. I was back to square one and hope had flown out of the window again.

On Tuesday, as I came in from a church meeting, Theo announced, 'Someone from *The Times* phoned when you were out.'

'*The Times*?' I said, not sure he hadn't meant *The Sunday Times*. They were different papers, Dipesh had told me, even in different buildings but with a common thread.

'I wrote it down here, Mum,' Theo said. 'His name is Martin Fletcher and there's his phone number.'

'Did he say anything? Or why he called? Did you tell him when I'd be home? Is he going to ring back?'

'I don't know, Mum, stop asking me questions. Just ring the number I wrote down,' Theo shouted in annoyance. He didn't like the intrusion of the press, and I was at a loss to make him understand it was our only hope.

Though it was ten in the evening, I dialed the mobile number Theo had written down. The phone went straight to voicemail and I left my name and number.

Wednesday morning I looked at the phone so many times I finally gave in and called *The Sunday Times* switchboard and asked for Martin Fletcher. 'He's not with us,' the operator said, 'try *The Times*.' Mystery solved. Calling *The Times* this time, I got through to his voicemail. If he was interested in talking to me, why didn't he phone back?

When Theo woke up I quizzed him again about the call and this time I extracted some more information. 'He said he was going to Libya and would e-mail you,' Theo said, rubbing his sleepy eyes.

'What, he told you he was going to Libya? When?'

'He was travelling last night and said he would e-mail you and asked when you were going to be in Libya.'

Exasperated, I switched on the computer and at once found an e-mail from the journalist. It said he was travelling to Libya on Wednesday and wanted to know whether, when I was back in Libya, I would be available for an interview. I e-mailed him straight back and told him I would be there on Saturday and gave him my Libyan mobile number.

It didn't dawn on me until afterwards that he had travelled in haste to Libya on the Wednesday morning to report on the story of al-Megrahi's release and return to Tripoli when he arrived in full glory on Thursday. I later discovered that he was the only journalist given permission to do an interview with the convicted terrorist when he returned to Tripoli; the article was titled 'I shook hands with a convicted terrorist'.

I decided to try his UK mobile on Thursday and I felt like clapping when he answered. His plan was to return to London on the weekend for a few days and then go back to Tripoli to report on the celebrations of Gaddafi's forty-year reign. The big day was the first of September, and it looked like I would miss him because as he flew back to London I would be leaving.

Friday saw me rushing around finishing my packing. My

friend Gina – a former teacher at the school in Tripoli – was coming that afternoon to stay, and then I was booked onto an early flight to Tripoli in the morning.

'I won't wake you in the morning,' I said that evening, hugging the children goodbye.

'We'll come with you to the airport if you want, Mum,' Tallena said. I had three suitcases to manage and would have appreciated their help, but I would manage.

'You sleep in, darling, I'll be fine,' I said, kissing my daughter on the forehead.

Fine turned out to be an inaccurate description; *devastated* would be more fitting. Because less than an hour of arriving at the airport I would be plunged into a nightmare.

Chapter 29

It was the crisp time of morning before the sun started to warm the air; I loved this time of day. I got up at six and the three hefty suitcases were lying by the front door waiting to be zipped up once I'd buried the contraband sausages and bacon rashers. The children rose in a sleepy state to kiss me goodbye and walked me down the alleyway to the waiting taxi.

'Bye, Mum. We love you,' they both said and hugged me again, even though they had done the ritual the night before. 'We can still come with you, if you need any help,' they offered. Sometimes they just wanted those last few minutes with their mother, knowing they wouldn't see me for months now.

'I'm fine,' I reassured them and gazed at the three suitcases. 'I'll manage okay. What can go wrong?' I kissed them again and got into the taxi. 'I'll ring you just before ten if you like, before the plane goes,' I offered.

Theo and Tallena looked at each other. Their thoughts were transparent: they didn't mind getting up to see me off but the thought of going back to sleep, undisturbed, was foremost on their minds now. 'Why don't you wait until you get to Libya and we'll phone you then?' Tallena suggested diplomatically.

At the airport I grabbed a trolley to haul my heavy bags and made a beeline to the check-in desk. After the usual wait and a game of luggage juggling to ensure each of my three cases did not exceed the permitted weight allowance, I was surprised to hear a familiar voice call my name.

Turning, I saw Rob Kernel, Carl's right-hand man at the Tripoli school, heading towards me.

'Felicity,' he said, hurrying towards me, 'you are not to get on the plane.'

I looked at him, startled, and said, 'What?'

'I've just had a message from Carl,' he said, 'and you're not to get on the plane until you've spoken to him.'

'I'm afraid I don't time for that! I have a plane to catch,' I said. Whatever it was could wait until I was back in Libya in a few hours.

But Rob was insistent. 'I'll call him on my phone,' he offered. Before I knew it Rob was on his phone telling Carl he was with me, and then passing the handset over to me.

'You have to speak to the head office before you do anything else,' Carl told me authoritatively.

This was a bizarre development – speak to the main managers that ran the school? 'You want me to speak to the head office. Why?'

'You have to speak to the main office. They'll explain everything to you,' was Carl's reply.

Tired of this riddle, I said, 'Look, Carl, I'm travelling to Libya now. Let's talk tomorrow when I'm back.'

'You are *not* to get on the plane!' Carl said, anger creeping in that I wasn't listening to him.

'No, I am coming back to Tripoli today. I've already booked in.'

It was the newspaper article, Carl explained; there was some issue with it at the school.

Now I was angry. 'Carl, you do not ring me at half eight on Saturday morning when I'm at Heathrow checking in my luggage and tell me not to get on the plane!' My voice had risen to above conversational level and Rob Kernel looked around in embarrassment at people staring nearby. 'That article came out last Sunday, six days ago. You've had plenty of time to ring me at home or send me an e-mail. If you're sacking me you're going to pay me a year's wages and the rest, and as soon as I put this phone down I'm ringing every national newspaper in the country. I am coming back to Libya *today*.'

I had no idea whether he had taken my threat seriously, but his next words shocked me again. 'There are issues about you having a Libyan lawyer to represent you here.'

'What? This is my personal life. It's nothing to do with the school, and besides, you've known all along that I was going to try to sue the state.'

'You need to speak to head office. Here's the number.' He started to recite a number but I interrupted him.

'If you want me to talk to them they need to ring me,' I said, fully against spending one penny making an international call on my mobile to find I had been sacked. 'Rob wants his phone back, or he'll miss the plane. I have to go,' I said to Carl, handing back the phone without saying anything to Rob.

Rob Kernel's phone went again, and it was Carl wanting to talk to me. I shook my head. I was not in any mind to talk to him. I had done an article for the paper, who had only printed a hundred words about the horrendous ordeal I had lived though, and somehow this was being used to block me returning to me job.

Half a minute later my phone rang and an unknown international number appeared across the screen. I guessed it was the head office number. They had my mobile number as I thought all along.

'Felicity, this is Miriam Lyell here. Did Carl tell you I was going to phone?' the woman began. There was no doubt even from her tone that she held a high-powered job.

'Yes, hello,' I answered wearily.

'There is a problem with you travelling back to Libya,' the woman started.

'No, there isn't,' I said, interrupting her.

'Let me speak,' the woman demanded. 'You are posing a security risk to the school and to the other teachers.'

'I am posing a security risk to the school!' I repeated, unable to believe my ears. 'What rubbish! I have lived there for a year and I have never been thought of as a security risk. Who thinks I'm a security risk? The Libyan government doesn't. I've always gone to Libya as a guest of the state!' I said, stretching the truth a little, but I was a guest of Libyan Arab Airlines when I went, which was state-owned. 'The Libyans don't think I'm any sort of threat! Do you want me to ring the Foreign Office here and ask them if they consider me a terrorist too?' I was livid at the accusation. If it had been a cold morning the steam coming from my ears would have been visible.

'Make no mistake, Felicity!' the woman said angrily, 'You will not be allowed on school premises. You are not allowed anywhere near the school grounds. You have put the school in danger.'

'I didn't even mention the school in the paper!'

'It says you work at an international school,' the woman said. The online version did but not the short piece in the Sunday paper, I thought.

'There are eight to ten international schools in Tripoli that I know of,' I said. 'I did not name the school; this is nothing to do with the school. I will sue you and I will sue the school for treating me like this,' I said furiously. 'You do not ring me at the airport, six days after the article comes out, and tell me that I am a security threat and cannot go back to Libya. You're treating me like a terrorist. Please believe me, I will contact the press about this. How do you think it looks when al-Megrahi, a convicted terrorist, is released on compassionate grounds and returns to Libya to a hero's welcome and you ring the widow of a British citizen who was shot down by a Libyan warplane to tell me I can't return to my job, my home there, because I'm a security risk? I am not the terrorist here, but I am being terrorized.' I was shouting now, overwhelmed by grief that the very small step I had made in securing public interest in my case was being blown to pieces by overzealous, powerful people. I knew the battle was lost, though.

The woman was angry that I had shouted at her and ended the conversation. 'Right,' she said, 'I will make a decision in three days about you and phone you.' She hung up.

'What did that mean?' I said to myself.

Rob was standing by, helpless, though he was running late for the flight now. I gave him some money to give to my friend Emad to feed my cats in Tripoli, then left him to queue for security.

I was trembling now with fury. This was nothing to do with the school, why were they interfering in my personal life? Didn't I have a right to ask why my husband had been killed and to find out who was responsible? As I walked towards the exit with my three suitcases again loaded on a trolley I despaired how I would manage on public transport. I couldn't face the ordeal, so I took a black cab that cost double what it had cost me to go out there. It was money I couldn't afford if I no longer had a job.

I wasn't off the phone all the way back. I started with Dipesh at *The Sunday Times*, but there was no answer. Then I called my daughter and then Gina, who was still at my house.

'I can't believe he's done that!' Gina kept saying. 'There was nothing in the article! It was just a sad story, that's all!'

Back home, my children gave me enormous hugs. 'I'll make you a cup of tea, Mum,' Theo said.

'I will have a cup of tea and then I'll ring the paper back. They aren't going to get away with this,' I said.

If the head of the school or their parent company thought I was bluffing when I said I would call the press, it was time for them to sit up and take me seriously. As far as I was concerned, I had done a bloody good job in my position as head of art, and had put myself out on many occasions for the school and the students. If they wanted to sack me they would have to do it within a school context, not because I was asking questions in Libya about my husband's death.

This time I got through to Dipesh. The deputy editor of *The Sunday Times* was dumbfounded by the consequence of the story and apologized immediately if it had caused any problems with my employer.

'No, it's not your fault at all. At no time did I mention the school, nor does it have anything to do with the school,' I reassured him. I did think the heading 'Widow moves to Libya in a last-ditch attempt to find answers to her husband's death' made it seem like I had gone to Libya solely to investigate Victor's death, but I knew, and the school well knew, that I was there to do my job primarily. 'Do you think there's a story there that I am being gagged and have been sacked because I asked questions in Libya?' I ventured. 'Could you ring the company and ask why they think I'm a security threat?'

Dipesh thought there might be a story, but he wanted to wait to see what I was told in three days. He pointed out that at this point I didn't know that I was being sacked. He would keep in touch, he said, to see what the developments were.

'What did he say?' Gina wanted to know as soon as I came off the phone.

I recounted the conversation. 'He can't really do anything until the woman phones back and I have something in writing,' I finished.

'If only Carl had e-mailed you in time so that you didn't go to the airport, it would be some type of proof.'

'You're right, Gina,' I said. 'He didn't put it in an e-mail because he knew I could then act on it. But why didn't he just wait until I got back to Libya and then try to silence me? It just doesn't make sense.'

'He doesn't want to see you face to face, and then there's the problem of arranging your exit visa,' Gina put in. 'No, he didn't want you back on Libyan soil, especially if you went and saw your lawyer.'

'My lawyer! That's it. I'm going to phone my lawyer now,' I said. Saturday was a work day for Mr. Khalid.

The lawyer listened to an abbreviated version of the morning's events and then told me that it would be against the law to sack me for an article that came out in the paper. He asked me to put the details in an e-mail and attach the article the press had written. He was adamant it was not grounds for dismissal. I told him firmly I would sue if I was, indeed, dismissed.

'Sue them anyway for treating you like this, Felicity!' Gina said when I got off the phone. 'What right do they have to treat anyone like this? How do they think you're a security threat exactly? You taught Gaddafi's niece and the prime minister's son and whoever else all last year, and now you're a security threat. Didn't Gaddafi's niece say her parents were going to invite you to Libya?' Gina was one of the very few people I had told that Gaddafi's sister had arranged visas and flights and were giving me and the children a villa to stay in for a month; which month? It was never set – just an empty promise. I had not wanted the others to know my private business; I hoped the stay would get me a meeting with Saif al-Islam Gaddafi, the son of the leader of Libya.

'Couldn't you ring her?' Gina offered.

'I don't have her number or e-mail,' I said. I wouldn't have used the contact in any case.

Dashing off the e-mail to the lawyer as quickly as possible, my mind was awash with whom to contact. I reached for the list of newspaper contact numbers I had and called a tabloid.

'Only the Sunday papers are in,' the operator told me, 'do you want me to put you through?'

I was put through to the *Mail on Sunday* and the man on the news desk told me I had two minutes of his time in which to tell my story. 'Keep it simple,' was the advice Dr. Jim Swire always gave for media liaison, and I was able to get the reporter's interest in under the two minutes given.

'I'm going to get someone to call you back straightaway,' the news desk told me and I gave him my mobile number.

Within ten minutes I was speaking to a reporter for the *Mail on Sunday*, who was taking down details. On his request, I gave him Carl's number, and he rang off to call my boss.

The phone buzzed on the table soon after. It was the *Mail on Sunday* reporter to say he had spoken to Carl in Libya and he said I wasn't sacked but that visa issues were preventing my return at present.

'He's lying, there are no visa issues. I was at the airport and told not to come back to Libya, that I wouldn't be allowed in,' I reiterated.

'Well, he says you're not sacked, so it's not the story we first thought it was,' the reporter said offhandedly as if I had wasted his time.

'Of course he's going to say that if he has the media ringing him up. He's going to cover his own back!' I pleaded with him to listen but his mind was made up.

Calmer now, I decided the sensible approach was to call the woman in the head office and apologize for losing my temper, but explained how unfair it had been to call me at the airport like that. I wanted her to know I was back home and had followed instructions, for the time being, not to get on a plane. Miriam said she appreciated that and would get back to me tomorrow, which was an improvement on waiting the three days. I estimated she must have spoken to their legal department and been warned of a potential lawsuit ahead of them.

Ringing Carl was the next hurdle to get over. 'Carl, it's Felicity,' I said. 'I understand you told the press that I wasn't sacked?'

'Felicity,' he said evasively, 'there are issues over safety now and we have to do what is best for the school.'

'I have spoken to my Libyan lawyer and he says you have no grounds to sack me. So make no mistake, I will sue you if you do.'

'Now, now, let's just wait until Sunday and see what Miriam Lyell says.'

'Could you put it in writing and e-mail me, please,' I asked. Carl refused.

'What's the problem with sending me an e-mail?' I asked. 'You just told the press you weren't sacking me, so why aren't you going to put that in writing?'

Carl changed the subject, 'Felicity, you need to be careful about political statements you make.'

'I haven't made any political statements!' I countered immediately. I wasn't interested in the political situation of the host country I worked in; I just wanted to search for the answers that had never been given to me.

'It says here that you called Leader Gaddafi a dictator,' Carl said. I imagined him sitting with a printout of the article on his desk and red pen highlighting different passages.

'What?' I said, disbelievingly. 'For one thing I didn't say Gaddafi was a dictator, it was a quote,' I blasted at him fiercely. It was like telling the Pope he wasn't a Catholic. 'And anyway, the whole world knows Gaddafi is a dictator.'

'You can't make statements like that,' Carl said sternly, and again I repeated that I had not said it and had no need to say it. 'You can't even say it in England,' Carl added.

'You can't tell me what I can say in England,' – or even in Libya, I thought. 'You can't tell me what I can or can't say to a journalist in my own home.'

'I am going to tell you again, you are not allowed to make any political statement at any time, anywhere!' Carl was angry now.

I stood my ground and replied, 'Carl, in this country we have what is known as freedom of speech. You cannot tell me what I'm allowed to say.' And I added for effect, 'I wonder what the press will make of this?' The conversation was going nowhere now and I was conscious that we were speaking on my bill and if I about to be unemployed I should watch the pennies.

As politely as I could, I said, 'Carl, please excuse me now. I am extremely tired and upset. I will wait to hear from Miriam tomorrow before I contact the press again.' I said goodbye and hung up.

After a glass or two of wine with Gina I checked my e-mails, only to find more bad news. Mr. Khalid had e-mailed to say he would not be able to represent me in any action against the school, due to a conflict of interests: his firm already actually acted for the company that owned the school. I was instantly alarmed: would the lawyer continue to seek answers about Victor's death now?

I dialed the lawyer's Libyan mobile and he picked up straightaway. Mr. Khalid was not happy. Though the article had not mentioned him or his firm, it had been clear I was seeing a Libyan lawyer, and he was very concerned that the quote about Gaddafi being a dictator would reflect badly on him, and put him in danger. The realization that the lawyer felt this way made me aware of the hidden undercurrents in Libyan society: you were safe only as long as you did not upset the regime.

'I am so sorry,' I said, and tried to explain my side of the story. 'What about my husband's case?' I said. It pained me to think that all the ground we had covered and the hope I had let creep back into my life was disintegrating before me.

He told me to come to his office when I returned to Libya to discuss the matter. At the airport I'd somehow, amid the emotion, had the foresight to change my ticket to Tuesday, the day on which Miriam Lyell had originally promised me an answer. Now, I decided I would go back to Libya that day, but not tell anyone that I was coming. I would go and see the lawyer then, and if he was withdrawing his services then at least I would know I had given it a shot. I didn't have a good feeling about the prospect of him continuing with my case.

Chapter 30

Sunday passed in a blur. Paranoia set in, and I found myself wondering whether the Libyans had leaned on my employer in an effort to silence me. I waited anxiously for the phone call, and went to the receiver several times to make sure the cord had not come loose and disconnected or the receiver misplaced. Finally, at seven p.m., the phone went.

'You can come back to school, Felicity,' Carl said, 'but you will have to meet the director of the company and sign a new contract.'

'What?' I blurted out.

'You will be taken to meet the company's director here in Libya to assure him that you will not be making any more political statements that could involve the company.'

'Carl, I am coming to Libya to do my job, and my contract stands for another year. My personal situation is nothing to do with the company or the school, and it is not their business or right to tell me I cannot pursue any legal case I have going on. I will be back before school starts, and I won't be signing anything.'

I must be mad to go back to work in Libya given the circumstances, I thought, but going back to Libya now was my only way of salvaging the damage the school had done to my cause. It would be difficult working for Carl now, but I saw no other option if I was to continue my fight for the truth.

This time I passed smoothly through Heathrow, and arrived quietly at Tripoli. I intended to lie low at my apartment for as long as possible. I slipped in through the side gate of my villa rather than use the main entrance where the guards stood, and gave my first smile of the day when my cats came leaping towards me.

The next morning Haj, the taxi driver, arrived to pick me up.

'My friend, it is so good to see you. Welcome back!' Haj said joyously. 'Why didn't you phone me to collect you from the airport?'

'Oh, Haj, I had an awful time coming to Tripoli,' I said.

'But why, what happened?' Haj asked, concerned that my usual smile was absent.

I wondered how much I should tell him, and gave him a brief précis of events.

'No way is this our government,' he said firmly. 'Why would they stop you coming here? For what reason? You are welcome here, you are my friend!'

I thanked Haj for his kindness, and off we set for the lawyer's office. Visiting the lawyer as a first port of call would at least spell out my position. I didn't hold out much hope that the meeting would go well, and looked at it as a matter of formality. I was determined to thank Mr. Khalid for all his efforts anyhow; it was the closest I had ever got to finding out hidden information, and I was grateful for that.

Entering the cool air-conditioned office from the fierce August heat outside sent shivers down my back. I sat in a leather armchair, waiting, in silence. I reflected at the irony of losing this lawyer. Over the summer my MP in England had written to me to say that the Foreign Office would not comment on my case or help me in any way because now that I had commissioned a lawyer it was a legal issue. It was clever, I had to admit – call me to the Embassy and encourage me to hire a lawyer, knowing that when I did so they could relinquish responsibility for my case. Now they couldn't help me because it was a legal issue – so what had been their reason for not helping for the sixteen years previous then?

Mr. Khalid arrived and invited me to the conference room. *At least he didn't just shake my hand and say there's nothing more he can do*, I thought as I sat down nervously at the huge wooden table. His secretary brought in a file and he took some documents out.

'We have to give up on the Human Rights Commission now; four months with no reply is not good news. And it seems we've come to the end of the line as far as exploring the high court,' the lawyer began. 'The prescripted time has worked against us, and you would have to get the court to overturn their previous decision and set a new prescripted time. This cannot be done unless you get the admission from the court about the trial where the military pilots were convicted. It would serve your interest better to get an international lawyer now to take on your case.'

It was as I thought; he was giving up my case against the state. I was not going to attempt to change his mind, it had been set from the start, but I wanted him to know my struggle.

'Try to find an international lawyer who will take on your case,' he advised again. 'We are willing to liaise with them on any technical point in law, but we are not able to comment any further than that.' He wasn't quite letting go, but standing back and waiting for me to pursue another avenue. 'But do it soon: much of the money set aside by the government to pay Lockerbie and the other cases has gone.'

Before finishing the meeting, Mr. Khalid delivered some final, surprising news. 'I can't represent you against the school, but I can't represent them either. I know too much about you both; representing either party is unethical.'

It felt like a small victory. I didn't have another lawyer yet but I could find one. The school, on the other hand, would have to find another too, and they didn't know that yet.

'Where do we go now, my friend?' Haj asked when I got dejectedly back into the waiting taxi.

'Can you find the Misda Hotel? We'll go there,' I told him. It was the hotel *The Times* journalist Martin Fletcher had said he was staying in while in Tripoli. I would take potluck and see whether I could find him rather than speak on the phone.

Haj found the hotel without too much trouble, but the receptionist said he had moved out of there and was staying somewhere else. Haj asked some workers and finally the doorman pointed us in the right direction.

At the next hotel, which was surprisingly modest, the receptionist confirmed Martin was a guest there and allowed me to call up to his room. He seemed surprised that I had tracked him down, but agreed to meet me in the lobby in fifteen minutes after he finished the copy he was writing.

I sat sipping a glass of water, and finally, just when I was beginning to think he wouldn't show, I saw a lean man walking towards me. Stretching out his hand, he introduced himself and sat down in the dark, cramped corner next to me.

'I am happy to talk to you,' the reporter began, 'but I can't promise that I'll be able to do anything concrete.' It was an honest approach but I felt the balloon burst again. Was there any point in reciting the whole tragic story again to a stranger who had seemed interested in my story a few days ago but now, meeting me face to face in the backstreets of Tripoli, was not so forthcoming?

He took out his notebook and started jotting down information: names, dates, places, spellings. I was familiar with the format by now. I had talked for about twenty minutes when my phone went off.

'I'll just turn this off,' I said, apologizing for the interruption, and then noticed it was Haj's number on the screen. 'Oh, it's my taxi driver,' I told him. 'I'll just let him know I'll be a few more minutes.' It had been over an hour and I had told him half an hour, so I understood his concern that he was still waiting outside in a busy street.

The reporter from *The Times* looked up from his notebook and astonished me with his next question: 'Can he take us to the grave?'

He had only seemed half interested in my story and the request threw me. 'I'm not sure I know where it is exactly,' I replied, thinking, *He's going to think I'm so stupid that I don't even know where my husband is buried.*

'Will the taxi driver know?' he asked, and I realized his interest in the story was growing rapidly if it revolved about a visit to the mass grave.

'It's possible,' I said, trying to rack my brains to think of the directions I had noted before. I remembered taking the airport road and travelling along it for twenty or thirty kilometers and then there was a set of traffic lights to turn left. The village was down several dirt tracks and the narrow opening to the road that led to the mass grave was partly hidden. The roads weren't signposted and they would only be written in Arabic if they were. I was apprehensive and unsure that I could find it again, or whether Haj actually knew the area at all. 'I'll ring him and ask,' I offered.

Taking the initiative, the reporter suggested, 'Let's go and ask him. He's just outside, isn't he?'

Again I was caught out by the reporter's enthusiasm. I had not expected to be going out to see my husband's grave and became a little shaky.

'Do you know Al Sabt?' I asked Haj, peering into the open window where he had been snoozing in his seat. Haj noticed the tall, lanky man standing next to me and his eyes rolled up and down, checking him out.

'Yes, I know it,' Haj answered. 'Do you want to go there?'

Again I was caught out by the urgency of the reporter when he asked, 'Do you think you can get us there in an hour and back by three?' It was after noon by now, and I remembered the time I had got lost with Sandra and we had driven for hours trying to find the grave and ended up at the wrong place.

Haj agreed to take us and said he could get us there and back in time. I was less sure that we would find the grave, but at least it had interested the reporter enough for us to make the journey.

'I will just go and get the photographer,' Martin told me. 'I won't be long.' He disappeared through the swing doors and I was left to take in the fact he had thought the story worthy of photographing the gravesite. For a long time I had thought the world should see where they had dumped my husband's body and poured concrete over it to bury the whole tragedy, a stark contrast to the beautiful graves at Arlington or Lockerbie.

The reporter emerged with a young-looking photographer and the reporter introduced him to us.

'Are you sure you know how to get there?' I asked Haj when we had left the bustle of Tripoli streets behind us and were approaching the airport road.

'Can you check at all where it is?' the reporter asked me.

'All I can do is ring the Ambassador's secretary and ask if I can speak to the driver who took me before to get directions, but even he had to double check,' I warned him. I dialed the number stored in my mobile phone. The secretary put me through to the right department but the driver wasn't working that day.

'Don't worry, I'll find it,' Haj said confidently. We had reached the turning at the traffic lights and it was hit and miss whether I would remember any landmarks after that.

As we drove, Martin asked me questions.

'Do you speak any Arabic, Felicity?'

'No,' I answered. 'Work is a completely English environment and all I really need is turn right, turn left and stop for the taxi driver.'

'What about your living conditions? Are they rather basic?' he continued.

'Well it's what you make it, isn't it?' I told him. 'I like it well enough, but I suppose you could say it's just a one-bedroom apartment.'

'What about friends? Do you have any friends here?'

'Well, your colleagues are your friends. You don't always like everyone, but there are always some you get on with and some you don't,' I answered.

He asked about the school, but I did not want to discuss my

working life. 'Please don't mention the name of the school; my boss is quite controlling, and besides, it's nothing to do with the school.' I didn't owe Carl any allegiance after what he had done to me at the airport, but I felt the issues at the school were nothing to do with Victor's case.

'Would it be alright just to say it's an international school?' Martin ventured.

'Yes, that's okay, so long as you don't say the name,' I said.

Finally, we were pulling up beside the iron gates of the cemetery.

'Are you sure this is the right place?' the reporter asked, because I had been so unsure of the way and then had found it without any problems.

'Yes, I recognize this new monument here,' I said, pointing to a new structure that had been put up to commemorate the people who had fallen when the Italians raided the area.

Haj had become agitated by the surroundings. 'Put that away,' he said to the photographer, pointing at the camera, as we got out of the car. The photographer ignored him, and carried on walking towards the entrance. I had never seen Haj so fidgety and restless. 'Don't be long, someone might see you,' he said nervously. 'We can't stay here long; you don't know who's about.' Haj was clearly worried that the trek out to Al Sabt had put him in a precarious position should any officials stop and question him.

The wind had stirred up and the hot breeze tickled my face. I brushed my long hair back from my face; today, I would not shield the tears that would flow down my face when I saw the grave again: I would lay my heart bare for all the world to see.

The tumbleweeds rolled aimlessly in the dirt as we entered the cemetery. I pointed to the corner that was immediately visible as we walked in. 'That's the mass grave, over there.' But they had already seen the chained-off section where concrete stretched like a car park. The place was silent but for a tattered flag blowing in the wind and the bell of the sheep herd beyond the walls.

Sensing that it was a culture shock to these men, I gave the little information I had on the place. 'Al-Megrahi gets a hero's welcome and I get this,' I said. As my arms fell open to gesture the photographer was taking shots to absorb the loneliness and melancholy of the place. 'My husband was shoveled into the earth here. I don't even know where, in what part of the grave. I don't even know what remains they found of him.'

The reporter was interested in my view on al-Megrahi's release and I bitterly said, 'Maybe his widow could bury him here, since he's dying. Do you think the Libyan people would like that?' Even a convicted bomber was not going to be forgotten in such a wasteland as this.

Martin was more interested in my political view than the grief of widowhood, and pressed the question several times. Making a statement to the press in the comfort of my own home was very different from standing at the side of my husband's ghastly grave and knowing that justice was only for those who could afford it.

'I would have no problem with the release of al-Megrahi,' I said carefully to the reporter, who did not take his eyes from me, 'if only they would show me the same compassion the West has shown him. There has to be some balance and equality here. The ball is completely in their court, and it would be fair if they showed me some compassion and recognized my suffering.'

We stayed at the grave for twenty minutes, Haj hovering anxiously around the entrance all the while.

'Maybe we should go,' Martin said, eyeing Haj, full of unease.

'He's very worried; I've never seen him like this before,' I told the two men.

The reporter was full of questions on the way back. Seeing the grave in which Victor lay seemed to have opened up his understanding of my situation.

'You are very brave, Felicity,' he said to me more than once.

Haj was relieved he was on the road again and put his foot

down to get away from the place as quickly as he could. The traffic had built up as we neared Tripoli, and the reporter was keen to get his copy off before the Internet played up. He promised to phone if *The Times* agreed to print the story, and I decided I had made the right move in contacting him. Despite Haj's pressing concern at being at the grave I was glad I had done that too: who knew when I would get the chance to go again, I told myself; the way things were going, I may soon be leaving Libya for good.

Chapter 31

When I arrived home after my trip to the cemetery I wanted nothing more than to have a quiet evening at home. Tomorrow I would need all my strength to start back at the school. Sitting in my garden after dinner, I was laughing at the cats darting in and out of my legs, showing off for their mistress who had returned to them, when I heard a voice singing out to me. It was Ryan, who lived in an apartment upstairs in the villa. He came down and welcomed me back, but there was a serious look on his face and I knew he had bad news.

'Felicity, Carl has been saying things about you at the staff meetings,' Ryan said. 'He's dragged your name through the mud, especially with all the new staff.'

I was surprised but not overly alarmed. 'What about the newspaper article?' I asked, not knowing why Ryan seemed so worried for me.

'He's said you've named the school and made their name dirt here in Tripoli.'

'What?' I exclaimed. 'But I've not even mentioned the school. It's nothing to do with them!' I said, devastated that lies had been spread about me. Lifting my head up, I said, 'Well, I don't know the new staff, but anyone who knows me will know I haven't done that. Besides, they just need to read the article online for themselves.'

Ryan hadn't finished. 'He spoke for more than fifteen minutes about you, telling us all your personal story. He had told Sandra and Lola and Lou not to attend. He made sure your three best friends at the school couldn't defend you.'

I appreciated Ryan's candid remarks. 'Have you seen the article?' I asked.

'Yeah, I have and yeah, I know there's nothing in it about the school; it's more about the lack of help from the British government, if anything. Listen, the new staff have been warned not to associate with you otherwise they could be in danger,' Ryan warned me.

'Well, thank you for telling me,' I said to my loyal friend. 'I really appreciate you letting me know.'

The news did not improve my feelings about going into school the next day, but I was determined to be professional and while I missed the morning briefing – I couldn't sit among the staff listening to Carl talk – I headed to my classroom the next morning to make preparations for the coming term. Racing up the steps to my department, I heard a voice calling after me. It was Jeanette, the French teacher.

'I must tell you something,' the woman said. 'Meeting after meeting Carl has dragged your name through the mud. Your name is dirt around here. Carl has destroyed your good name.' The teacher was clear and concise and there was no mistaking the distaste in her tone.

'Thank you for letting me know,' I said to the petite teacher, who indicated that she had to hurry or she would be late for her next meeting. I was relieved that Ryan had broken this news to me already, and that his story was already corroborated.

In my classroom, I sat with my head in my hands. Had I made a mistake in coming back? My heart was no longer in my job and I could see little hope in salvaging the small strides to knowing the truth. The phone ringing made me jump. I contemplated ignoring it, thinking it would be Carl, but when I looked at the screen I didn't recognize the number.

It was Martin Fletcher. Before I could greet him, he said, 'You have a full page to yourself.'

My red blotchy face broke into a smile. 'A whole page?' I repeated. 'How many words did you do? Did you use any images?' I questioned, my voice becoming lighter all the time.

'It's about eight hundred words. There's one large picture at the grave and the small family one on the front page of the paper,' he let me know cheerfully. I could tell he was pleased with himself.

'Martin, I can't thank you enough,' I said, elated.

'No, it was my pleasure. You are a very brave person, and I wish you success and hope the article will help you.'

I was dying to get onto the Internet to check the article. Leaving my desk, I went into my office and tried to connect without any luck. After trying several times, I knew it was useless; it was often down for hours or even days. I would just have to try later.

I was busying myself with paperwork when the classroom door was flung open. I looked up, startled, to see Carl and Roma, the head of secondary, coming towards me.

Without saying hello Carl came and stood over me. 'You are meant to be at the meetings,' he said gruffly.

I carried on shuffling the papers and did not even look at him as I said quietly, 'No, Carl, I am not going to any of your meetings until you apologize to me in front of everyone for what you have said about me, without me even being there to defend myself. You have no right to talk to anyone about me, let alone the whole staff, and slander my name like you have.'

'You came back two days ago, where have you been?' Roma demanded.

'I had an appointment to see my lawyer,' I answered truthfully, leaving out any mention of the interview with the journalist from *The Times* or the article in that day's paper.

'You have put the school in a very precarious position,' Carl said. 'Potentially this could have been dangerous for the company.'

'That's nonsense; this has nothing to do with the company. The school was one of many ventures the parent company owned. There's no way they're implicated or have anything to do with my husband's case. You're talking a lot of rot!' I told him calmly. I was proud of my self-control.

'I will let you know when you have to go and see the director,' Carl said.

'I don't know if I want to go to that,' I replied. 'I will think about it.'

With that, they left me alone.

The rest of the day passed uneventfully. The Internet was still down, and I did not tell anyone about the article in *The Times*, though I did text the children in London and ask them to buy a copy of the paper. Tallena called me, puzzled by the request, and I explained about the interview the day before and the article being printed that day. I told her things were not good at school, but I played down the bitter and twisted things that had been said about me.

That evening, I gathered my courage and went to a barbecue arranged for the staff. 'How was your day?' a couple of old friends asked as I sat down with them and I bounced back, 'Better than expected!' I was dying to tell someone about the latest article but didn't want anyone to overhear me. 'I'll tell you about it later,' I said.

Then two friends, James and Emma, arrived. As he kissed me hello on the cheek, James whispered in my ear, 'We've been reading all about you!' He smiled knowingly and my eyes opened wide at his revelation.

'You read the article?'

'Yes, you're on the front page of the world section,' he smiled. 'We've just flown in; *The Times* was on board the plane.'

Excitement raced through me. 'Have you still got it?' I wanted to know, unable to contain my excitement that I might see the actual paper instead on the online version.

James' wife Emma confirmed it was back at their apartment, and I managed to contain my desire to rush right over and agreed I would go round to see it the next day. When I finally got my hands on the paper and read the article, I laughed at how the journalist had portrayed my position in Libya. I had answered his questions truthfully, and the truth was what he had written. The lead-in read: 'Widow leaves her family and lives alone in one-bedroom apartment in foreign land, to seek justice for her husband. She speaks no Arabic and has few friends...' – he had carefully summarized our conversation in the car on the way to the cemetery. The picture of me made me squirm; my face looked withered and drooped with age. The photographer had caught the moment I had said, 'Megrahi gets a hero's welcome, and I get this,' with my hands outspread and the mass grave in the background. Overall, I was pleased with the coverage; it was an improvement on *The Sunday Times* article.

As far as I was aware, Carl was still not aware of the new article. He sent me a message to say that my meeting with the company director was arranged for Tuesday, and to set cover for the afternoon. At the prescribed time I duly waited in the reception area, but after half an hour I gave up and asked the receptionist if anyone was in the office with the head.

'No, he's gone out for the afternoon,' the Libyan girl told me.

The meeting had been cancelled, and no one had told me. I had the uneasy feeling that I was being played, which intensified when one of my Year 12 students, Louise, stopped me in the corridor.

'Excuse me, miss,' she said, 'I just wanted to tell you how much I enjoyed your class. I'm sorry we aren't doing it any more.'

'What? Who told you that, Louise?' I questioned her carefully.

'Mr. Murray was in the lesson today when we normally would have had you and told us the timetable had been restructured and the school could no longer offer us the art class.'

'We'll see about that,' I said.

'It's too late, miss,' Louise apologized. 'Everyone had to choose another option and we start tomorrow. They said it was in the system now and the other classes depended on the numbers.'

I was fuming. My students had been lied to, and forced to change to a different subject. Had I been sent to wait for the meeting that never happened to get me out of the way? I had already had to give up my Year 13 class to a new teacher coming in who had arrived from Zimbabwe with her husband. She had taught lower school art for the past six years there but the school had never had a sixth form college and she had come in as a primary teacher. Or had she, I wondered. Had it been in Carl's mind to sack me for some time? Had the other art teacher been lined up to replace me?

Because I could not find him, I e-mailed the head of sixth form who had told my students to switch classes, copying the e-mail to Carl and Roma also. It was an underhanded thing to do, to take my Year 12 class from me without even informing me, and I knew I needed as much written evidence as possible. As I opened my desk drawer to take out a pen, I saw the list of lawyers that the British Embassy had originally given me. I took it out and studied the names and the specializations that were listed. There was a nagging feeling that all these changes to my working life added up to harassment and bullying. I would keep the list of lawyers in a safe place.

The return e-mail from Ian Murray sent me charging straight over to Carl's office. The head of sixth form had looked again at my timetable now that it was lighter because I no longer had a year 12 class to teach and informed me that I would have to spend seven periods supervising in the sixth form study room.

'You can't take both my sixth form classes off me and then tell me I have to do cover!' I said. 'Why do we now have to supervise the sixth form study room? It's up to them if they study or not; you don't find supervision in any other schools. And this is a new post – you have to advertise for it. You can't just allot this job to me. My job is to teach art! This seems like bullying and harassment to me,' I said to him.

'I would be very careful what you say, Felicity,' Carl warned me.

'No, Carl, it's you who need to be careful. I have *The Sunday Times* editor e-mailing me, asking if this school is trying to push me out or silence me, and offering to do a follow-up story.' I wanted to add, *Do you really think I wouldn't name the school then?* but decided I had said enough to antagonize him for the moment. 'Please have another look at this cover and rework it,' I said and then left before he could answer.

I had meant to keep the communication from Dipesh at *The Sunday Times* to myself, but I couldn't resist using it to warn Carl. Dipesh had twice e-mailed since I had arrived back. The first congratulated me for the superb piece *The Times* had done and said his superiors were extremely annoyed that they had not done the full feature on me. I had replied, filling Dipesh in on recent events, and his second e-mail in reply had said, 'If you are gagged in any way, let me know.'

That afternoon I called the lawyer on the Embassy list whose specialty was listed as being employment law. He was interested, and agreed to see me the following week.

Chapter 32

Some reprieve came when Carl sent an e-mail to say he had looked at the cover I was expected to do for the sixth form study and had cut it back to two extra lessons. I decided to meet him halfway, glad that he had listened to me. Perhaps the incidents at the school were coincidences without malice intended; perhaps things would quiet down now and go back to normal.

Carl phoned on Tuesday morning to say the meeting with the director would happen straight after lunch. He was unusually cheery when I got to his office. I didn't wait in the reception area this time but knocked loudly on his office door to make sure he was in. He drove me to the director's office, maintaining a friendly demeanor throughout. I was wary of him; the last thing I wanted to do was get into a conversation with him. Ryan had told me to just go along and get my wrist slapped and it would all blow over. I would have to bite my tongue but I supposed he could be right.

The road was windy. The brick-walled road kept hidden from view the stately villas beyond. After a while we came to a building that looked like a factory, and Carl pulled over and spoke to the security guard on duty. Automatically, the barrier went up and he parked the car and went into the office to get me a security pass. I was directed to a reception area to wait while Carl went in to see the director first. There was a company magazine on the table and I flicked through it, noticing the number of facets that the company had in operation. There were offices everywhere, including London. I knew this was a powerful firm and the school was just one of its many sidelines.

'Come in, Mr. Diaz is ready for you now,' Carl announced from the office doorway. The director, Mr. Diaz, was sitting at his computer with his back to me and Steven motioned for me to sit down around the big round table. It reminded me of the one in the lawyer's office, and how I had sat at it just two weeks ago having hope torn from me. I was sturdier than that now: the grueling first week at school had toughened me and I had steeled myself for this meeting.

The director, a lean, authoritative man, came to shake hands with me. He began a speech on how they had to live by the Libyan ways and knew any authority could shut them down at a whim. I listened attentively, but eventually felt I had to say my piece.

'A country like Libya is above the law...' the director was saying.

'Actually, Libya isn't above the law, Mr. Diaz, as we have just seen when it had to pay each of the Lockerbie victims ten million dollars each,' I said, expressionless.

The director glared at me. 'That's from the outside world, Mrs. Prazak. I can assure you, once inside the country, it is a very different matter.' I knew what he was getting at. If someone disappeared, you knew you would never see them again. One of the primary teachers had tutored Gaddafi's grandchild at his house and had heard shots fired the day their driver was reported killed in a car crash.

'And even the Lockerbie people have not been entirely successful in getting their compensation,' the director continued.

'Actually, they have just received the last tranche,' I said, 'but to an extent you are right because the lawyers took a third of their money, three million dollars each. That's quite a payout when there are only three main law firms, two in the States and one in the UK. Three million dollars times two hundred and seventy people. My lawyer was one of them. He feels very, very sorry for me that I received nothing from Libya for my husband's unexplained death.'

'We have your file and indeed we are very sympathetic to what happened to you, Mrs. Prazak,' the director said.

Twitching in my seat, I rubbed my ankles together under the

large wooden table, thinking, *He has my file, what file is he talking about?* I decided to say nothing.

'We're prepared to give your file to someone very important who can help you,' he said expectantly.

Carl broke in then, to my annoyance, bringing to the director's attention the new contract that they had drawn up for the staff. He passed it over for the director's approval, who then showed it to me. It was written in English and I barely looked at it, which annoyed Carl greatly. He turned the document back towards me and started reading out the new conditions for working at the school.

'You will not be allowed to speak to the press or bring them onto the school grounds without prior permission. The company's name can never be mentioned. No one is allowed to participate in any interviews while they are employed by us. No one will use the word "dictator" with reference to Colonel Gaddafi,' Carl read on, emphasizing clause after clause.

'Who is the contract for?' I asked.

'These are the new contracts for all the staff,' Carl replied.

'Do you mean the new staff that have just arrived?'

'No, every member of staff will have to sign it on Sunday at the meeting,' Carl informed me.

'I won't be signing it, Carl. My two-year contract stands. The deputy editor of *The Sunday Times* has e-mailed wanting to know how I am and if I am being gagged.' I looked at both of the men around the table. 'I would call this gagging and taking away my civil liberties, wouldn't you?'

'We are just trying to work this out for all our benefits, Mrs. Prazak,' the director said with composure.

'Mrs. Al Hasi saw your article last Thursday in *The Times* and the one before where you said you came to Libya to find answers for your husband's death,' Carl said, and I switched immediately to the defensive at hearing one of the parents' names. 'She thought you came to Libya to teach the students first, not go looking for answers here, and I had to explain to her that I have no control over what the papers say. You are sending the wrong message to the students and parents.'

I kicked back my chair, letting the screeching noise of the movement echo around the room. 'That shows me the level of compassion that she has: my personal life is none of her business. She obviously doesn't care about my tragedy, but I have done everything in my power to teach her daughter and do a good job, and that's all Mrs. Al Hasi needs to be concerned with!'

'Mrs. Prazak, no one is questioning your dedication to the students. You clearly care a lot about them. It is just from the position of the company that we must be certain where our employees' loyalties lie. This is Libya and we could be shut down without any reasons given,' the director said softly.

'This is my position, Mr. Diaz,' I told him. 'I was widowed under very tragic circumstances with two very young children to bring up on my own. It was not my choice. I had a husband I loved and the children had a father that adored them. I was grief stricken for years; it was hard enough to get by day by day, let alone take on the British or Libyan government. I did what I could at the time. It has taken me sixteen years before I have been strong enough and in a position to find out about suing either the military, that blew up the plane, or Libyan Arab Airlines, both of which are state-owned. Can you tell me I don't have a right to sue either of them or both of them for the unlawful death of my husband?'

Mr. Diaz had listened to every word and he gave an answer that surprised me. 'You sue the state, Mrs. Prazak. The state is responsible. I can see you are a very intelligent woman, Mrs. Prazak. Leave everything with me and I will do what I can for you.'

It was a turn of events that I had not expected, and a humble 'thank you' was all I could muster.

The interrogation was over. As we drove back to school, I

didn't know whether I'd had my knuckles rapped or my hand shaken.

Chapter 33

Tripoli was abuzz with happenings and the press were all over the city. I kept an eye on other stories that *The Times* journalist was writing day after day. Dipesh from *The Sunday Times* e-mailed me again after I told him of the contract that I was asked, and refused, to sign. When the other teachers were given the contract to sign after my meeting any English had been completely removed: the new contract was written in Arabic only. Most signed it.

On the day I was to meet with my new lawyer, Theo called, brimming with news that a reporter had just been to see him.

'What's that?' I asked my son, who was jubilant at the news.

'A reporter from the *Standard* came around and wanted to do a story with me,' he repeated gleefully.

Still puzzled as to how the meeting had come about, I listened to Theo explain how the reporter had told him she'd read the story in the paper at the time of al-Megrahi's release and wanted to know what had happened since then. Theo was proud of himself, saying he had handled the interview very well.

'What did you tell her?' I gasped. 'Did you say I'm having problems at work?'

'Yes, Mum, I did. And she wants to phone you.'

'Thanks for letting me know, darling,' I told my son. It was good to see interest in the story still. 'I have to go now. I have a meeting.'

The meeting was with Carl, who had called me to his office. Roma, the head of secondary, was also there when I arrived.

'We have called you here on a matter of competency,' Carl began. 'This is a letter that sets out the conditions you need to fulfill for the criteria of competency. You need to read it and sign it.' Carl shuffled a two-page document towards me. Then he gave a long speech saying that having taken advice from the head office he had decided I was not an adequate teacher to be employed by the school.

My head was screaming, *What are you on about?* Just three days ago he had taken me to the director of the company who'd said he would do what he could to help me. What had changed in three days? Then the penny dropped that Gaddafi's fortieth anniversary had passed and the press were pulling out of Tripoli. I had seen the celebrations: the lights, the parades, the gaiety, the flyover of military aircraft and Gaddafi's private plane coloring the sky with vibrant smoke. It was all over now and the media had all but gone home, and now here I was sitting in Carl's office once again being grilled about my status at the school. The offer to help me had bought them time as they waited for the media to leave.

Carl sat waiting for me to reach out and pick up the document. He took the pen that was on the table and thrust it towards me.

'Well, what's in it?' I said, not even picking up the document.

'It has been agreed that you will have a ten-week observation period to assess your competency level as a teacher.'

'What!' I exclaimed.

Carl explained that the exam fails in my A level class were the problem. I pointed out to him that there were failures across all the subjects, not just art. And, I reminded him, I had been to Roma many times to warn her that they would not pass because they were not doing the work and meeting the criteria of the exam board. Carl was not moved.

'We have decided, and the head office have agreed to it, that you will undergo a ten-week observation period with four senior members of staff observing you.'

'Four member of staff? What are you talking about Carl? You know that isn't allowed, that's harassment,' I bounced back. 'You are allowed to observe me two or three times a year. Like last year, when I had two lesson observations that were both excellent.' I looked at him carefully. 'And what happens at the end of the ten-week period?'

'After ten weeks, when you are found to be incompetent, you will be dismissed.' *When, not if.*

'If this was a matter of competency, Carl, you would have seen a problem from day one. Not congratulated me time and time again on the good work other students were producing. And you would have sent me on the IB to give me the training. You cannot do this to me alone. If this is about exam passes, then you have to observe every teacher whose students failed.'

At best I had ten weeks left at the school. It was a hard blow to take, especially as I had momentarily allowed myself to think the director would help me. I had to get out of there; I had nothing else to say. As if on cue my phone rang. It was Haj letting me know he was outside my place.

'I have to go now,' I said politely.

Carl said, 'You need to sign and take your copy of the document.'

Getting up out of my chair I answered, 'No, Carl, I don't agree with it. I am not signing anything.'

Carl's face dropped. 'You need to take the letter!'

I had not even read it and I didn't want to do anything that could be construed as acceptance of his terms. 'I have to go,' I said. 'I am on my way to see a lawyer. If you want him to have a copy of this, then it is you who will be giving it to him. I am not taking it. Please excuse me now.'

As soon as I shut the door I felt like I was going to collapse. The unscheduled meeting had lasted about forty minutes and I was in shock at what had been planned, probably all along, for me. In the taxi on the way to the new lawyer's office the phone rang. It was the journalist Theo had told me about. Listening to the journalist say how well Theo had conducted himself in the interview, I was extremely proud of my son.

'I've arranged for a photographer to come and take the children's photos,' the journalist told me. 'Is that alright with you?'

'Yes, of course, if they've agreed to it,' I said.

'How is it going for you back in Libya?' the journalist asked, and I told her honestly that things were not good.

'My boss just tried to impose on me a ten-week observational period to establish my competency! I didn't agree to it and am on my way to see a lawyer,' I told her.

'Good for you!' the journalist said cheerfully. 'Would you say your boss is trying to silence you?'

'I certainly would say that. He tried to get me to sign a new contract to say I wouldn't speak to the press, but I wouldn't do it.' I related the meeting with the director.

'How can he do a thing like that?' The journalist was staggered at the suggestion.

The journalist took some more details and before I realized it Haj had pulled up outside the lawyer's office. The journalist said she would ring back later.

The lawyer, Mr. Ali, spoke in excellent English. I quickly realized from his youth that he was not one of the main lawyers in the law firm, but he was dressed impeccably and he listened attentively, making a few notes from time to time, as I talked.

'This man cannot do this,' Mr. Ali told me. 'Did you bring a copy of your contract?' After studying it, he told me, 'You know, there are many mistakes with this contract.' He had his secretary take a photocopy of it. 'I will go and see if Mr. Zwara is still here and take advice from him,' the young lawyer said. He was away for about ten minutes and I hoped I would get some constructive advice before I left.

Mr. Ali came back into the room, and ushered me along to meet the senior partner. I must have been something of a ghost to him; he had represented many of the Libyan families after the disaster.

'We can help you,' he said, 'but first you must wait until after the ten weeks and see what they do to you. You do not have to do the lesson observations, they are not in your contract, but until you have something put in writing we cannot act.'

At first I felt a little disappointed that I could not just launch a harassment suit against my employer. 'Should I have taken the letter telling me about the planned observations?'

The lawyer assured me it did not matter, and then told me pointedly, 'Do not even discuss it further with them. They can take it up with us if they try to force you to do this. And now, I need you to go home and put into writing everything you have told me – write down every meeting, every issue you have had.'

So after the meeting I sat at my laptop and wrote everything I could remember of my problems at the school. When my friend Sandra stopped by, I was typing away furiously.

Listening to my story attentively, Sandra waited until I finished before saying, 'You know he expected you to say you would leave rather allow the observations? Are you sure you really want to stay and do this, Felicity?'

'I'm not going. Why should I go! I'll need the money; at least I have up until Christmas.'

'But all these people coming into your lessons! It's so disruptive, and they'll be there to catch you out,' Sandra said.

'There's no way I am letting anyone come in to observe me. If he tried that in the UK I'd be straight on to my union; there's no way any management can make you go through such a grueling, belittling process.'

Sandra came back with, 'But this is Libya! He can do anything he wants!'

'No, he can't!' I said emphatically.

When Sandra left I looked around my apartment – the large rugs spread over the floors, the decorative baskets and lights I had bought in the desert, my paintings hanging all along the wide hallway. Surveying the belongings I had collected, I wondered what I would do in ten weeks. Sell them off? Ship them back to the UK? There would be no happy ending to this. I had to face that I would soon be ousted from the place I had called home and that my search for justice would end. What I did not know, though, was quite how soon I would be cast out.

Chapter 34

On Sunday, my last in Libya, Haj drove me to the lawyer to give him the minutes and other paperwork he had asked for. They were making a file for the day the ten-week period ended and I would be forced out of my job. It was a weight off my mind knowing all the information I had typed up was now at a lawyer's office just waiting for the day that Carl confronted me again. But it was not ten weeks before I returned there; it was mere days.

On Tuesday, there was a guest at the staff briefing from the company: Miriam Lyell. After the meeting, I went over to introduce myself. She went white when she realized who I was. I handed her a copy of the minutes I had written of my last meeting with Carl. 'My lawyer also has a copy,' I said before heading off to class.

At lunchtime the *Standard* journalist called again, wanting to clarify a couple of points. I explained that things had deteriorated since I had last spoken to her, but that I couldn't talk at that minute because my class was just about to come in. I asked the journalist to call at three p.m. when I would be free. Carl had left a message telling me to come to his office immediately, but with just five minutes of my lunch hour left, I decided to ignore it and turned my phone off. I went directly home as soon as my class was over to have the conversation with the journalist in private. No sooner had I closed the door behind me than Roma was banging on it.

'We've been trying to get you all day!' she reprimanded me.

'Did you try my art room?' I said, mockingly.

'Carl wants you to come over to my office now.' I was slightly taken aback that he wanted to meet me in Roma's office and not his.

'Alright, Roma, I will come over to your office, but I am not discussing the observational period. If you want to talk about it, I need my lawyer present.'

Carl was sitting at Roma's small table tapping the wood in a nervous manner when I came in. He indicated that I sit, but I responded that I needed to know what the meeting was about and stayed standing. He was holding an envelope and thrust it at me.

'Just open the letter, it explains everything,' he said.

I quickly scanned the letter, picking up the gist in seconds. I looked up at Carl with a half-smile on my face and said, 'Thank you for this. It is exactly what my lawyer is waiting for.'

Carl's face sagged in disbelief. No doubt he had been expecting rage and tears, but all he got was the back of my head as I exited.

My phone rang as I walked through the office door into the corridor, and I told the journalist calling from London that I had just been sacked.

'What does the letter say exactly, Mrs. Prazak?' the journalist asked, wanting to get the wording correct.

'It says due to breaches of protocol my employment is terminated with immediate effect...' And then I gasped, because my eyes had scanned over the next sentence and I now grasped its meaning. 'And I'm to leave the country in two days, by Thursday!'

'Can he make you do that?' the journalist asked.

'It says a final exit visa will be issued and they will buy me a one-way ticket home.' I read the whole letter to the journalist.

'What will you do?' the journalist asked.

I explained that once a final exit visa was issued you had to leave, plus you could not come back for three years. 'He's effectively stopping me from visiting my husband's grave or taking up the law case again against the state.'

And then I named the school and offered to give the journalist Carl's number so he could confirm my story.

'No, that's alright.' The journalist reassured me that she believed every last word, and then offered her sincere apologies that this had happened to me and said that she had every confidence that her editor would run the story in the paper the next day.

I had stood in the corridor two or three minutes talking to the journalist and couldn't resist a final stand. Flinging open the door to Roma's office, I said, 'By the way, that was the press, and I've told them you've sacked me and I've named the school.' I just had time to register Carl's appalled expression before I let the door swing shut behind me and bang against the frame.

Immediately I phoned Haj to come and collect me, and I travelled directly to the lawyer's office. Mr. Ali greeted me at the door and read the letter of termination. He took me straight to the senior partner's office. We sat in the leather seats in front of the lawyer's desk and waited patiently while Mr. Zwara read the short letter.

His first words to me were, 'This man is stupid! We have labor laws in Libya. We will file suit straightaway.' He spoke in Arabic to the aide to take some further details and the only question he asked me was, 'Have you had much time off sick?' I replied that I'd had two days off that year and two days off the previous year. The motion of his hand waving the air across his desk indicated it was not cause for the dismissal and the only factor that could have affected my case, I guessed.

I asked Mr. Zwara, 'What if I don't leave? What if I just stay in Libya to fight my case and stay in my apartment?'

Earnestly, he clasped his hands together and said they would take care of all the legal issues with the case and it was unlikely that I would even be needed to appear in court. 'What you don't want are problems with immigration if you have a lawsuit going on. Once a final exit visa is issued you have to leave Libya,' he said.

Haj took me to the nearest ATM, and I took out enough

money to pay the lawyer's starting fee. The firm would take the rest of their fee as a percentage of the outcome of the settlement in the case. Counting out every dinar, I felt like I was breaking chains binding me. When we returned to the lawyer's office, Mr. Zwara asked me to write a synopsis of my financial loss and the emotional strain and stress I was suffering. I agreed, my head buzzing with ideas and feelings. *How could they possibly pay me enough to know what it is to be treated as a security treat and prevented from seeking recompense for the life of my husband?* I thought. The release of the convicted bomber and the elation of the Libyan people had heightened the emotion of the whole drama, and I had been unbearably humiliated. Had the observations gone ahead, it would have ruined my credibility as a teacher; no school would employ me if they knew that I'd been observed in such a manner.

When I left the lawyer's office, I asked Haj to take me to the Wadan. It was a new seven-star hotel, one I'd been wanting to explore, and now, with the clock ticking, there was no better chance. I would nestle there, have something to eat and draft my letter for the lawyer, I decided.

I was pleasantly surprised to find a familiar face behind the reception desk: the manageress I had been talking to at the garden party and who used to send her son to the school.

'Felicity, how are you?' she greeted me warmly.

'Well, I've just been sacked and my lawyer wants me to write an account of what happened because I'm suing the school.'

'Wonderful!' the manageress sang back, to my delight. 'I'm glad someone's finally standing up to him.' The manageress had taken her son out of the school because of the attitude Carl displayed to the parents.

The woman couldn't do enough for me, and guided me around the hotel, pointing out features and décor, and then settled me in a spacious courtyard with a cascading water feature. 'Anything you want, just call.'

Cheekily, I asked, 'Could I just get some paper to draft a letter on, please?'

The demure, slim manageress smiled elegantly back at me and said, 'Felicity, if we had champagne I would give it to you.'

It took about two hours to draft the letter that I would hand to the lawyer the next day. It outlined my financial loss but also pointed out my age and the problems now of obtaining employment without a reference that I knew would not be given to me. It explained the good work I had done, citing praise from both Carl and Roma that had been recorded in my file. I emphasized the knock-on effect of displacing me and the belongings that I had acquired in good faith believing that I would be staying at a school. Even when I returned to the UK I effectively had nowhere to stay; I had rented my room in London to a tenant so that Theo and Tallena had a source of income.

I arrived home near seven p.m. and no sooner had I fed the cats than there was a knock at my door. It was Ryan and Ellie from the floor above, wanting to show me their support. They were not the only ones: my phone rang constantly with staff lending their sympathy. Finally, I got enough space to call Theo and Tallena. I was dreading telling them that I had been sacked and would be evicted from the country that had killed their father, but I discovered at once that they already knew.

'The journalist rang to get our comments on how we were coping with our mother being thrown out of a regime that had covered up our father's death,' Tallena told me. 'It will be in the paper tomorrow, Mum. We gave them a photo of you also.'

My daughter and son were concerned, and would not rest until their mother was safely back with them. The decision not to try to fight the extradition was not only sensible from the lawyer's point of view; my family would have been on tenterhooks the whole time.

The next morning I was doing my best to organize my departure. Emad had agreed to take my cats, and I was throwing clothes into suitcases. When the clock hand had moved to five past nine I dialed the Ambassador's number and asked for his secretary.

'I'm very sorry to hear this, Felicity,' said the Ambassador with genuine concern after I related my story. 'We will of course to continue to pursue your case and do all we can for you.'

'This is meant to be in the press today. I'm certain that the media and the British public will look at this as the Libyan government ousting me from Libya. Carl hasn't thought about this enough. How does it look when al-Megrahi, a convicted terrorist, has just come home to Libya to a hero's welcome, and the widow of a British citizen who was killed in very tragic circumstances by a Libyan military plane is kicked out of Libya for openly pursuing justice for her husband's death?' I said.

The Ambassador listened attentively and said he would look at the article online today. I imagined his fingers already tapping away at the search engine as he wished me well for the future. It had been the right move to tell him. No doubt Carl had colored in the competency fantasy to him, but there could be a backlash of calls from the media to the Embassy and I wanted my side heard.

As soon as I came off the phone to the Ambassador, I quickly searched for the story and triumphantly shouted praises when I saw the article. 'Wow!' I said to myself. 'It's a long time since I looked like that.' The children had given the press a photo of me and Victor on holiday together in Bali. The journalist had got the words spot on, and I relished reading the school's name in the paper. The stupid man, it had been nothing to do with the school.

Though students sadly thanked me for my time with them and friends gave me a lovely send-off at my 'deportation party', as I packed to leave Libya, loneliness engulfed me. I despaired that I would ever get closure on Victor's death. It would be far too risky to pursue a case against the state if I was to sue the school. It was gutting to know that I would have to put the case against the state on hold, when I had finally begun to make some progress on it. I had thought it had been fate that I landed a job in Libya so that I could be near my husband's resting place and find some answers. I had thought it had been some divine intervention. Now what would I do? I was unemployed, and banished from Libya. What chance did I have now of uncovering the truth and securing justice at last?

As the plane lifted off from Tripoli Airport bound for London, I looked out of the window and thought of Victor, beloved Victor. Today would have been our twenty-first wedding anniversary. I was going home to our children, but oh how I wished I was going home to him too. Then all would have been well in the world. As the British Airways pilot came over the loudspeaker to welcome us to the flight, my mind recited over and over again the words Mohammed had told me were in the crash report I had never seen, the very last words my husband ever heard:

The pilot cried out to Allah and said, 'We are finished.'

Martin Fletcher, journalist discovers the board with the LN1103 atrocity while reporting on the civil war in Benghazi.

Epilogue

Dubai, London, Benghazi, 2011

A quick glance at the clock on my art room wall as I positioned myself in front of my computer confirmed that I had five minutes before the morning briefing. I tapped my foot, frustrated, as the computer warmed up. My new role as head of creative arts had landed me for the past six months in Dubai in the United Arab Emirates, and the large studio I sat in would soon be filled with a clashing of students' chatter and clanging chairs. The school day began early in the Middle East, and if the Internet played up now it would be nearing five p.m. by the time I could go back into my own private, troubled world.

'Come on,' I urged impatiently, as if the computer wasn't an inanimate object and could choose to humor my tense mood. The routine of checking my private e-mails first thing in the morning had become overshadowed by my compulsion to read every inch of the news on the screen about Libya and the latest crisis going on. I had even started setting my alarm earlier than six a.m. and taking in as much of the information seeping out Libya as my mind could digest before the sun blasted onto the open Dubai skies.

Scanning the headlines displayed on the computer, I knew I had seen most of the breaking news just half an hour beforehand when I had left my apartment. I been glued for days to the news broadcast about the Arab uprising that the media had dubbed the Arab Spring. Egypt and Tunisia had seen their radical leaders fall within days of civil unrest as people took control of the streets and their lives. Libya, I knew, would never fall so easily from the lecherous tentacles of Gaddafi. My mind was shredded with grief and guilt that I was not there to experience firsthand the fear and panic that I knew former colleagues and friends were enduring since the rebels in Benghazi began their fight for freedom on the

17th February 2011. The world's cameras had followed the unprecedented events, capturing what I should have been experiencing, as Tripoli became a battle scene.

March had passed and I had seen familiar faces on the news retelling their ordeals of escaping the war zone. The evacuation from Tripoli was the only focus. One by one I caught a glimpse of a former student or colleague being interviewed or embracing a worried relative at the airport after their escape from the regime. If I hadn't seen them on TV, I banged on the keyboard, looking for an e-mail from others who were letting me know they were safe. There were still people unaccounted for and I was searching the news for word. On that April morning I just had time to scan through my e-mails, hoping the night had brought e-mails from others still stuck in Tripoli.

But nothing could have prepared me for what I read when I clicked open an e-mail from the journalist who had interviewed me in Tripoli in 2009. Keywords kept jumping out at me as if a knife's blade was shooting out of the computer scene: *rebels... accounting for atrocity... shot down plane... Gaddafi regime.* I read the e-mail again, aware the seconds were slipping by:

Dear Felicity... I am now in Benghazi. I thought you would like to know that one of the atrocities of the Gaddafi regime for which the rebels want a full accounting is the plane crash that killed your husband. They believe Gaddafi shot the plane down, then said it was an accident caused by international sanctions. There is a list of names, including your husband's, hanging on a wall outside the courthouse. Martin.

My mind at once flitted to the labor case that earlier this year had finally culminated in a court ruling that the school had broken Libyan labor law in ousting me from my position at the school in Tripoli. Compensation would account for a year's wages, expenses and damages. But the unrest in Libya had derailed the legal process, and I'd had to accept that I would have to wait until the regime toppled and some form of normality resumed before a sum would be set and secured from the school.

Now, Martin's short message sent electrical signals to my brain cells and joy and hope of which I didn't know I was capable flooded back into the void I had become. I read the message twice, nearly jumping for joy at such devastating news. Then I hit the off switch and practically danced down the corridor. All the lies would be exposed now, because the rebels had always known the truth and the pieces of the jigsaw that had been missing all these years were finally found.

Strangely, hysterically and overwhelmingly, I was elated at the horrific news, and my soul was bursting to shout it out. But I shared so little of myself in my new job. I had told no one of my forced ejection from Libya, though there was no shame to my hurried departure. But what I had taken at the time as a straight-forward case of bullying was turning out to be suspiciously political. I had touched too close to a nerve center of a dictatorial regime by asking questions. It was easy for them back in September 2009 to kick me out of Tripoli, but as things evolved, by July 2011, it was impossible to keep me out of Benghazi where the revolution had begun.

Some weeks later Martin sent on the images that his photographer had taken in Benghazi. The plain five-by-three board that hung outside Benghazi courthouse listed the atrocity defiantly, saying in English that Criminal Gaddafi had shot down the plane LN1103 and listing the names of the martyrs. Victor's name was there. It was an awe-inspiring moment for me to see his name there, in black and white.

The words printed in the center of the board must have jolted Martin into remembering our conversation at the mass grave in 2009.

'Of course,' I had said as we stepped over the tumbleweeds that rolled around the barren wasteland entrapping the souls in a stateless purgatory, 'there are reports that there were live missiles fired at the plane.'

The enquiring journalist searched my face, looking for an explanation. 'How do you know that, Felicity?' he asked, in near disbelief at the revelation.

'I've always known,' I told him matter-of-factly.

But even I had barely considered the idea that Gaddafi himself was responsible; that was beyond all our comprehension. The most my mind, for all these years, had been able to cope with was the suggestion that it had been an attempted coup and that the wrong plane had been shot down on the approach to Tripoli Airport. Gaddafi's personal plane, I was told, had been half an hour late, and the wrong plane had been sacrificed.

Now I was enticed by the truth and the overwhelming desire to see the board that stated the facts and my husband's name written in Arabic. The war in Libya had raged full scale for the past five months, with NATO bombing Tripoli, and the rebels, as the anti-Gaddafi opposers were called, fought resiliently for their freedom. 'They're not rebels,' I would say in their defense, 'they're reformers.' The untrained freedom fighters now had no choice but to fight to the end. And once the full scale of Gaddafi's atrocities was uncovered, then the world would understand there was no going back.

My quick response to Martin was that I must see the board. It felt like a shrine to me, to all those innocents who had been murdered, Victor among them. I knew that seeing the shrine would quench my soul. But my mind was in turmoil, convinced it wouldn't be even a remote possibility to go to Libya until the long months of the civil war had ended and only if Gaddafi was ousted. And he had better be, I thought: if he survived the civil unrest and the war that gripped his country then Benghazi would be annihilated. There was no question in my mind that his ruthlessness and despotic anger would be quenched only when the second largest city in the country was razed to the ground.

I was astonished when Martin e-mailed back to say I did not

need a visa to enter Libya, and I could avoid the no-fly zone by entering Benghazi via a long bus ride from Cairo. This world-class journalist made going to Libya in wartime sound as easy as getting the bus to Clapham Junction. I called Martin in July when I got back to England for the summer, and said, 'Surely you can only get in because you're a journalist and it's different for the press!'

'Anyone can go,' he assured me, and he offered to send me contact details of a driver who would taxi me all the way from Cairo to Benghazi. It's two hundred dollars by taxi, or fifty dollars or so if you can put up with the bus.'

Going into a war zone wouldn't be everyone's dream holiday, but I felt there was no place I'd rather be. 'If you go there,' I was told, 'you don't usually come out.' But it was the only thing I wanted to do that holiday, so that my spiritual life would get back on track.

Amid making arrangements for my trip, I wrote the following letter to Foreign Secretary William Hague.

Dear Mr. Hague,
RE: THE MURDER OF VICTOR PRAZAK IN LIBYA 22/12/1992

I am writing to ask for your intervention in seeking a resolution to the injustice that a British citizen, my husband, has been murdered by the Gaddafi regime and the previous governments so far have not sought justice for the atrocity in which he lost his precious life.

In a recent meeting with the heads of state for Britain, the leader of the opposition, Mahmoud Gebril, brought a list of atrocities committed by the Gaddafi regime for which they are seeking justice and recompense. Among these atrocities is the shooting down of flight LN1103 on 22nd December 1992, which my husband, VICTOR CHARLES PRAZAK, was on. Missiles packed with live explosives were fired at the civilian carrier, killing a hundred and fifty-seven people on board. The Libyan warplane that shot the aircraft down then collided with the passenger plane while the MiG pilots ejected safely.

My husband was buried the following day in a mass grave outside Tripoli without my permission and without his family being allowed to be there.

Outside the courthouse in Benghazi is a list of the victims of this atrocity, including my husband. I have repeatedly requested a crash report, an inquest and an inquiry into the death of my husband. I have also asked for a transcript for the closed trial where the pilot was found to be responsible. His orders would have come directly from Gaddafi and the now recognized government of Libya believe Gaddafi's act of barbarism was to get sympathy for the UN sanctions on Libya.

I have written to my MP Jane Ellison three times, without any response, and stated that the Prime Minister David Cameron cannot do a deal with Gaddafi until this atrocity is resolved for myself and the Libyan people and others who lost their loved ones on this sacrificial flight.

I would like to request a meeting with you and the Prime Minister to help stop the oppression of the Libyan people and find justice for me and them. I am prepared to take out a private prosecution for an international arrest warrant for crimes against humanities for any defector of the Libyan regime who should be answerable for their heinous crimes.

Yours sincerely,
Felicity Prazak

The response? There was none.

Theo and Tallena had mixed feelings about my upcoming trip to Benghazi. My daughter protested and said not to go. I was abroad most of the year and losing even a week of their precious time with me did not sit well with her. I pondered whether I should take Theo and quizzed him on this, but he was indifferent to the idea. I wondered for their sakes whether I tried too hard to find answers and ask questions that were never taken seriously.

My sister was more than a little alarmed at my proposal to travel to a country engaged in a civil war. 'NATO are bombing Libya, Felicity!' she reminded me. 'It's just a plaque! Why do you want to see it?'

'NATO isn't bombing Benghazi,' I replied to my sister, who I knew only had my safety at heart, but who couldn't understand the need to be part of news that was affecting the world. I never even tried to explain my feelings that I should have been part of the evacuation and experienced the fear and ordeal people went through leaving Tripoli. How could she understand it would have been real to me, where nothing else was? For nineteen years I had lived in a fog of lies. Gaddafi's propaganda had nearly worked on me. I had blamed sanctions and the West for a murder he had committed and orchestrated down to the last detail of changing the flight number from 400 to 1103 to coincide with Lockerbie.

The Libyan uprising had released the truth that they all knew but were never able to talk about for fear their own lives would be taken from them. Six months before, no one even dared breathe the dictator's name for fear of arrest and imprisonment or worse. Now freedom oozed from everyone's lips and the truth was gushing out like water tumbling down a waterfall, gaining power and momentum with every day. Nothing would stop the flow of freedom that had come to Benghazi.

Initially, I was hesitant in contacting Adel, my former colleague, but I knew he was from Benghazi originally and I'd had a sense, while working with him in the school in Libya, that he had history, as did I. It turned out I was right: Adel was one of the Libyans shot outside the Libyan Embassy when Yvonne Fletcher was killed. Adel e-mailed back, saying he was well and that he and his family, his wife and two young children, were safe in the UK after the evacuation. Adel offered that I could travel with him and his family when they went to Benghazi; they would fly to Cairo and then travel overland to Benghazi. They would be staying there for the month of Ramadan. His offer sealed it for me: I knew it must be reasonably safe because Adel would never put his family at risk, especially as they were now safe in the UK. He had already done the trip so knew what was in store and I needed to trust him. I would not be fazed by the idea of travelling to a country locked in a brutal civil war. If I was to uncover the truth then I knew I had to make this journey. No flaming arrows or missiles or anti-aircraft guns were going to stand as a blockade.

The Arab Uprising was the springboard to my freedom at last. Outside the courthouse in Benghazi, I stood my ground as I looked directly into the cameras of a large TV network while the interviewer teased, 'What would you say to Gaddafi if you could see him right now?'

I smiled as I answered, calmly, quietly, seriously. 'You did not get away with this mass murder. You thought you would suppress your people and massacre them as you pleased. But now the truth is spoken, and I want you to know that I know what you did. And I will have the satisfaction of seeing you accountable and responsible for this execution and be brought to justice for it.'

The thief who took my husband from me will face his judgment day. If it takes me another nineteen years, I will not rest until justice is done. The journey to a civil war submerged me in an ocean of truth and unearthed the hell that the Libyan people suffered. United to fight together now, Libya's Unknown Atrocity will be told.

BOOKS

O is a symbol of the world, of oneness and unity. In different
cultures it also means the "eye," symbolizing knowledge and
insight. We aim to publish books that are accessible, constructive
and that challenge accepted opinion, both that of academia and
the "moral majority."

Our books are available in all good English language
bookstores worldwide. If you don't see the book on the shelves
ask the bookstore to order it for you, quoting the ISBN number
and title. Alternatively you can order online (all major online
retail sites carry our titles) or contact the distributor in the
relevant country, listed on the copyright page.

See our website **www.o-books.net** for a full list of over 500
titles, growing by 100 a year.

And tune in to myspiritradio.com for our book review radio show,
hosted by June-Elleni Laine, where you can listen to the authors
discussing their books.